Building Machine Learning Systems with Python

Second Edition

Get more from your data through creating practical machine learning systems with Python

Luis Pedro Coelho

Willi Richert

[PACKT] PUBLISHING

open source *
community experience distilled

BIRMINGHAM - MUMBAI

Building Machine Learning Systems with Python
Second Edition

First published: July 2013

Second edition: March 2015

Production reference: 1230315

Published by Packt Publishing Ltd.
Livery Place
35 Livery Street
Birmingham B3 2PB, UK.

ISBN 978-1-78439-277-2

www.packtpub.com

Credits

Authors
Luis Pedro Coelho
Willi Richert

Reviewers
Matthieu Brucher
Maurice HT Ling
Radim Řehůřek

Commissioning Editor
Kartikey Pandey

Acquisition Editors
Greg Wild
Richard Harvey
Kartikey Pandey

Content Development Editor
Arun Nadar

Technical Editor
Pankaj Kadam

Copy Editors
Relin Hedly
Sameen Siddiqui
Laxmi Subramanian

Project Coordinator
Nikhil Nair

Proofreaders
Simran Bhogal
Lawrence A. Herman
Linda Morris
Paul Hindle

Indexer
Hemangini Bari

Graphics
Sheetal Aute
Abhinash Sahu

Production Coordinator
Arvindkumar Gupta

Cover Work
Arvindkumar Gupta

About the Authors

Luis Pedro Coelho is a computational biologist: someone who uses computers as a tool to understand biological systems. In particular, Luis analyzes DNA from microbial communities to characterize their behavior. Luis has also worked extensively in bioimage informatics — the application of machine learning techniques for the analysis of images of biological specimens. His main focus is on the processing and integration of large-scale datasets.

Luis has a PhD from Carnegie Mellon University, one of the leading universities in the world in the area of machine learning. He is the author of several scientific publications.

Luis started developing open source software in 1998 as a way to apply real code to what he was learning in his computer science courses at the Technical University of Lisbon. In 2004, he started developing in Python and has contributed to several open source libraries in this language. He is the lead developer on the popular computer vision package for Python and mahotas, as well as the contributor of several machine learning codes.

Luis currently divides his time between Luxembourg and Heidelberg.

I thank my wife, Rita, for all her love and support and my daughter, Anna, for being the best thing ever.

Willi Richert has a PhD in machine learning/robotics, where he used reinforcement learning, hidden Markov models, and Bayesian networks to let heterogeneous robots learn by imitation. Currently, he works for Microsoft in the Core Relevance Team of Bing, where he is involved in a variety of ML areas such as active learning, statistical machine translation, and growing decision trees.

This book would not have been possible without the support of my wife, Natalie, and my sons, Linus and Moritz. I am especially grateful for the many fruitful discussions with my current or previous managers, Andreas Bode, Clemens Marschner, Hongyan Zhou, and Eric Crestan, as well as my colleagues and friends, Tomasz Marciniak, Cristian Eigel, Oliver Niehoerster, and Philipp Adelt. The interesting ideas are most likely from them; the bugs belong to me.

About the Reviewers

Matthieu Brucher holds an engineering degree from the Ecole Supérieure d'Electricité (Information, Signals, Measures), France and has a PhD in unsupervised manifold learning from the Université de Strasbourg, France. He currently holds an HPC software developer position in an oil company and is working on the next generation reservoir simulation.

Maurice HT Ling has been programming in Python since 2003. Having completed his PhD in Bioinformatics and BSc (Hons.) in Molecular and Cell Biology from The University of Melbourne, he is currently a Research Fellow at Nanyang Technological University, Singapore, and an Honorary Fellow at The University of Melbourne, Australia. Maurice is the Chief Editor for *Computational and Mathematical Biology*, and co-editor for *The Python Papers*. Recently, Maurice cofounded the first synthetic biology start-up in Singapore, AdvanceSyn Pte. Ltd., as the Director and Chief Technology Officer. His research interests lies in life — biological life, artificial life, and artificial intelligence — using computer science and statistics as tools to understand life and its numerous aspects. In his free time, Maurice likes to read, enjoy a cup of coffee, write his personal journal, or philosophize on various aspects of life. His website and LinkedIn profile are `http://maurice.vodien.com` and `http://www.linkedin.com/in/mauriceling`, respectively.

Radim Řehůřek is a tech geek and developer at heart. He founded and led the research department at Seznam.cz, a major search engine company in central Europe. After finishing his PhD, he decided to move on and spread the machine learning love, starting his own privately owned R&D company, RaRe Consulting Ltd. RaRe specializes in made-to-measure data mining solutions, delivering cutting-edge systems for clients ranging from large multinationals to nascent start-ups.

Radim is also the author of a number of popular open source projects, including gensim and smart_open.

A big fan of experiencing different cultures, Radim has lived around the globe with his wife for the past decade, with his next steps leading to South Korea. No matter where he stays, Radim and his team always try to evangelize data-driven solutions and help companies worldwide make the most of their machine learning opportunities.

www.PacktPub.com

Support files, eBooks, discount offers, and more

For support files and downloads related to your book, please visit www.PacktPub.com.

Did you know that Packt offers eBook versions of every book published, with PDF and ePub files available? You can upgrade to the eBook version at www.PacktPub.com and as a print book customer, you are entitled to a discount on the eBook copy. Get in touch with us at service@packtpub.com for more details.

At www.PacktPub.com, you can also read a collection of free technical articles, sign up for a range of free newsletters and receive exclusive discounts and offers on Packt books and eBooks.

https://www2.packtpub.com/books/subscription/packtlib

Do you need instant solutions to your IT questions? PacktLib is Packt's online digital book library. Here, you can search, access, and read Packt's entire library of books.

Why subscribe?

- Fully searchable across every book published by Packt
- Copy and paste, print, and bookmark content
- On demand and accessible via a web browser

Free access for Packt account holders

If you have an account with Packt at www.PacktPub.com, you can use this to access PacktLib today and view 9 entirely free books. Simply use your login credentials for immediate access.

Table of Contents

Preface

One could argue that it is a fortunate coincidence that you are holding this book in your hands (or have it on your eBook reader). After all, there are millions of books printed every year, which are read by millions of readers. And then there is this book read by you. One could also argue that a couple of machine learning algorithms played their role in leading you to this book—or this book to you. And we, the authors, are happy that you want to understand more about the hows and whys.

Most of the book will cover the *how*. How has data to be processed so that machine learning algorithms can make the most out of it? How should one choose the right algorithm for a problem at hand?

Occasionally, we will also cover the *why*. Why is it important to measure correctly? Why does one algorithm outperform another one in a given scenario?

We know that there is much more to learn to be an expert in the field. After all, we only covered some *hows* and just a tiny fraction of the *whys*. But in the end, we hope that this mixture will help you to get up and running as quickly as possible.

What this book covers

Chapter 1, Getting Started with Python Machine Learning, introduces the basic idea of machine learning with a very simple example. Despite its simplicity, it will challenge us with the risk of overfitting.

Chapter 2, Classifying with Real-world Examples, uses real data to learn about classification, whereby we train a computer to be able to distinguish different classes of flowers.

Chapter 3, Clustering – Finding Related Posts, teaches how powerful the bag of words approach is, when we apply it to finding similar posts without really "understanding" them.

Chapter 4, Topic Modeling, moves beyond assigning each post to a single cluster and assigns them to several topics as a real text can deal with multiple topics.

Chapter 5, Classification – Detecting Poor Answers, teaches how to use the bias-variance trade-off to debug machine learning models though this chapter is mainly on using a logistic regression to find whether a user's answer to a question is good or bad.

Chapter 6, Classification II – Sentiment Analysis, explains how Naïve Bayes works, and how to use it to classify tweets to see whether they are positive or negative.

Chapter 7, Regression, explains how to use the classical topic, regression, in handling data, which is still relevant today. You will also learn about advanced regression techniques such as the Lasso and ElasticNets.

Chapter 8, Recommendations, builds recommendation systems based on costumer product ratings. We will also see how to build recommendations just from shopping data without the need for ratings data (which users do not always provide).

Chapter 9, Classification – Music Genre Classification, makes us pretend that someone has scrambled our huge music collection, and our only hope to create order is to let a machine learner classify our songs. It will turn out that it is sometimes better to trust someone else's expertise than creating features ourselves.

Chapter 10, Computer Vision, teaches how to apply classification in the specific context of handling images by extracting features from data. We will also see how these methods can be adapted to find similar images in a collection.

Chapter 11, Dimensionality Reduction, teaches us what other methods exist that can help us in downsizing data so that it is chewable by our machine learning algorithms.

Chapter 12, Bigger Data, explores some approaches to deal with larger data by taking advantage of multiple cores or computing clusters. We also have an introduction to using cloud computing (using Amazon Web Services as our cloud provider).

Appendix, Where to Learn More Machine Learning, lists many wonderful resources available to learn more about machine learning.

What you need for this book

This book assumes you know Python and how to install a library using easy_install or pip. We do not rely on any advanced mathematics such as calculus or matrix algebra.

We are using the following versions throughout the book, but you should be fine with any more recent ones:

- Python 2.7 (all the code is compatible with version 3.3 and 3.4 as well)
- NumPy 1.8.1
- SciPy 0.13
- scikit-learn 0.14.0

Who this book is for

This book is for Python programmers who want to learn how to perform machine learning using open source libraries. We will walk through the basic modes of machine learning based on realistic examples.

This book is also for machine learners who want to start using Python to build their systems. Python is a flexible language for rapid prototyping, while the underlying algorithms are all written in optimized C or C++. Thus the resulting code is fast and robust enough to be used in production as well.

Conventions

In this book, you will find a number of styles of text that distinguish between different kinds of information. Here are some examples of these styles, and an explanation of their meaning.

Code words in text, database table names, folder names, filenames, file extensions, pathnames, dummy URLs, user input, and Twitter handles are shown as follows: "We then use `poly1d()` to create a model function from the model parameters."

A block of code is set as follows:

```
[aws info]
AWS_ACCESS_KEY_ID =  AAKIIT7HHF6IUSN3OCAA
AWS_SECRET_ACCESS_KEY = <your secret key>
```

Any command-line input or output is written as follows:

```
>>> import numpy
>>> numpy.version.full_version
1.8.1
```

New terms and **important words** are shown in bold. Words that you see on the screen, in menus or dialog boxes for example, appear in the text like this: "Once the machine is stopped, the **Change instance type** option becomes available."

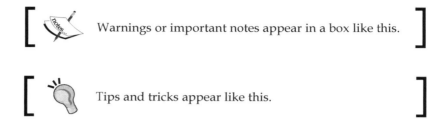

Warnings or important notes appear in a box like this.

Tips and tricks appear like this.

Reader feedback

Feedback from our readers is always welcome. Let us know what you think about this book—what you liked or may have disliked. Reader feedback is important for us to develop titles that you really get the most out of.

To send us general feedback, simply send an e-mail to feedback@packtpub.com, and mention the book title via the subject of your message. If there is a topic that you have expertise in and you are interested in either writing or contributing to a book, see our author guide on www.packtpub.com/authors.

Customer support

Now that you are the proud owner of a Packt book, we have a number of things to help you to get the most from your purchase.

Downloading the example code

You can download the example code files from your account at http://www.packtpub.com for all the Packt Publishing books you have purchased. If you purchased this book elsewhere, you can visit http://www.packtpub.com/support and register to have the files e-mailed directly to you.

The code for this book is also available on GitHub at https://github.com/luispedro/BuildingMachineLearningSystemsWithPython. This repository is kept up-to-date so that it will incorporate both errata and any necessary updates for newer versions of Python or of the packages we use in the book.

Errata

Although we have taken every care to ensure the accuracy of our content, mistakes do happen. If you find a mistake in one of our books—maybe a mistake in the text or the code—we would be grateful if you could report this to us. By doing so, you can save other readers from frustration and help us improve subsequent versions of this book. If you find any errata, please report them by visiting http://www.packtpub.com/submit-errata, selecting your book, clicking on the **Errata Submission Form** link, and entering the details of your errata. Once your errata are verified, your submission will be accepted and the errata will be uploaded to our website or added to any list of existing errata under the Errata section of that title.

To view the previously submitted errata, go to https://www.packtpub.com/books/content/support and enter the name of the book in the search field. The required information will appear under the **Errata** section.

Another excellent way would be to visit www.TwoToReal.com where the authors try to provide support and answer all your questions.

Piracy

Piracy of copyright material on the Internet is an ongoing problem across all media. At Packt, we take the protection of our copyright and licenses very seriously. If you come across any illegal copies of our works, in any form, on the Internet, please provide us with the location address or website name immediately so that we can pursue a remedy.

Please contact us at copyright@packtpub.com with a link to the suspected pirated material.

We appreciate your help in protecting our authors, and our ability to bring you valuable content.

Questions

You can contact us at questions@packtpub.com if you are having a problem with any aspect of the book, and we will do our best to address it.

1
Getting Started with Python Machine Learning

Machine learning teaches machines to learn to carry out tasks by themselves. It is that simple. The complexity comes with the details, and that is most likely the reason you are reading this book.

Maybe you have too much data and too little insight. You hope that using machine learning algorithms you can solve this challenge, so you started digging into the algorithms. But after some time you were puzzled: Which of the myriad of algorithms should you actually choose?

Alternatively, maybe you are in general interested in machine learning and for some time you have been reading blogs and articles about it. Everything seemed to be magic and cool, so you started your exploration and fed some toy data into a decision tree or a support vector machine. However, after you successfully applied it to some other data, you wondered: Was the whole setting right? Did you get the optimal results? And how do you know whether there are no better algorithms? Or whether your data was the right one?

Welcome to the club! Both of us (authors) were at those stages looking for information that tells the stories behind the theoretical textbooks about machine learning. It turned out that much of that information was "black art" not usually taught in standard text books. So in a sense, we wrote this book to our younger selves. A book that not only gives a quick introduction into machine learning, but also teaches lessons we learned along the way. We hope that it will also give you a smoother entry to one of the most exciting fields in Computer Science.

Machine learning and Python – a dream team

The goal of machine learning is to teach machines (software) to carry out tasks by providing them a couple of examples (how to do or not do the task). Let's assume that each morning when you turn on your computer, you do the same task of moving e-mails around so that only e-mails belonging to the same topic end up in the same folder. After some time, you might feel bored and think of automating this chore. One way would be to start analyzing your brain and write down all rules your brain processes while you are shuffling your e-mails. However, this will be quite cumbersome and always imperfect. While you will miss some rules, you will over-specify others. A better and more future-proof way would be to automate this process by choosing a set of e-mail meta info and body/folder name pairs and let an algorithm come up with the best rule set. The pairs would be your training data, and the resulting rule set (also called model) could then be applied to future e-mails that we have not yet seen. This is machine learning in its simplest form.

Of course, machine learning (often also referred to as Data Mining or Predictive Analysis) is not a brand new field in itself. Quite the contrary, its success over the recent years can be attributed to the pragmatic way of using rock-solid techniques and insights from other successful fields like statistics. There the purpose is for us humans to get insights into the data, for example, by learning more about the underlying patterns and relationships. As you read more and more about successful applications of machine learning (you have checked out www.kaggle.com already, haven't you?), you will see that applied statistics is a common field among machine learning experts.

As you will see later, the process of coming up with a decent ML approach is never a waterfall-like process. Instead, you will see yourself going back and forth in your analysis, trying out different versions of your input data on diverse sets of ML algorithms. It is this explorative nature that lends itself perfectly to Python. Being an interpreted high-level programming language, it seems that Python has been designed exactly for this process of trying out different things. What is more, it does this even fast. Sure, it is slower than C or similar statically typed programming languages. Nevertheless, with the myriad of easy-to-use libraries that are often written in C, you don't have to sacrifice speed for agility.

What the book will teach you (and what it will not)

This book will give you a broad overview of what types of learning algorithms are currently most used in the diverse fields of machine learning, and where to watch out when applying them. From our own experience, however, we know that doing the "cool" stuff, that is, using and tweaking machine learning algorithms such as support vector machines, nearest neighbor search, or ensembles thereof, will only consume a tiny fraction of the overall time of a good machine learning expert. Looking at the following typical workflow, we see that most of the time will be spent in rather mundane tasks:

- Reading in the data and cleaning it
- Exploring and understanding the input data
- Analyzing how best to present the data to the learning algorithm
- Choosing the right model and learning algorithm
- Measuring the performance correctly

When talking about exploring and understanding the input data, we will need a bit of statistics and basic math. However, while doing that, you will see that those topics that seemed to be so dry in your math class can actually be really exciting when you use them to look at interesting data.

The journey starts when you read in the data. When you have to answer questions such as how to handle invalid or missing values, you will see that this is more an art than a precise science. And a very rewarding one, as doing this part right will open your data to more machine learning algorithms and thus increase the likelihood of success.

With the data being ready in your program's data structures, you will want to get a real feeling of what animal you are working with. Do you have enough data to answer your questions? If not, you might want to think about additional ways to get more of it. Do you even have too much data? Then you probably want to think about how best to extract a sample of it.

Often you will not feed the data directly into your machine learning algorithm. Instead you will find that you can refine parts of the data before training. Many times the machine learning algorithm will reward you with increased performance. You will even find that a simple algorithm with refined data generally outperforms a very sophisticated algorithm with raw data. This part of the machine learning workflow is called **feature engineering**, and is most of the time a very exciting and rewarding challenge. You will immediately see the results of being creative and intelligent.

Choosing the right learning algorithm, then, is not simply a shootout of the three or four that are in your toolbox (there will be more you will see). It is more a thoughtful process of weighing different performance and functional requirements. Do you need a fast result and are willing to sacrifice quality? Or would you rather spend more time to get the best possible result? Do you have a clear idea of the future data or should you be a bit more conservative on that side?

Finally, measuring the performance is the part where most mistakes are waiting for the aspiring machine learner. There are easy ones, such as testing your approach with the same data on which you have trained. But there are more difficult ones, when you have imbalanced training data. Again, data is the part that determines whether your undertaking will fail or succeed.

We see that only the fourth point is dealing with the fancy algorithms. Nevertheless, we hope that this book will convince you that the other four tasks are not simply chores, but can be equally exciting. Our hope is that by the end of the book, you will have truly fallen in love with data instead of learning algorithms.

To that end, we will not overwhelm you with the theoretical aspects of the diverse ML algorithms, as there are already excellent books in that area (you will find pointers in the Appendix). Instead, we will try to provide an intuition of the underlying approaches in the individual chapters—just enough for you to get the idea and be able to undertake your first steps. Hence, this book is by no means *the definitive guide* to machine learning. It is more of a starter kit. We hope that it ignites your curiosity enough to keep you eager in trying to learn more and more about this interesting field.

In the rest of this chapter, we will set up and get to know the basic Python libraries NumPy and SciPy and then train our first machine learning using scikit-learn. During that endeavor, we will introduce basic ML concepts that will be used throughout the book. The rest of the chapters will then go into more detail through the five steps described earlier, highlighting different aspects of machine learning in Python using diverse application scenarios.

What to do when you are stuck

We try to convey every idea necessary to reproduce the steps throughout this book. Nevertheless, there will be situations where you are stuck. The reasons might range from simple typos over odd combinations of package versions to problems in understanding.

In this situation, there are many different ways to get help. Most likely, your problem will already be raised and solved in the following excellent Q&A sites:

`http://metaoptimize.com/qa`: This Q&A site is laser-focused on machine learning topics. For almost every question, it contains above average answers from machine learning experts. Even if you don't have any questions, it is a good habit to check it out every now and then and read through some of the answers.

`http://stats.stackexchange.com`: This Q&A site is named Cross Validated, similar to MetaOptimize, but is focused more on statistical problems.

`http://stackoverflow.com`: This Q&A site is much like the previous ones, but with broader focus on general programming topics. It contains, for example, more questions on some of the packages that we will use in this book, such as SciPy or matplotlib.

`#machinelearning` on `https://freenode.net/`: This is the IRC channel focused on machine learning topics. It is a small but very active and helpful community of machine learning experts.

`http://www.TwoToReal.com`: This is the instant Q&A site written by the authors to support you in topics that don't fit in any of the preceding buckets. If you post your question, one of the authors will get an instant message if he is online and be drawn in a chat with you.

As stated in the beginning, this book tries to help you get started quickly on your machine learning journey. Therefore, we highly encourage you to build up your own list of machine learning related blogs and check them out regularly. This is the best way to get to know what works and what doesn't.

The only blog we want to highlight right here (more in the Appendix) is `http://blog.kaggle.com`, the blog of the Kaggle company, which is carrying out machine learning competitions. Typically, they encourage the winners of the competitions to write down how they approached the competition, what strategies did not work, and how they arrived at the winning strategy. Even if you don't read anything else, this is a must.

Getting started

Assuming that you have Python already installed (everything at least as recent as 2.7 should be fine), we need to install NumPy and SciPy for numerical operations, as well as matplotlib for visualization.

Introduction to NumPy, SciPy, and matplotlib

Before we can talk about concrete machine learning algorithms, we have to talk about how best to store the data we will chew through. This is important as the most advanced learning algorithm will not be of any help to us if it will never finish. This may be simply because accessing the data is too slow. Or maybe its representation forces the operating system to swap all day. Add to this that Python is an interpreted language (a highly optimized one, though) that is slow for many numerically heavy algorithms compared to C or FORTRAN. So we might ask why on earth so many scientists and companies are betting their fortune on Python even in highly computation-intensive areas?

The answer is that, in Python, it is very easy to off-load number crunching tasks to the lower layer in the form of C or FORTRAN extensions. And that is exactly what NumPy and SciPy do (http://scipy.org/Download). In this tandem, NumPy provides the support of highly optimized multidimensional arrays, which are the basic data structure of most state-of-the-art algorithms. SciPy uses those arrays to provide a set of fast numerical recipes. Finally, matplotlib (http://matplotlib.org/) is probably the most convenient and feature-rich library to plot high-quality graphs using Python.

Installing Python

Luckily, for all major operating systems, that is, Windows, Mac, and Linux, there are targeted installers for NumPy, SciPy, and matplotlib. If you are unsure about the installation process, you might want to install Anaconda Python distribution (which you can access at https://store.continuum.io/cshop/anaconda/), which is driven by Travis Oliphant, a founding contributor of SciPy. What sets Anaconda apart from other distributions such as Enthought Canopy (which you can download from https://www.enthought.com/downloads/) or Python(x,y) (accessible at http://code.google.com/p/pythonxy/wiki/Downloads), is that Anaconda is already fully Python 3 compatible — the Python version we will be using throughout the book.

Chewing data efficiently with NumPy and intelligently with SciPy

Let's walk quickly through some basic NumPy examples and then take a look at what SciPy provides on top of it. On the way, we will get our feet wet with plotting using the marvelous Matplotlib package.

For an in-depth explanation, you might want to take a look at some of the more interesting examples of what NumPy has to offer at `http://www.scipy.org/Tentative_NumPy_Tutorial`.

You will also find the *NumPy Beginner's Guide - Second Edition*, *Ivan Idris*, by Packt Publishing, to be very valuable. Additional tutorial style guides can be found at `http://scipy-lectures.github.com`, and the official SciPy tutorial at `http://docs.scipy.org/doc/scipy/reference/tutorial`.

 In this book, we will use NumPy in version 1.8.1 and SciPy in version 0.14.0.

Learning NumPy

So let's import NumPy and play a bit with it. For that, we need to start the Python interactive shell:

```
>>> import numpy
>>> numpy.version.full_version
1.8.1
```

As we do not want to pollute our namespace, we certainly should not use the following code:

```
>>> from numpy import *
```

Because, for instance, `numpy.array` will potentially shadow the array package that is included in standard Python. Instead, we will use the following convenient shortcut:

```
>>> import numpy as np
>>> a = np.array([0,1,2,3,4,5])
>>> a
array([0, 1, 2, 3, 4, 5])
>>> a.ndim
1
>>> a.shape
(6,)
```

So, we just created an array like we would create a list in Python. However, the NumPy arrays have additional information about the shape. In this case, it is a one-dimensional array of six elements. No surprise so far.

We can now transform this array to a two-dimensional matrix:

```
>>> b = a.reshape((3,2))
>>> b
array([[0, 1],
       [2, 3],
       [4, 5]])
>>> b.ndim
2
>>> b.shape
(3, 2)
```

The funny thing starts when we realize just how much the NumPy package is optimized. For example, doing this avoids copies wherever possible:

```
>>> b[1][0] = 77
>>> b
array([[ 0,  1],
       [77,  3],
       [ 4,  5]])
>>> a
array([ 0,  1, 77,  3,  4,  5])
```

In this case, we have modified value 2 to 77 in b, and immediately see the same change reflected in a as well. Keep in mind that whenever you need a true copy, you can always perform:

```
>>> c = a.reshape((3,2)).copy()
>>> c
array([[ 0,  1],
       [77,  3],
       [ 4,  5]])
>>> c[0][0] = -99
>>> a
array([ 0,  1, 77,  3,  4,  5])
>>> c
array([[-99,   1],
       [ 77,   3],
       [  4,   5]])
```

Note that here, c and a are totally independent copies.

Another big advantage of NumPy arrays is that the operations are propagated to the individual elements. For example, multiplying a NumPy array will result in an array of the same size with all of its elements being multiplied:

```
>>> d = np.array([1,2,3,4,5])
>>> d*2
array([ 2,  4,  6,  8, 10])
```

Similarly, for other operations:

```
>>> d**2
array([ 1,  4,  9, 16, 25])
```

Contrast that to ordinary Python lists:

```
>>> [1,2,3,4,5]*2
[1, 2, 3, 4, 5, 1, 2, 3, 4, 5]
>>> [1,2,3,4,5]**2
Traceback (most recent call last):
  File "<stdin>", line 1, in <module>
TypeError: unsupported operand type(s) for ** or pow(): 'list' and 'int'
```

Of course by using NumPy arrays, we sacrifice the agility Python lists offer. Simple operations such as adding or removing are a bit complex for NumPy arrays. Luckily, we have both at our hands and we will use the right one for the task at hand.

Indexing

Part of the power of NumPy comes from the versatile ways in which its arrays can be accessed.

In addition to normal list indexing, it allows you to use arrays themselves as indices by performing:

```
>>> a[np.array([2,3,4])]
array([77,  3,  4])
```

Together with the fact that conditions are also propagated to individual elements, we gain a very convenient way to access our data:

```
>>> a>4
array([False, False,  True, False, False,  True], dtype=bool)
>>> a[a>4]
array([77,  5])
```

By performing the following command, this can be used to trim outliers:

```
>>> a[a>4] = 4
>>> a
array([0, 1, 4, 3, 4, 4])
```

As this is a frequent use case, there is the special clip function for it, clipping the values at both ends of an interval with one function call:

```
>>> a.clip(0,4)
array([0, 1, 4, 3, 4, 4])
```

Handling nonexisting values

The power of NumPy's indexing capabilities comes in handy when preprocessing data that we have just read in from a text file. Most likely, that will contain invalid values that we will mark as not being a real number using numpy.NAN:

```
>>> c = np.array([1, 2, np.NAN, 3, 4]) # let's pretend we have read this
from a text file
>>> c
array([ 1.,   2.,   nan,   3.,   4.])
>>> np.isnan(c)
array([False, False,  True, False, False], dtype=bool)
>>> c[~np.isnan(c)]
array([ 1.,   2.,   3.,   4.])
>>> np.mean(c[~np.isnan(c)])
2.5
```

Comparing the runtime

Let's compare the runtime behavior of NumPy compared with normal Python lists. In the following code, we will calculate the sum of all squared numbers from 1 to 1000 and see how much time it will take. We perform it 10,000 times and report the total time so that our measurement is accurate enough.

```
import timeit
normal_py_sec = timeit.timeit('sum(x*x for x in range(1000))',
                              number=10000)
naive_np_sec = timeit.timeit(
                'sum(na*na)',
                setup="import numpy as np; na=np.arange(1000)",
                number=10000)
good_np_sec = timeit.timeit(
                'na.dot(na)',
                setup="import numpy as np; na=np.arange(1000)",
                number=10000)

print("Normal Python: %f sec" % normal_py_sec)
print("Naive NumPy: %f sec" % naive_np_sec)
print("Good NumPy: %f sec" % good_np_sec)

Normal Python: 1.050749 sec
Naive NumPy: 3.962259 sec
Good NumPy: 0.040481 sec
```

We make two interesting observations. Firstly, by just using NumPy as data storage (Naive NumPy) takes 3.5 times longer, which is surprising since we believe it must be much faster as it is written as a C extension. One reason for this is that the access of individual elements from Python itself is rather costly. Only when we are able to apply algorithms inside the optimized extension code is when we get speed improvements. The other observation is quite a tremendous one: using the dot() function of NumPy, which does exactly the same, allows us to be more than 25 times faster. In summary, in every algorithm we are about to implement, we should always look how we can move loops over individual elements from Python to some of the highly optimized NumPy or SciPy extension functions.

However, the speed comes at a price. Using NumPy arrays, we no longer have the incredible flexibility of Python lists, which can hold basically anything. NumPy arrays always have only one data type.

```
>>> a = np.array([1,2,3])
>>> a.dtype
dtype('int64')
```

If we try to use elements of different types, such as the ones shown in the following code, NumPy will do its best to coerce them to be the most reasonable common data type:

```
>>> np.array([1, "stringy"])
array(['1', 'stringy'], dtype='<U7')
>>> np.array([1, "stringy", set([1,2,3])])
array([1, stringy, {1, 2, 3}], dtype=object)
```

Learning SciPy

On top of the efficient data structures of NumPy, SciPy offers a magnitude of algorithms working on those arrays. Whatever numerical heavy algorithm you take from current books on numerical recipes, most likely you will find support for them in SciPy in one way or the other. Whether it is matrix manipulation, linear algebra, optimization, clustering, spatial operations, or even fast Fourier transformation, the toolbox is readily filled. Therefore, it is a good habit to always inspect the `scipy` module before you start implementing a numerical algorithm.

For convenience, the complete namespace of NumPy is also accessible via SciPy. So, from now on, we will use NumPy's machinery via the SciPy namespace. You can check this easily comparing the function references of any base function, such as:

```
>>> import scipy, numpy
>>> scipy.version.full_version
0.14.0
>>> scipy.dot is numpy.dot
True
```

The diverse algorithms are grouped into the following toolboxes:

SciPy packages	Functionalities
cluster	• Hierarchical clustering (cluster.hierarchy)
	• Vector quantization / k-means (cluster.vq)

SciPy packages	Functionalities
constants	• Physical and mathematical constants • Conversion methods
fftpack	Discrete Fourier transform algorithms
integrate	Integration routines
interpolate	Interpolation (linear, cubic, and so on)
io	Data input and output
linalg	Linear algebra routines using the optimized BLAS and LAPACK libraries
ndimage	n-dimensional image package
odr	Orthogonal distance regression
optimize	Optimization (finding minima and roots)
signal	Signal processing
sparse	Sparse matrices
spatial	Spatial data structures and algorithms
special	Special mathematical functions such as Bessel or Jacobian
stats	Statistics toolkit

The toolboxes most interesting to our endeavor are `scipy.stats`, `scipy.interpolate`, `scipy.cluster`, and `scipy.signal`. For the sake of brevity, we will briefly explore some features of the stats package and leave the others to be explained when they show up in the individual chapters.

Our first (tiny) application of machine learning

Let's get our hands dirty and take a look at our hypothetical web start-up, MLaaS, which sells the service of providing machine learning algorithms via HTTP. With increasing success of our company, the demand for better infrastructure increases to serve all incoming web requests successfully. We don't want to allocate too many resources as that would be too costly. On the other side, we will lose money, if we have not reserved enough resources to serve all incoming requests. Now, the question is, when will we hit the limit of our current infrastructure, which we estimated to be at 100,000 requests per hour. We would like to know in advance when we have to request additional servers in the cloud to serve all the incoming requests successfully without paying for unused ones.

Reading in the data

We have collected the web stats for the last month and aggregated them in ch01/ data/web_traffic.tsv (.tsv because it contains tab-separated values). They are stored as the number of hits per hour. Each line contains the hour consecutively and the number of web hits in that hour.

The first few lines look like the following:

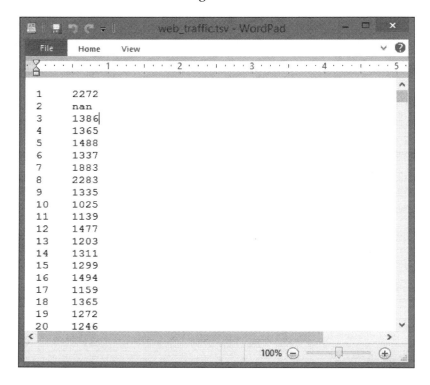

Using SciPy's genfromtxt(), we can easily read in the data using the following code:

```
>>> import scipy as sp
>>> data = sp.genfromtxt("web_traffic.tsv", delimiter="\t")
```

We have to specify tab as the delimiter so that the columns are correctly determined.

A quick check shows that we have correctly read in the data:

```
>>> print(data[:10])
[[   1.00000000e+00    2.27200000e+03]
 [   2.00000000e+00                nan]
 [   3.00000000e+00    1.38600000e+03]
 [   4.00000000e+00    1.36500000e+03]
 [   5.00000000e+00    1.48800000e+03]
 [   6.00000000e+00    1.33700000e+03]
 [   7.00000000e+00    1.88300000e+03]
 [   8.00000000e+00    2.28300000e+03]
 [   9.00000000e+00    1.33500000e+03]
 [   1.00000000e+01    1.02500000e+03]]
>>> print(data.shape)
(743, 2)
```

As you can see, we have 743 data points with two dimensions.

Preprocessing and cleaning the data

It is more convenient for SciPy to separate the dimensions into two vectors, each of size 743. The first vector, x, will contain the hours, and the other, y, will contain the Web hits in that particular hour. This splitting is done using the special index notation of SciPy, by which we can choose the columns individually:

```
x = data[:,0]
y = data[:,1]
```

There are many more ways in which data can be selected from a SciPy array. Check out http://www.scipy.org/Tentative_NumPy_Tutorial for more details on indexing, slicing, and iterating.

One caveat is still that we have some values in y that contain invalid values, nan. The question is what we can do with them. Let's check how many hours contain invalid data, by running the following code:

```
>>> sp.sum(sp.isnan(y))
```

8

As you can see, we are missing only 8 out of 743 entries, so we can afford to remove them. Remember that we can index a SciPy array with another array. Sp.isnan(y) returns an array of Booleans indicating whether an entry is a number or not. Using ~, we logically negate that array so that we choose only those elements from x and y where y contains valid numbers:

```
>>> x = x[~sp.isnan(y)]
>>> y = y[~sp.isnan(y)]
```

To get the first impression of our data, let's plot the data in a scatter plot using matplotlib. matplotlib contains the pyplot package, which tries to mimic MATLAB's interface, which is a very convenient and easy to use one as you can see in the following code:

```
>>> import matplotlib.pyplot as plt
>>> # plot the (x,y) points with dots of size 10
>>> plt.scatter(x, y, s=10)
>>> plt.title("Web traffic over the last month")
>>> plt.xlabel("Time")
>>> plt.ylabel("Hits/hour")
>>> plt.xticks([w*7*24 for w in range(10)],
                ['week %i' % w for w in range(10)])
>>> plt.autoscale(tight=True)
>>> # draw a slightly opaque, dashed grid
>>> plt.grid(True, linestyle='-', color='0.75')
>>> plt.show()
```

 You can find more tutorials on plotting at http://matplotlib.org/users/pyplot_tutorial.html.

In the resulting chart, we can see that while in the first weeks the traffic stayed more or less the same, the last week shows a steep increase:

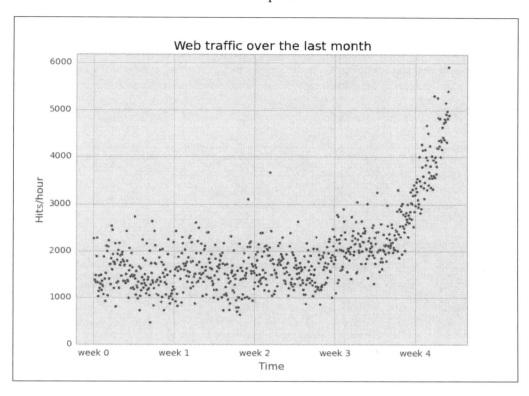

Choosing the right model and learning algorithm

Now that we have a first impression of the data, we return to the initial question: How long will our server handle the incoming web traffic? To answer this we have to do the following:

1. Find the real model behind the noisy data points.

2. Following this, use the model to extrapolate into the future to find the point in time where our infrastructure has to be extended.

Before building our first model...

When we talk about models, you can think of them as simplified theoretical approximations of complex reality. As such there is always some inferiority involved, also called the approximation error. This error will guide us in choosing the right model among the myriad of choices we have. And this error will be calculated as the squared distance of the model's prediction to the real data; for example, for a learned model function f, the error is calculated as follows:

```
def error(f, x, y):
    return sp.sum((f(x)-y)**2)
```

The vectors x and y contain the web stats data that we have extracted earlier. It is the beauty of SciPy's vectorized functions that we exploit here with f(x). The trained model is assumed to take a vector and return the results again as a vector of the same size so that we can use it to calculate the difference to y.

Starting with a simple straight line

Let's assume for a second that the underlying model is a straight line. Then the challenge is how to best put that line into the chart so that it results in the smallest approximation error. SciPy's polyfit() function does exactly that. Given data x and y and the desired order of the polynomial (a straight line has order 1), it finds the model function that minimizes the error function defined earlier:

```
fp1, residuals, rank, sv, rcond = sp.polyfit(x, y, 1, full=True)
```

The polyfit() function returns the parameters of the fitted model function, fp1. And by setting full=True, we also get additional background information on the fitting process. Of this, only residuals are of interest, which is exactly the error of the approximation:

```
>>> print("Model parameters: %s" % fp1)
Model parameters: [   2.59619213   989.02487106]
>>> print(residuals)
[   3.17389767e+08]
```

This means the best straight line fit is the following function

```
f(x) = 2.59619213 * x + 989.02487106.
```

We then use poly1d() to create a model function from the model parameters:

```
>>> f1 = sp.poly1d(fp1)
>>> print(error(f1, x, y))
317389767.34
```

We have used `full=True` to retrieve more details on the fitting process. Normally, we would not need it, in which case only the model parameters would be returned.

We can now use `f1()` to plot our first trained model. In addition to the preceding plotting instructions, we simply add the following code:

```
fx = sp.linspace(0,x[-1], 1000) # generate X-values for plotting
plt.plot(fx, f1(fx), linewidth=4)
plt.legend(["d=%i" % f1.order], loc="upper left")
```

This will produce the following plot:

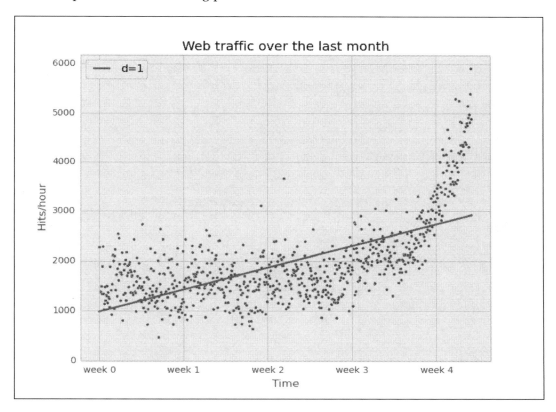

It seems like the first 4 weeks are not that far off, although we clearly see that there is something wrong with our initial assumption that the underlying model is a straight line. And then, how good or how bad actually is the error of 317,389,767.34?

The absolute value of the error is seldom of use in isolation. However, when comparing two competing models, we can use their errors to judge which one of them is better. Although our first model clearly is not the one we would use, it serves a very important purpose in the workflow. We will use it as our baseline until we find a better one. Whatever model we come up with in the future, we will compare it against the current baseline.

Towards some advanced stuff

Let's now fit a more complex model, a polynomial of degree 2, to see whether it better understands our data:

```
>>> f2p = sp.polyfit(x, y, 2)
>>> print(f2p)
array([  1.05322215e-02,  -5.26545650e+00,   1.97476082e+03])
>>> f2 = sp.poly1d(f2p)
>>> print(error(f2, x, y))
179983507.878
```

You will get the following plot:

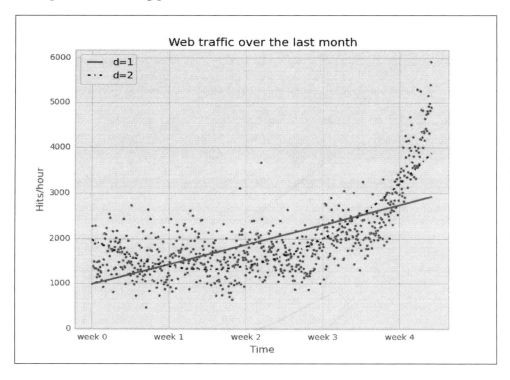

The error is 179,983,507.878, which is almost half the error of the straight line model. This is good but unfortunately this comes with a price: We now have a more complex function, meaning that we have one parameter more to tune inside `polyfit()`. The fitted polynomial is as follows:

```
f(x) = 0.0105322215 * x**2  - 5.26545650 * x + 1974.76082
```

So, if more complexity gives better results, why not increase the complexity even more? Let's try it for degrees 3, 10, and 100.

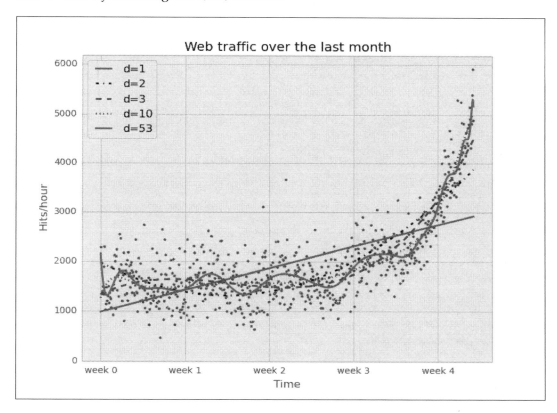

Interestingly, we do not see `d=53` for the polynomial that had been fitted with 100 degrees. Instead, we see lots of warnings on the console:

`RankWarning: Polyfit may be poorly conditioned`

This means because of numerical errors, polyfit cannot determine a good fit with 100 degrees. Instead, it figured that 53 must be good enough.

It seems like the curves capture and better the fitted data the more complex they get. And also, the errors seem to tell the same story:

```
Error d=1: 317,389,767.339778
Error d=2: 179,983,507.878179
Error d=3: 139,350,144.031725
Error d=10: 121,942,326.363461
Error d=53: 109,318,004.475556
```

However, taking a closer look at the fitted curves, we start to wonder whether they also capture the true process that generated that data. Framed differently, do our models correctly represent the underlying mass behavior of customers visiting our website? Looking at the polynomial of degree 10 and 53, we see wildly oscillating behavior. It seems that the models are fitted too much to the data. So much that it is now capturing not only the underlying process but also the noise. This is called **overfitting**.

At this point, we have the following choices:

- Choosing one of the fitted polynomial models.
- Switching to another more complex model class. Splines?
- Thinking differently about the data and start again.

Out of the five fitted models, the first order model clearly is too simple, and the models of order 10 and 53 are clearly overfitting. Only the second and third order models seem to somehow match the data. However, if we extrapolate them at both borders, we see them going berserk.

Switching to a more complex class seems also not to be the right way to go. What arguments would back which class? At this point, we realize that we probably have not fully understood our data.

Stepping back to go forward – another look at our data

So, we step back and take another look at the data. It seems that there is an inflection point between weeks 3 and 4. So let's separate the data and train two lines using week 3.5 as a separation point:

```
inflection = 3.5*7*24 # calculate the inflection point in hours
xa = x[:inflection] # data before the inflection point
ya = y[:inflection]
xb = x[inflection:] # data after
```

```
yb = y[inflection:]

fa = sp.poly1d(sp.polyfit(xa, ya, 1))
fb = sp.poly1d(sp.polyfit(xb, yb, 1))

fa_error = error(fa, xa, ya)
fb_error = error(fb, xb, yb)
print("Error inflection=%f" % (fa_error + fb_error))
Error inflection=132950348.197616
```

From the first line, we train with the data up to week 3, and in the second line we train with the remaining data.

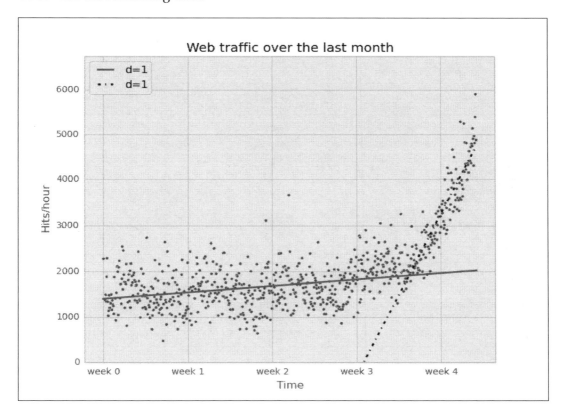

Clearly, the combination of these two lines seems to be a much better fit to the data than anything we have modeled before. But still, the combined error is higher than the higher order polynomials. Can we trust the error at the end?

Asked differently, why do we trust the straight line fitted only at the last week of our data more than any of the more complex models? It is because we assume that it will capture future data better. If we plot the models into the future, we see how right we are (**d=1** is again our initial straight line).

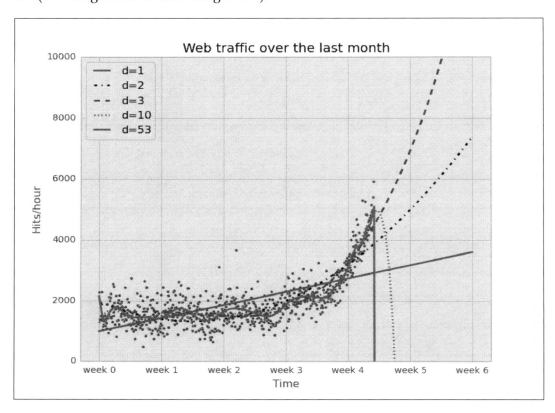

The models of degree 10 and 53 don't seem to expect a bright future of our start-up. They tried so hard to model the given data correctly that they are clearly useless to extrapolate beyond. This is called overfitting. On the other hand, the lower degree models seem not to be capable of capturing the data good enough. This is called **underfitting**.

So let's play fair to models of degree 2 and above and try out how they behave if we fit them only to the data of the last week. After all, we believe that the last week says more about the future than the data prior to it. The result can be seen in the following psychedelic chart, which further shows how badly the problem of overfitting is.

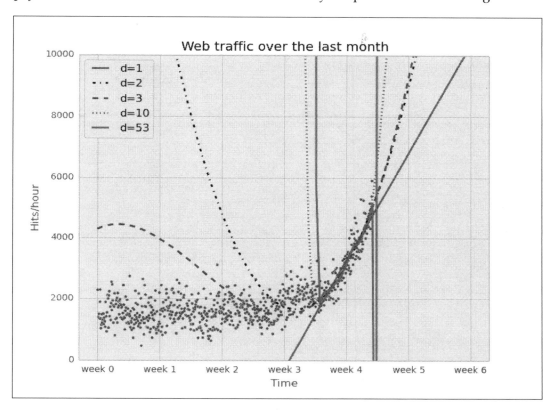

Still, judging from the errors of the models when trained only on the data from week 3.5 and later, we still should choose the most complex one (note that we also calculate the error only on the time after the inflection point):

```
Error d=1:    22,143,941.107618
Error d=2:    19,768,846.989176
Error d=3:    19,766,452.361027
Error d=10:   18,949,339.348539
Error d=53:   18,300,702.038119
```

Training and testing

If we only had some data from the future that we could use to measure our models against, then we should be able to judge our model choice only on the resulting approximation error.

Although we cannot look into the future, we can and should simulate a similar effect by holding out a part of our data. Let's remove, for instance, a certain percentage of the data and train on the remaining one. Then we used the held-out data to calculate the error. As the model has been trained not knowing the held-out data, we should get a more realistic picture of how the model will behave in the future.

The test errors for the models trained only on the time after inflection point now show a completely different picture:

```
Error d=1:  6397694.386394

Error d=2:  6010775.401243

Error d=3:  6047678.658525

Error d=10: 7037551.009519

Error d=53: 7052400.001761
```

Have a look at the following plot:

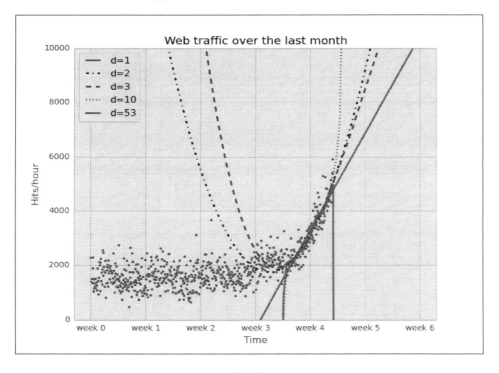

It seems that we finally have a clear winner: The model with degree 2 has the lowest test error, which is the error when measured using data that the model did not see during training. And this gives us hope that we won't get bad surprises when future data arrives.

Answering our initial question

Finally we have arrived at a model which we think represents the underlying process best; it is now a simple task of finding out when our infrastructure will reach 100,000 requests per hour. We have to calculate when our model function reaches the value 100,000.

Having a polynomial of degree 2, we could simply compute the inverse of the function and calculate its value at 100,000. Of course, we would like to have an approach that is applicable to any model function easily.

This can be done by subtracting 100,000 from the polynomial, which results in another polynomial, and finding its root. SciPy's `optimize` module has the function `fsolve` that achieves this, when providing an initial starting position with parameter `x0`. As every entry in our input data file corresponds to one hour, and we have 743 of them, we set the starting position to some value after that. Let `fbt2` be the winning polynomial of degree 2.

```
>>> fbt2 = sp.poly1d(sp.polyfit(xb[train], yb[train], 2))
>>> print("fbt2(x)= \n%s" % fbt2)
fbt2(x)=
        2
0.086 x - 94.02 x + 2.744e+04
>>> print("fbt2(x)-100,000= \n%s" % (fbt2-100000))
fbt2(x)-100,000=
        2
0.086 x - 94.02 x - 7.256e+04
>>> from scipy.optimize import fsolve
>>> reached_max = fsolve(fbt2-100000, x0=800)/(7*24)
>>> print("100,000 hits/hour expected at week %f" % reached_max[0])
```

It is expected to have 100,000 hits/hour at week 9.616071, so our model tells us that, given the current user behavior and traction of our start-up, it will take another month until we have reached our capacity threshold.

Of course, there is a certain uncertainty involved with our prediction. To get a real picture of it, one could draw in more sophisticated statistics to find out about the variance we have to expect when looking farther and farther into the future.

And then there are the user and underlying user behavior dynamics that we cannot model accurately. However, at this point, we are fine with the current predictions. After all, we can prepare all time-consuming actions now. If we then monitor our web traffic closely, we will see in time when we have to allocate new resources.

Summary

Congratulations! You just learned two important things, of which the most important one is that as a typical machine learning operator, you will spend most of your time in understanding and refining the data—exactly what we just did in our first tiny machine learning example. And we hope that this example helped you to start switching your mental focus from algorithms to data. Then you learned how important it is to have the correct experiment setup and that it is vital to not mix up training and testing.

Admittedly, the use of polynomial fitting is not the coolest thing in the machine learning world. We have chosen it to not distract you by the coolness of some shiny algorithm when we conveyed the two most important messages we just summarized earlier.

So, let's move to the next chapter in which we will dive deep into scikit-learn, the marvelous machine learning toolkit, give an overview of different types of learning, and show you the beauty of feature engineering.

2
Classifying with Real-world Examples

The topic of this chapter is **classification**. You have probably already used this form of machine learning as a consumer, even if you were not aware of it. If you have any modern e-mail system, it will likely have the ability to automatically detect spam. That is, the system will analyze all incoming e-mails and mark them as either spam or not-spam. Often, you, the end user, will be able to manually tag e-mails as spam or not, in order to improve its spam detection ability. This is a form of machine learning where the system is taking examples of two types of messages: spam and ham (the typical term for "non spam e-mails") and using these examples to automatically classify incoming e-mails.

The general method of classification is to use a set of examples of each class to learn rules that can be applied to new examples. This is one of the most important machine learning modes and is the topic of this chapter.

Working with text such as e-mails requires a specific set of techniques and skills, and we discuss those in the next chapter. For the moment, we will work with a smaller, easier-to-handle dataset. The example question for this chapter is, "Can a machine distinguish between flower species based on images?" We will use two datasets where measurements of flower morphology are recorded along with the species for several specimens.

We will explore these small datasets using a few simple algorithms. At first, we will write classification code ourselves in order to understand the concepts, but we will quickly switch to using scikit-learn whenever possible. The goal is to first understand the basic principles of classification and then progress to using a state-of-the-art implementation.

The Iris dataset

The Iris dataset is a classic dataset from the 1930s; it is one of the first modern examples of statistical classification.

The dataset is a collection of morphological measurements of several Iris flowers. These measurements will enable us to distinguish multiple species of the flowers. Today, species are identified by their DNA fingerprints, but in the 1930s, DNA's role in genetics had not yet been discovered.

The following four attributes of each plant were measured:

- sepal length
- sepal width
- petal length
- petal width

In general, we will call the individual numeric measurements we use to describe our data **features**. These features can be directly measured or computed from intermediate data.

This dataset has four features. Additionally, for each plant, the species was recorded. The problem we want to solve is, "Given these examples, if we see a new flower out in the field, could we make a good prediction about its species from its measurements?"

This is the **supervised learning** or **classification** problem: given labeled examples, can we design a rule to be later applied to other examples? A more familiar example to modern readers who are not botanists is spam filtering, where the user can mark e-mails as spam, and systems use these as well as the non-spam e-mails to determine whether a new, incoming message is spam or not.

Later in the book, we will look at problems dealing with text (starting in the next chapter). For the moment, the Iris dataset serves our purposes well. It is small (150 examples, four features each) and can be easily visualized and manipulated.

Visualization is a good first step

Datasets, later in the book, will grow to thousands of features. With only four in our starting example, we can easily plot all two-dimensional projections on a single page. We will build intuitions on this small example, which can then be extended to large datasets with many more features. As we saw in the previous chapter, visualizations are excellent at the initial exploratory phase of the analysis as they allow you to learn the general features of your problem as well as catch problems that occurred with data collection early.

Each subplot in the following plot shows all points projected into two of the dimensions. The outlying group (triangles) are the Iris Setosa plants, while Iris Versicolor plants are in the center (circle) and Iris Virginica are plotted with *x* marks. We can see that there are two large groups: one is of Iris Setosa and another is a mixture of Iris Versicolor and Iris Virginica.

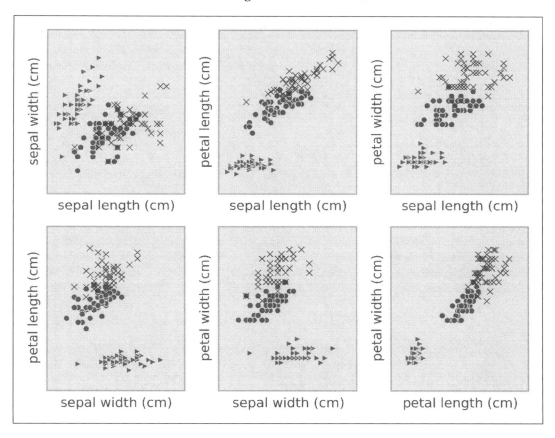

In the following code snippet, we present the code to load the data and generate the plot:

```
>>> from matplotlib import pyplot as plt
>>> import numpy as np

>>> # We load the data with load_iris from sklearn
>>> from sklearn.datasets import load_iris
```

```
>>> data = load_iris()

>>> # load_iris returns an object with several fields
>>> features = data.data
>>> feature_names = data.feature_names
>>> target = data.target
>>> target_names = data.target_names

>>> for t in range(3):
...     if t == 0:
...         c = 'r'
...         marker = '>'
...     elif t == 1:
...         c = 'g'
...         marker = 'o'
...     elif t == 2:
...         c = 'b'
...         marker = 'x'
...     plt.scatter(features[target == t,0],
...                 features[target == t,1],
...                 marker=marker,
...                 c=c)
```

Building our first classification model

If the goal is to separate the three types of flowers, we can immediately make a few suggestions just by looking at the data. For example, petal length seems to be able to separate Iris Setosa from the other two flower species on its own. We can write a little bit of code to discover where the cut-off is:

```
>>> # We use NumPy fancy indexing to get an array of strings:
>>> labels = target_names[target]

>>> # The petal length is the feature at position 2
>>> plength = features[:, 2]

>>> # Build an array of booleans:
```

```
>>> is_setosa = (labels == 'setosa')


>>> # This is the important step:
>>> max_setosa =plength[is_setosa].max()
>>> min_non_setosa = plength[~is_setosa].min()
>>> print('Maximum of setosa: {0}.'.format(max_setosa))
Maximum of setosa: 1.9.


>>> print('Minimum of others: {0}.'.format(min_non_setosa))
Minimum of others: 3.0.
```

Therefore, we can build a simple model: if the petal length is smaller than 2, then this is an Iris Setosa flower; otherwise it is either Iris Virginica or Iris Versicolor. This is our first model and it works very well in that it separates Iris Setosa flowers from the other two species without making any mistakes. In this case, we did not actually do any machine learning. Instead, we looked at the data ourselves, looking for a separation between the classes. Machine learning happens when we write code to look for this separation automatically.

The problem of recognizing Iris Setosa apart from the other two species was very easy. However, we cannot immediately see what the best threshold is for distinguishing Iris Virginica from Iris Versicolor. We can even see that we will never achieve perfect separation with these features. We could, however, look for the best possible separation, the separation that makes the fewest mistakes. For this, we will perform a little computation.

We first select only the non-Setosa features and labels:

```
>>> # ~ is the boolean negation operator
>>> features = features[~is_setosa]
>>> labels = labels[~is_setosa]
>>> # Build a new target variable, is_virginica
>>> is_virginica = (labels == 'virginica')
```

Here we are heavily using NumPy operations on arrays. The is_setosa array is a Boolean array and we use it to select a subset of the other two arrays, features and labels. Finally, we build a new boolean array, virginica, by using an equality comparison on labels.

Now, we run a loop over all possible features and thresholds to see which one results in better accuracy. Accuracy is simply the fraction of examples that the model classifies correctly.

```
>>> # Initialize best_acc to impossibly low value
>>> best_acc = -1.0
>>> for fi in range(features.shape[1]):
...    # We are going to test all possible thresholds
...    thresh = features[:,fi]
...    for t in thresh:
...       # Get the vector for feature `fi`
...       feature_i = features[:, fi]
...       # apply threshold `t`
...       pred = (feature_i > t)
...       acc = (pred == is_virginica).mean()
...       rev_acc = (pred == ~is_virginica).mean()
...       if rev_acc > acc:
...          reverse = True
...          acc = rev_acc
...       else:
...          reverse = False
...
...       if acc > best_acc:
...          best_acc = acc
...          best_fi = fi
...          best_t = t
...          best_reverse = reverse
```

We need to test two types of thresholds for each feature and value: we test a *greater than threshold* and the reverse comparison. This is why we need the rev_acc variable in the preceding code; it holds the accuracy of reversing the comparison.

The last few lines select the best model. First, we compare the predictions, pred, with the actual labels, is_virginica. The little trick of computing the mean of the comparisons gives us the fraction of correct results, the accuracy. At the end of the for loop, all the possible thresholds for all the possible features have been tested, and the variables best_fi, best_t, and best_reverse hold our model. This is all the information we need to be able to classify a new, unknown object, that is, to assign a class to it. The following code implements exactly this method:

```
def is_virginica_test(fi, t, reverse, example):
    "Apply threshold model to a new example"
    test = example[fi] > t
    if reverse:
        test = not test
    return test
```

What does this model look like? If we run the code on the whole data, the model that is identified as the best makes decisions by splitting on the petal width. One way to gain intuition about how this works is to visualize the **decision boundary**. That is, we can see which feature values will result in one decision versus the other and exactly where the boundary is. In the following screenshot, we see two regions: one is white and the other is shaded in grey. Any datapoint that falls on the white region will be classified as Iris Virginica, while any point that falls on the shaded side will be classified as Iris Versicolor.

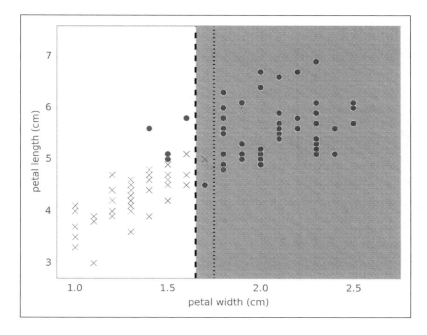

In a threshold model, the decision boundary will always be a line that is parallel to one of the axes. The plot in the preceding screenshot shows the decision boundary and the two regions where points are classified as either white or grey. It also shows (as a dashed line) an alternative threshold, which will achieve exactly the same accuracy. Our method chose the first threshold it saw, but that was an arbitrary choice.

Evaluation – holding out data and cross-validation

The model discussed in the previous section is a simple model; it achieves 94 percent accuracy of the whole data. However, this evaluation may be overly optimistic. We used the data to define what the threshold will be, and then we used the same data to evaluate the model. Of course, the model will perform better than anything else we tried on this dataset. The reasoning is circular.

What we really want to do is estimate the ability of the model to generalize to new instances. We should measure its performance in instances that the algorithm has not seen at training. Therefore, we are going to do a more rigorous evaluation and use held-out data. For this, we are going to break up the data into two groups: on one group, we'll train the model, and on the other, we'll test the one we held out of training. The full code, which is an adaptation of the code presented earlier, is available on the online support repository. Its output is as follows:

```
Training accuracy was 96.0%.
Testing accuracy was 90.0% (N = 50).
```

The result on the training data (which is a subset of the whole data) is apparently even better than before. However, what is important to note is that the result in the testing data is lower than that of the training error. While this may surprise an inexperienced machine learner, it is expected that testing accuracy will be lower than the training accuracy. To see why, look back at the plot that showed the decision boundary. Consider what would have happened if some of the examples close to the boundary were not there or that one of them between the two lines was missing. It is easy to imagine that the boundary will then move a little bit to the right or to the left so as to put them on the *wrong* side of the border.

> The accuracy on the training data, the **training accuracy**, is almost always an overly optimistic estimate of how well your algorithm is doing. We should always measure and report the **testing accuracy**, which is the accuracy on a collection of examples that were not used for training.

These concepts will become more and more important as the models become more complex. In this example, the difference between the accuracy measured on training data and on testing data is not very large. When using a complex model, it is possible to get 100 percent accuracy in training and do no better than random guessing on testing!

One possible problem with what we did previously, which was to hold out data from training, is that we only used half the data for training. Perhaps it would have been better to use more training data. On the other hand, if we then leave too little data for testing, the error estimation is performed on a very small number of examples. Ideally, we would like to use all of the data for training and all of the data for testing as well, which is impossible.

We can achieve a good approximation of this impossible ideal by a method called **cross-validation**. One simple form of cross-validation is *leave-one-out cross-validation*. We will take an example out of the training data, learn a model without this example, and then test whether the model classifies this example correctly. This process is then repeated for all the elements in the dataset.

The following code implements exactly this type of cross-validation:

```
>>> correct = 0.0
>>> for ei in range(len(features)):
        # select all but the one at position `ei`:
        training = np.ones(len(features), bool)
        training[ei] = False
        testing = ~training
        model = fit_model(features[training], is_virginica[training])
        predictions = predict(model, features[testing])
        correct += np.sum(predictions == is_virginica[testing])
>>> acc = correct/float(len(features))
>>> print('Accuracy: {0:.1%}'.format(acc))
Accuracy: 87.0%
```

At the end of this loop, we will have tested a series of models on all the examples and have obtained a final average result. When using cross-validation, there is no circularity problem because each example was tested on a model which was built without taking that datapoint into account. Therefore, the cross-validated estimate is a reliable estimate of how well the models would generalize to new data.

The major problem with leave-one-out cross-validation is that we are now forced to perform many times more work. In fact, you must learn a whole new model for each and every example and this cost will increase as our dataset grows.

We can get most of the benefits of leave-one-out at a fraction of the cost by using x-fold cross-validation, where *x* stands for a small number. For example, to perform five-fold cross-validation, we break up the data into five groups, so-called five folds.

Then you learn five models: each time you will leave one fold out of the training data. The resulting code will be similar to the code given earlier in this section, but we leave 20 percent of the data out instead of just one element. We test each of these models on the left-out fold and average the results.

Dataset	Fold 1	Fold 2	Fold 3	Fold 4	Fold 5
1	Test	Train	Train	Train	Train
2	Train	Test	Train	Train	Train
3	Train	Train	Test	Train	Train
4	Train	Train	Train	Test	Train
5	Train	Train	Train	Train	Test

The preceding figure illustrates this process for five blocks: the dataset is split into five pieces. For each fold, you hold out one of the blocks for testing and train on the other four. You can use any number of folds you wish. There is a trade-off between computational efficiency (the more folds, the more computation is necessary) and accurate results (the more folds, the closer you are to using the whole of the data for training). Five folds is often a good compromise. This corresponds to training with 80 percent of your data, which should already be close to what you will get from using all the data. If you have little data, you can even consider using 10 or 20 folds. In the extreme case, if you have as many folds as datapoints, you are simply performing leave-one-out cross-validation. On the other hand, if computation time is an issue and you have more data, 2 or 3 folds may be the more appropriate choice.

When generating the folds, you need to be careful to keep them balanced. For example, if all of the examples in one fold come from the same class, then the results will not be representative. We will not go into the details of how to do this, because the machine learning package scikit-learn will handle them for you.

We have now generated several models instead of just one. So, "What final model do we return and use for new data?" The simplest solution is now to train a single overall model on all your training data. The cross-validation loop gives you an estimate of how well this model should generalize.

 A cross-validation schedule allows you to use all your data to estimate whether your methods are doing well. At the end of the cross-validation loop, you can then use all your data to train a final model.

Although it was not properly recognized when machine learning was starting out as a field, nowadays, it is seen as a very bad sign to even discuss the training accuracy of a classification system. This is because the results can be very misleading and even just presenting them marks you as a newbie in machine learning. We always want to measure and compare either the error on a held-out dataset or the error estimated using a cross-validation scheme.

Building more complex classifiers

In the previous section, we used a very simple model: a threshold on a single feature. Are there other types of systems? Yes, of course! Many others. Throughout this book, you will see many other types of models and we're not even going to cover everything that is out there.

To think of the problem at a higher abstraction level, "What makes up a classification model?" We can break it up into three parts:

- **The structure of the model**: How exactly will a model make decisions? In this case, the decision depended solely on whether a given feature was above or below a certain threshold value. This is too simplistic for all but the simplest problems.

- **The search procedure**: How do we find the model we need to use? In our case, we tried every possible combination of feature and threshold. You can easily imagine that as models get more complex and datasets get larger, it rapidly becomes impossible to attempt all combinations and we are forced to use approximate solutions. In other cases, we need to use advanced optimization methods to find a good solution (fortunately, scikit-learn already implements these for you, so using them is easy even if the code behind them is very advanced).

- **The gain or loss function**: How do we decide which of the possibilities tested should be returned? Rarely do we find the perfect solution, the model that never makes any mistakes, so we need to decide which one to use. We used accuracy, but sometimes it will be better to optimize so that the model makes fewer errors of a specific kind. For example, in spam filtering, it may be worse to delete a good e-mail than to erroneously let a bad e-mail through. In that case, we may want to choose a model that is conservative in throwing out e-mails rather than the one that just makes the fewest mistakes overall. We can discuss these issues in terms of gain (which we want to maximize) or loss (which we want to minimize). They are equivalent, but sometimes one is more convenient than the other.

We can play around with these three aspects of classifiers and get different systems. A simple threshold is one of the simplest models available in machine learning libraries and only works well when the problem is very simple, such as with the Iris dataset. In the next section, we will tackle a more difficult classification task that requires a more complex structure.

In our case, we optimized the threshold to minimize the number of errors. Alternatively, we might have different loss functions. It might be that one type of error is much costlier than the other. In a medical setting, false negatives and false positives are not equivalent. A **false negative** (when the result of a test comes back negative, but that is false) might lead to the patient not receiving treatment for a serious disease. A **false positive** (when the test comes back positive even though the patient does not actually have that disease) might lead to additional tests to confirm or unnecessary treatment (which can still have costs, including side effects from the treatment, but are often less serious than missing a diagnostic). Therefore, depending on the exact setting, different trade-offs can make sense. At one extreme, if the disease is fatal and the treatment is cheap with very few negative side-effects, then you want to minimize false negatives as much as you can.

What the **gain/cost** function should be is always dependent on the exact problem you are working on. When we present a general-purpose algorithm, we often focus on minimizing the number of mistakes, achieving the highest accuracy. However, if some mistakes are costlier than others, it might be better to accept a lower overall accuracy to minimize the overall costs.

A more complex dataset and a more complex classifier

We will now look at a slightly more complex dataset. This will motivate the introduction of a new classification algorithm and a few other ideas.

Learning about the Seeds dataset

We now look at another agricultural dataset, which is still small, but already too large to plot exhaustively on a page as we did with Iris. This dataset consists of measurements of wheat seeds. There are seven features that are present, which are as follows:

- area A
- perimeter P
- compactness $C = 4\pi A/P^2$
- length of kernel
- width of kernel
- asymmetry coefficient
- length of kernel groove

There are three classes, corresponding to three wheat varieties: Canadian, Koma, and Rosa. As earlier, the goal is to be able to classify the species based on these morphological measurements. Unlike the Iris dataset, which was collected in the 1930s, this is a very recent dataset and its features were automatically computed from digital images.

This is how image pattern recognition can be implemented: you can take images, in digital form, compute a few relevant features from them, and use a generic classification system. In *Chapter 10, Computer Vision*, we will work through the computer vision side of this problem and compute features in images. For the moment, we will work with the features that are given to us.

UCI Machine Learning Dataset Repository

The University of California at Irvine (UCI) maintains an online repository of machine learning datasets (at the time of writing, they list 233 datasets). Both the Iris and the Seeds dataset used in this chapter were taken from there.

The repository is available online at http://archive.ics.uci.edu/ml/.

Features and feature engineering

One interesting aspect of these features is that the compactness feature is not actually a new measurement, but a function of the previous two features, area and perimeter. It is often very useful to derive new combined features. Trying to create new features is generally called **feature engineering**. It is sometimes seen as less glamorous than algorithms, but it often matters more for performance (a simple algorithm on well-chosen features will perform better than a fancy algorithm on not-so-good features).

In this case, the original researchers computed the **compactness**, which is a typical feature for shapes. It is also sometimes called **roundness**. This feature will have the same value for two kernels, one of which is twice as big as the other one, but with the same shape. However, it will have different values for kernels that are very round (when the feature is close to one) when compared to kernels that are elongated (when the feature is closer to zero).

The goals of a good feature are to simultaneously vary with what matters (the desired output) and be invariant with what does not. For example, compactness does not vary with size, but varies with the shape. In practice, it might be hard to achieve both objectives perfectly, but we want to approximate this ideal.

You will need to use background knowledge to design good features. Fortunately, for many problem domains, there is already a vast literature of possible features and feature-types that you can build upon. For images, all of the previously mentioned features are typical and computer vision libraries will compute them for you. In text-based problems too, there are standard solutions that you can mix and match (we will also see this in the next chapter). When possible, you should use your knowledge of the problem to design a specific feature or to select which ones from the literature are more applicable to the data at hand.

Even before you have data, you must decide which data is worthwhile to collect. Then, you hand all your features to the machine to evaluate and compute the best classifier.

A natural question is whether we can select good features automatically. This problem is known as **feature selection**. There are many methods that have been proposed for this problem, but in practice very simple ideas work best. For the small problems we are currently exploring, it does not make sense to use feature selection, but if you had thousands of features, then throwing out most of them might make the rest of the process much faster.

Nearest neighbor classification

For use with this dataset, we will introduce a new classifier: **the nearest neighbor classifier**. The nearest neighbor classifier is very simple. When classifying a new element, it looks at the training data for the object that is closest to it, its nearest neighbor. Then, it returns its label as the answer. Notice that this model performs perfectly on its training data! For each point, its closest neighbor is itself, and so its label matches perfectly (unless two examples with different labels have exactly the same feature values, which will indicate that the features you are using are not very descriptive). Therefore, it is essential to test the classification using a cross-validation protocol.

The nearest neighbor method can be generalized to look not at a single neighbor, but to multiple ones and take a vote amongst the neighbors. This makes the method more robust to outliers or mislabeled data.

Classifying with scikit-learn

We have been using handwritten classification code, but Python is a very appropriate language for machine learning because of its excellent libraries. In particular, scikit-learn has become the standard library for many machine learning tasks, including classification. We are going to use its implementation of nearest neighbor classification in this section.

The scikit-learn classification API is organized around classifier objects. These objects have the following two essential methods:

- `fit(features, labels)`: This is the learning step and fits the parameters of the model
- `predict(features)`: This method can only be called after fit and returns a prediction for one or more inputs

Here is how we could use its implementation of k-nearest neighbors for our data. We start by importing the `KneighborsClassifier` object from the `sklearn.neighbors` submodule:

```
>>> from sklearn.neighbors import KNeighborsClassifier
```

The scikit-learn module is imported as sklearn (sometimes you will also find that scikit-learn is referred to using this short name instead of the full name). All of the sklearn functionality is in submodules, such as `sklearn.neighbors`.

We can now instantiate a classifier object. In the constructor, we specify the number of neighbors to consider, as follows:

```
>>> classifier = KNeighborsClassifier(n_neighbors=1)
```

If we do not specify the number of neighbors, it defaults to 5, which is often a good choice for classification.

We will want to use cross-validation (of course) to look at our data. The scikit-learn module also makes this easy:

```
>>> from sklearn.cross_validation import KFold

>>> kf = KFold(len(features), n_folds=5, shuffle=True)
>>> # `means` will be a list of mean accuracies (one entry per fold)
>>> means = []
>>> for training,testing in kf:
...     # We fit a model for this fold, then apply it to the
...     # testing data with `predict`:
...     classifier.fit(features[training], labels[training])
...     prediction = classifier.predict(features[testing])
...
...     # np.mean on an array of booleans returns fraction
...      # of correct decisions for this fold:
...     curmean = np.mean(prediction == labels[testing])
...     means.append(curmean)
>>> print("Mean accuracy: {:.1%}".format(np.mean(means)))
Mean accuracy: 90.5%
```

Using five folds for cross-validation, for this dataset, with this algorithm, we obtain 90.5 percent accuracy. As we discussed in the earlier section, the cross-validation accuracy is lower than the training accuracy, but this is a more credible estimate of the performance of the model.

Looking at the decision boundaries

We will now examine the decision boundary. In order to plot these on paper, we will simplify and look at only two dimensions. Take a look at the following plot:

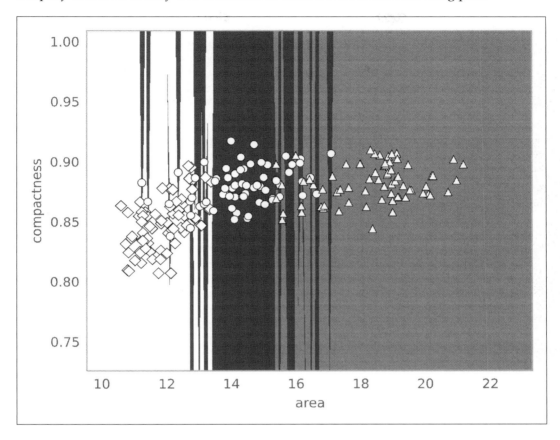

Canadian examples are shown as diamonds, Koma seeds as circles, and Rosa seeds as triangles. Their respective areas are shown as white, black, and grey. You might be wondering why the regions are so horizontal, almost weirdly so. The problem is that the x axis (area) ranges from 10 to 22, while the y axis (compactness) ranges from 0.75 to 1.0. This means that a small change in x is actually much larger than a small change in y. So, when we compute the distance between points, we are, for the most part, only taking the x axis into account. This is also a good example of why it is a good idea to visualize our data and look for red flags or surprises.

If you studied physics (and you remember your lessons), you might have already noticed that we had been summing up lengths, areas, and dimensionless quantities, mixing up our units (which is something you never want to do in a physical system). We need to normalize all of the features to a common scale. There are many solutions to this problem; a simple one is to *normalize to z-scores*. The z-score of a value is how far away from the mean it is, in units of standard deviation. It comes down to this operation:

$$f' = \frac{f - \mu}{\sigma}$$

In this formula, f is the old feature value, f' is the normalized feature value, μ is the mean of the feature, and σ is the standard deviation. Both μ and σ are estimated from training data. Independent of what the original values were, after z-scoring, a value of zero corresponds to the training mean, positive values are above the mean, and negative values are below it.

The scikit-learn module makes it very easy to use this normalization as a preprocessing step. We are going to use a pipeline of transformations: the first element will do the transformation and the second element will do the classification. We start by importing both the pipeline and the feature scaling classes as follows:

```
>>> from sklearn.pipeline import Pipeline
>>> from sklearn.preprocessing import StandardScaler
```

Now, we can combine them.

```
>>> classifier = KNeighborsClassifier(n_neighbors=1)
>>> classifier = Pipeline([('norm', StandardScaler()), ('knn',
classifier)])
```

The Pipeline constructor takes a list of pairs `(str, clf)`. Each pair corresponds to a step in the pipeline: the first element is a string naming the step, while the second element is the object that performs the transformation. Advanced usage of the object uses these names to refer to different steps.

After normalization, every feature is in the same units (technically, every feature is now dimensionless; it has no units) and we can more confidently mix dimensions. In fact, if we now run our nearest neighbor classifier, we obtain 93 percent accuracy, estimated with the same five-fold cross-validation code shown previously!

Look at the decision space again in two dimensions:

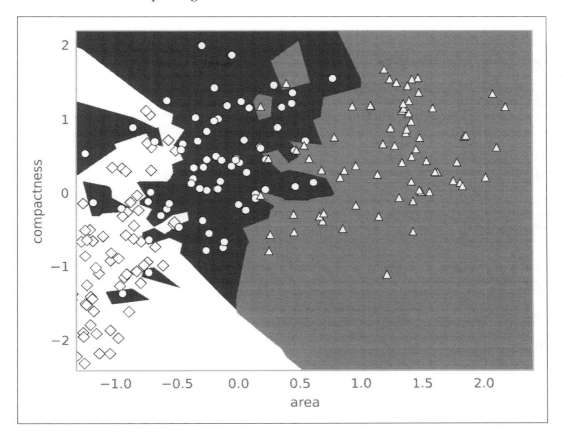

The boundaries are now different and you can see that both dimensions make a difference for the outcome. In the full dataset, everything is happening on a seven-dimensional space, which is very hard to visualize, but the same principle applies; while a few dimensions are dominant in the original data, after normalization, they are all given the same importance.

Binary and multiclass classification

The first classifier we used, the threshold classifier, was a simple binary classifier. Its result is either one class or the other, as a point is either above the threshold value or it is not. The second classifier we used, the nearest neighbor classifier, was a natural multiclass classifier, its output can be one of the several classes.

It is often simpler to define a simple binary method than the one that works on multiclass problems. However, we can reduce any multiclass problem to a series of binary decisions. This is what we did earlier in the Iris dataset, in a haphazard way: we observed that it was easy to separate one of the initial classes and focused on the other two, reducing the problem to two binary decisions:

1. Is it an Iris Setosa (yes or no)?
2. If not, check whether it is an Iris Virginica (yes or no).

Of course, we want to leave this sort of reasoning to the computer. As usual, there are several solutions to this multiclass reduction.

The simplest is to use a series of *one versus the rest* classifiers. For each possible label ℓ, we build a classifier of the type *is this ℓ or something else?* When applying the rule, exactly one of the classifiers will say *yes* and we will have our solution. Unfortunately, this does not always happen, so we have to decide how to deal with either multiple positive answers or no positive answers.

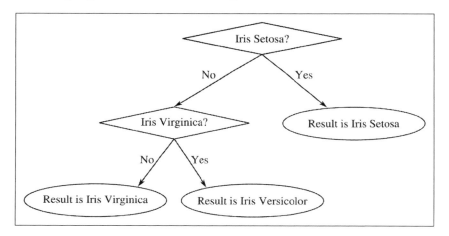

Alternatively, we can build a classification tree. Split the possible labels into two, and build a classifier that asks, "Should this example go in the left or the right bin?" We can perform this splitting recursively until we obtain a single label. The preceding diagram depicts the tree of reasoning for the Iris dataset. Each diamond is a single binary classifier. It is easy to imagine that we could make this tree larger and encompass more decisions. This means that any classifier that can be used for binary classification can also be adapted to handle any number of classes in a simple way.

There are many other possible ways of turning a binary method into a multiclass one. There is no single method that is clearly better in all cases. The scikit-learn module implements several of these methods in the `sklearn.multiclass` submodule.

 Some classifiers are binary systems, while many real-life problems are naturally multiclass. Several simple protocols reduce a multiclass problem to a series of binary decisions and allow us to apply the binary models to our multiclass problem. This means methods that are apparently only for binary data can be applied to multiclass data with little extra effort.

Summary

Classification means generalizing from examples to build a model (that is, a rule that can automatically be applied to new, unclassified objects). It is one of the fundamental tools in machine learning and we will see many more examples of this in the forthcoming chapters.

In a sense, this was a very theoretical chapter, as we introduced generic concepts with simple examples. We went over a few operations with the Iris dataset. This is a small dataset. However, it has the advantage that we were able to plot it out and see what we were doing in detail. This is something that will be lost when we move on to problems with many dimensions and many thousands of examples. The intuitions we gained here will all still be valid.

You also learned that the training error is a misleading, over-optimistic estimate of how well the model does. We must, instead, evaluate it on testing data that has not been used for training. In order to not waste too many examples in testing, a cross-validation schedule can get us the best of both worlds (at the cost of more computation).

We also had a look at the problem of feature engineering. Features are not predefined for you, but choosing and designing features is an integral part of designing a machine learning pipeline. In fact, it is often the area where you can get the most improvements in accuracy, as better data beats fancier methods. The chapters on text-based classification, music genre recognition, and computer vision will provide examples for these specific settings.

The next chapter looks at how to proceed when your data does not have predefined classes for classification.

3

Clustering – Finding Related Posts

In the previous chapter, you learned how to find the classes or categories of individual datapoints. With a handful of training data items that were paired with their respective classes, you learned a model, which we can now use to classify future data items. We called this supervised learning because the learning was guided by a teacher; in our case, the teacher had the form of correct classifications.

Let's now imagine that we do not possess those labels by which we can learn the classification model. This could be, for example, because they were too expensive to collect. Just imagine the cost if the only way to obtain millions of labels will be to ask humans to classify those manually. What could we have done in that case?

Well, of course, we will not be able to learn a classification model. Still, we could find some pattern within the data itself. That is, let the data describe itself. This is what we will do in this chapter, where we consider the challenge of a question and answer website. When a user is browsing our site, perhaps because they were searching for particular information, the search engine will most likely point them to a specific answer. If the presented answers are not what they were looking for, the website should present (at least) the related answers so that they can quickly see what other answers are available and hopefully stay on our site.

The naïve approach will be to simply take the post, calculate its similarity to all other posts and display the top n most similar posts as links on the page. Quickly, this will become very costly. Instead, we need a method that quickly finds all the related posts.

We will achieve this goal in this chapter using clustering. This is a method of arranging items so that similar items are in one cluster and dissimilar items are in distinct ones. The tricky thing that we have to tackle first is how to turn text into something on which we can calculate similarity. With such a similarity measurement, we will then proceed to investigate how we can leverage that to quickly arrive at a cluster that contains similar posts. Once there, we will only have to check out those documents that also belong to that cluster. To achieve this, we will introduce you to the marvelous SciKit library, which comes with diverse machine learning methods that we will also use in the following chapters.

Measuring the relatedness of posts

From the machine learning point of view, raw text is useless. Only if we manage to transform it into meaningful numbers, can we then feed it into our machine learning algorithms, such as clustering. This is true for more mundane operations on text such as similarity measurement.

How not to do it

One text similarity measure is the Levenshtein distance, which also goes by the name Edit Distance. Let's say we have two words, "machine" and "mchiene". The similarity between them can be expressed as the minimum set of edits that are necessary to turn one word into the other. In this case, the edit distance will be 2, as we have to add an "a" after the "m" and delete the first "e". This algorithm is, however, quite costly as it is bound by the length of the first word times the length of the second word.

Looking at our posts, we could cheat by treating whole words as characters and performing the edit distance calculation on the word level. Let's say we have two posts (let's concentrate on the following title, for simplicity's sake) called "How to format my hard disk" and "Hard disk format problems", we will need an edit distance of 5 because of removing "how", "to", "format", "my" and then adding "format" and "problems" in the end. Thus, one could express the difference between two posts as the number of words that have to be added or deleted so that one text morphs into the other. Although we could speed up the overall approach quite a bit, the time complexity remains the same.

But even if it would have been fast enough, there is another problem. In the earlier post, the word "format" accounts for an edit distance of 2, due to deleting it first, then adding it. So, our distance seems to be not robust enough to take word reordering into account.

How to do it

More robust than edit distance is the so-called **bag of word** approach. It totally ignores the order of words and simply uses word counts as their basis. For each word in the post, its occurrence is counted and noted in a vector. Not surprisingly, this step is also called vectorization. The vector is typically huge as it contains as many elements as words occur in the whole dataset. Take, for instance, two example posts with the following word counts:

Word	Occurrences in post 1	Occurrences in post 2
disk	1	1
format	1	1
how	1	0
hard	1	1
my	1	0
problems	0	1
to	1	0

The columns Occurrences in post 1 and Occurrences in post 2 can now be treated as simple vectors. We can simply calculate the Euclidean distance between the vectors of all posts and take the nearest one (too slow, as we have found out earlier). And as such, we can use them later as our feature vectors in the clustering steps according to the following procedure:

1. Extract salient features from each post and store it as a vector per post.
2. Then compute clustering on the vectors.
3. Determine the cluster for the post in question.
4. From this cluster, fetch a handful of posts having a different similarity to the post in question. This will increase diversity.

But there is some more work to be done before we get there. Before we can do that work, we need some data to work on.

Preprocessing – similarity measured as a similar number of common words

As we have seen earlier, the bag of word approach is both fast and robust. It is, though, not without challenges. Let's dive directly into them.

Converting raw text into a bag of words

We do not have to write custom code for counting words and representing those counts as a vector. SciKit's `CountVectorizer` method does the job not only efficiently but also has a very convenient interface. SciKit's functions and classes are imported via the `sklearn` package:

```
>>> from sklearn.feature_extraction.text import CountVectorizer
>>> vectorizer = CountVectorizer(min_df=1)
```

The `min_df` parameter determines how `CountVectorizer` treats seldom words (minimum document frequency). If it is set to an integer, all words occurring less than that value will be dropped. If it is a fraction, all words that occur in less than that fraction of the overall dataset will be dropped. The `max_df` parameter works in a similar manner. If we print the instance, we see what other parameters SciKit provides together with their default values:

```
>>> print(vectorizer)
CountVectorizer(analyzer='word', binary=False, charset=None,
        charset_error=None, decode_error='strict',
        dtype=<class 'numpy.int64'>, encoding='utf-8',
input='content',
        lowercase=True, max_df=1.0, max_features=None, min_df=1,
        ngram_range=(1, 1), preprocessor=None, stop_words=None,
        strip_accents=None, token_pattern='(?u)\\b\\w\\w+\\b',
        tokenizer=None, vocabulary=None)
```

We see that, as expected, the counting is done at word level (`analyzer=word`) and words are determined by the regular expression pattern `token_pattern`. It will, for example, tokenize "cross-validated" into "cross" and "validated". Let's ignore the other parameters for now and consider the following two example subject lines:

```
>>> content = ["How to format my hard disk", " Hard disk format
problems "]
```

We can now put this list of subject lines into the `fit_transform()` function of our vectorizer, which does all the hard vectorization work.

```
>>> X = vectorizer.fit_transform(content)
>>> vectorizer.get_feature_names()
[u'disk', u'format', u'hard', u'how', u'my', u'problems', u'to']
```

The vectorizer has detected seven words for which we can fetch the counts individually:

```
>>> print(X.toarray().transpose())
[[1 1]
 [1 1]
 [1 1]
 [1 0]
 [1 0]
 [0 1]
 [1 0]]
```

This means that the first sentence contains all the words except "problems", while the second contains all but "how", "my", and "to". In fact, these are exactly the same columns as we have seen in the preceding table. From X, we can extract a feature vector that we will use to compare two documents with each other.

We will start with a naïve approach first, to point out some preprocessing peculiarities we have to account for. So let's pick a random post, for which we then create the count vector. We will then compare its distance to all the count vectors and fetch the post with the smallest one.

Counting words

Let's play with the toy dataset consisting of the following posts:

Post filename	Post content
01.txt	This is a toy post about machine learning. Actually, it contains not much interesting stuff.
02.txt	Imaging databases can get huge.
03.txt	Most imaging databases save images permanently.
04.txt	Imaging databases store images.
05.txt	Imaging databases store images. Imaging databases store images. Imaging databases store images.

In this post dataset, we want to find the most similar post for the short post "imaging databases".

Assuming that the posts are located in the directory `DIR`, we can feed `CountVectorizer` with it:

```
>>> posts = [open(os.path.join(DIR, f)).read() for f in
os.listdir(DIR)]
>>> from sklearn.feature_extraction.text import CountVectorizer
>>> vectorizer = CountVectorizer(min_df=1)
```

We have to notify the vectorizer about the full dataset so that it knows upfront what words are to be expected:

```
>>> X_train = vectorizer.fit_transform(posts)
>>> num_samples, num_features = X_train.shape
>>> print("#samples: %d, #features: %d" % (num_samples,
num_features))
#samples: 5, #features: 25
```

Unsurprisingly, we have five posts with a total of 25 different words. The following words that have been tokenized will be counted:

```
>>> print(vectorizer.get_feature_names())
[u'about', u'actually', u'capabilities', u'contains', u'data',
u'databases', u'images', u'imaging', u'interesting', u'is', u'it',
u'learning', u'machine', u'most', u'much', u'not', u'permanently',
u'post', u'provide', u'save', u'storage', u'store', u'stuff',
u'this', u'toy']
```

Now we can vectorize our new post.

```
>>> new_post = "imaging databases"
>>> new_post_vec = vectorizer.transform([new_post])
```

Note that the count vectors returned by the `transform` method are sparse. That is, each vector does not store one count value for each word, as most of those counts will be zero (the post does not contain the word). Instead, it uses the more memory-efficient implementation `coo_matrix` (for "COOrdinate"). Our new post, for instance, actually contains only two elements:

```
>>> print(new_post_vec)
  (0, 7)    1
  (0, 5)    1
```

Via its `toarray()` member, we can once again access the full `ndarray`:

```
>>> print(new_post_vec.toarray())
[[0 0 0 0 0 1 0 1 0 0 0 0 0 0 0 0 0 0 0 0 0 0 0 0 0]]
```

We need to use the full array, if we want to use it as a vector for similarity calculations. For the similarity measurement (the naïve one), we calculate the Euclidean distance between the count vectors of the new post and all the old posts:

```
>>> import scipy as sp
>>> def dist_raw(v1, v2):
...     delta = v1-v2
...     return sp.linalg.norm(delta.toarray())
```

The `norm()` function calculates the Euclidean norm (shortest distance). This is just one obvious first pick and there are many more interesting ways to calculate the distance. Just take a look at the paper *Distance Coefficients between Two Lists or Sets* in The Python Papers Source Codes, in which Maurice Ling nicely presents 35 different ones.

With `dist_raw`, we just need to iterate over all the posts and remember the nearest one:

```
>>> import sys
>>> best_doc = None
>>> best_dist = sys.maxint
>>> best_i = None
>>> for i, post in enumerate(num_samples):
...     if post == new_post:
...         continue
...     post_vec = X_train.getrow(i)
...     d = dist_raw(post_vec, new_post_vec)
...     print("=== Post %i with dist=%.2f: %s"%(i, d, post))
...     if d<best_dist:
...         best_dist = d
...         best_i = i
>>> print("Best post is %i with dist=%.2f"%(best_i, best_dist))


=== Post 0 with dist=4.00: This is a toy post about machine learning.
Actually, it contains not much interesting stuff.
=== Post 1 with dist=1.73: Imaging databases provide storage
capabilities.
```

```
=== Post 2 with dist=2.00: Most imaging databases save images
permanently.
=== Post 3 with dist=1.41: Imaging databases store data.
=== Post 4 with dist=5.10: Imaging databases store data. Imaging
databases store data. Imaging databases store data.
Best post is 3 with dist=1.41
```

Congratulations, we have our first similarity measurement. Post 0 is most dissimilar from our new post. Quite understandably, it does not have a single word in common with the new post. We can also understand that Post 1 is very similar to the new post, but not the winner, as it contains one word more than Post 3, which is not contained in the new post.

Looking at Post 3 and Post 4, however, the picture is not so clear any more. Post 4 is the same as Post 3 duplicated three times. So, it should also be of the same similarity to the new post as Post 3.

Printing the corresponding feature vectors explains why:

```
>>> print(X_train.getrow(3).toarray())
[[0 0 0 0 1 1 0 1 0 0 0 0 0 0 0 0 0 0 0 0 0 1 0 0 0]]
>>> print(X_train.getrow(4).toarray())
[[0 0 0 0 3 3 0 3 0 0 0 0 0 0 0 0 0 0 0 0 0 3 0 0 0]]
```

Obviously, using only the counts of the raw words is too simple. We will have to normalize them to get vectors of unit length.

Normalizing word count vectors

We will have to extend dist_raw to calculate the vector distance not on the raw vectors but on the normalized instead:

```
>>> def dist_norm(v1, v2):
...     v1_normalized = v1/sp.linalg.norm(v1.toarray())
...     v2_normalized = v2/sp.linalg.norm(v2.toarray())
...     delta = v1_normalized - v2_normalized
...     return sp.linalg.norm(delta.toarray())
```

This leads to the following similarity measurement:

```
=== Post 0 with dist=1.41: This is a toy post about machine learning.
Actually, it contains not much interesting stuff.
=== Post 1 with dist=0.86: Imaging databases provide storage
capabilities.
```

```
=== Post 2 with dist=0.92: Most imaging databases save images
permanently.
=== Post 3 with dist=0.77: Imaging databases store data.
=== Post 4 with dist=0.77: Imaging databases store data. Imaging
databases store data. Imaging databases store data.
Best post is 3 with dist=0.77
```

This looks a bit better now. Post 3 and Post 4 are calculated as being equally similar. One could argue whether that much repetition would be a delight to the reader, but from the point of counting the words in the posts this seems to be right.

Removing less important words

Let's have another look at Post 2. Of its words that are not in the new post, we have "most", "save", "images", and "permanently". They are actually quite different in the overall importance to the post. Words such as "most" appear very often in all sorts of different contexts and are called stop words. They do not carry as much information and thus should not be weighed as much as words such as "images", which doesn't occur often in different contexts. The best option would be to remove all the words that are so frequent that they do not help to distinguish between different texts. These words are called stop words.

As this is such a common step in text processing, there is a simple parameter in `CountVectorizer` to achieve that:

```
>>> vectorizer = CountVectorizer(min_df=1, stop_words='english')
```

If you have a clear picture of what kind of stop words you would want to remove, you can also pass a list of them. Setting `stop_words` to `english` will use a set of 318 English stop words. To find out which ones, you can use `get_stop_words()`:

```
>>> sorted(vectorizer.get_stop_words())[0:20]
```

```
['a', 'about', 'above', 'across', 'after', 'afterwards', 'again',
'against', 'all', 'almost', 'alone', 'along', 'already', 'also',
'although', 'always', 'am', 'among', 'amongst', 'amoungst']
```

The new word list is seven words lighter:

```
[u'actually', u'capabilities', u'contains', u'data', u'databases',
u'images', u'imaging', u'interesting', u'learning', u'machine',
u'permanently', u'post', u'provide', u'save', u'storage', u'store',
u'stuff', u'toy']
```

Without stop words, we arrive at the following similarity measurement:

```
=== Post 0 with dist=1.41: This is a toy post about machine learning.
Actually, it contains not much interesting stuff.
=== Post 1 with dist=0.86: Imaging databases provide storage
capabilities.
=== Post 2 with dist=0.86: Most imaging databases save images
permanently.
=== Post 3 with dist=0.77: Imaging databases store data.
=== Post 4 with dist=0.77: Imaging databases store data. Imaging
databases store data. Imaging databases store data.
Best post is 3 with dist=0.77
```

Post 2 is now on par with Post 1. It has, however, changed not much overall since our posts are kept short for demonstration purposes. It will become vital when we look at real-world data.

Stemming

One thing is still missing. We count similar words in different variants as different words. Post 2, for instance, contains "imaging" and "images". It will make sense to count them together. After all, it is the same concept they are referring to.

We need a function that reduces words to their specific word stem. SciKit does not contain a stemmer by default. With the **Natural Language Toolkit** (**NLTK**), we can download a free software toolkit, which provides a stemmer that we can easily plug into CountVectorizer.

Installing and using NLTK

How to install NLTK on your operating system is described in detail at http://nltk.org/install.html. Unfortunately, it is not yet officially supported for Python 3, which means that also pip install will not work. We can, however, download the package from http://www.nltk.org/nltk3-alpha/ and install it manually after uncompressing using Python's setup.py install.

To check whether your installation was successful, open a Python interpreter and type:

```
>>> import nltk
```

You will find a very nice tutorial to NLTK in the book *Python 3 Text Processing with NLTK 3 Cookbook, Jacob Perkins, Packt Publishing*. To play a little bit with a stemmer, you can visit the web page http://text-processing.com/demo/stem/.

NLTK comes with different stemmers. This is necessary, because every language has a different set of rules for stemming. For English, we can take SnowballStemmer.

```
>>> import nltk.stem
>>> s = nltk.stem.SnowballStemmer('english')
>>> s.stem("graphics")
u'graphic'
>>> s.stem("imaging")
u'imag'
>>> s.stem("image")
u'imag'
>>> s.stem("imagination")
u'imagin'
>>> s.stem("imagine")
u'imagin'
```

 Note that stemming does not necessarily have to result in valid English words.

It also works with verbs:

```
>>> s.stem("buys")
u'buy'
>>> s.stem("buying")
u'buy'
```

This means, it works most of the time:

```
>>> s.stem("bought")
u'bought'
```

Extending the vectorizer with NLTK's stemmer

We need to stem the posts before we feed them into CountVectorizer. The class provides several hooks with which we can customize the stage's preprocessing and tokenization. The preprocessor and tokenizer can be set as parameters in the constructor. We do not want to place the stemmer into any of them, because we will then have to do the tokenization and normalization by ourselves. Instead, we overwrite the build_analyzer method:

```
>>> import nltk.stem
>>> english_stemmer = nltk.stem.SnowballStemmer('english'))
>>> class StemmedCountVectorizer(CountVectorizer):
...     def build_analyzer(self):
...         analyzer = super(StemmedCountVectorizer,
self).build_analyzer()
...         return lambda doc: (english_stemmer.stem(w) for w in
analyzer(doc))
>>> vectorizer = StemmedCountVectorizer(min_df=1,
stop_words='english')
```

This will do the following process for each post:

1. The first step is lower casing the raw post in the preprocessing step (done in the parent class).

2. Extracting all individual words in the tokenization step (done in the parent class).

3. This concludes with converting each word into its stemmed version.

As a result, we now have one feature less, because "images" and "imaging" collapsed to one. Now, the set of feature names is as follows:

```
[u'actual', u'capabl', u'contain', u'data', u'databas', u'imag',
u'interest', u'learn', u'machin', u'perman', u'post', u'provid',
u'save', u'storag', u'store', u'stuff', u'toy']
```

Running our new stemmed vectorizer over our posts, we see that collapsing "imaging" and "images", revealed that actually Post 2 is the most similar post to our new post, as it contains the concept "imag" twice:

```
=== Post 0 with dist=1.41: This is a toy post about machine learning.
Actually, it contains not much interesting stuff.
=== Post 1 with dist=0.86: Imaging databases provide storage
capabilities.
```

```
=== Post 2 with dist=0.63: Most imaging databases save images
permanently.

=== Post 3 with dist=0.77: Imaging databases store data.

=== Post 4 with dist=0.77: Imaging databases store data. Imaging
databases store data. Imaging databases store data.

Best post is 2 with dist=0.63
```

Stop words on steroids

Now that we have a reasonable way to extract a compact vector from a noisy textual post, let's step back for a while to think about what the feature values actually mean.

The feature values simply count occurrences of terms in a post. We silently assumed that higher values for a term also mean that the term is of greater importance to the given post. But what about, for instance, the word "subject", which naturally occurs in each and every single post? Alright, we can tell CountVectorizer to remove it as well by means of its max_df parameter. We can, for instance, set it to 0.9 so that all words that occur in more than 90 percent of all posts will always be ignored. But, what about words that appear in 89 percent of all posts? How low will we be willing to set max_df? The problem is that however we set it, there will always be the problem that some terms are just more discriminative than others.

This can only be solved by counting term frequencies for every post and in addition discount those that appear in many posts. In other words, we want a high value for a given term in a given value, if that term occurs often in that particular post and very seldom anywhere else.

This is exactly what **term frequency – inverse document frequency (TF-IDF)** does. TF stands for the counting part, while IDF factors in the discounting. A naïve implementation will look like this:

```
>>> import scipy as sp
>>> def tfidf(term, doc, corpus):
...     tf = doc.count(term) / len(doc)
...     num_docs_with_term = len([d for d in corpus if term in d])
...     idf = sp.log(len(corpus) / num_docs_with_term)
...     return tf * idf
```

You see that we did not simply count the terms, but also normalize the counts by the document length. This way, longer documents do not have an unfair advantage over shorter ones.

For the following documents, D, consisting of three already tokenized documents, we can see how the terms are treated differently, although all appear equally often per document:

```
>>> a, abb, abc = ["a"], ["a", "b", "b"], ["a", "b", "c"]
>>> D = [a, abb, abc]
>>> print(tfidf("a", a, D))
0.0
>>> print(tfidf("a", abb, D))
0.0
>>> print(tfidf("a", abc, D))
0.0
>>> print(tfidf("b", abb, D))
0.270310072072
>>> print(tfidf("a", abc, D))
0.0
>>> print(tfidf("b", abc, D))
0.135155036036
>>> print(tfidf("c", abc, D))
0.366204096223
```

We see that a carries no meaning for any document since it is contained everywhere. The b term is more important for the document abb than for abc as it occurs there twice.

In reality, there are more corner cases to handle than the preceding example does. Thanks to SciKit, we don't have to think of them as they are already nicely packaged in TfidfVectorizer, which is inherited from CountVectorizer. Sure enough, we don't want to miss our stemmer:

```
>>> from sklearn.feature_extraction.text import TfidfVectorizer
>>> class StemmedTfidfVectorizer(TfidfVectorizer):
...     def build_analyzer(self):
...         analyzer = super(TfidfVectorizer,
                             self).build_analyzer()
...         return lambda doc: (
                 english_stemmer.stem(w) for w in analyzer(doc))
>>> vectorizer = StemmedTfidfVectorizer(min_df=1,
                stop_words='english', decode_error='ignore')
```

The resulting document vectors will not contain counts any more. Instead they will contain the individual TF-IDF values per term.

Our achievements and goals

Our current text pre-processing phase includes the following steps:

1. Firstly, tokenizing the text.
2. This is followed by throwing away words that occur way too often to be of any help in detecting relevant posts.
3. Throwing away words that occur way so seldom so that there is only little chance that they occur in future posts.
4. Counting the remaining words.
5. Finally, calculating TF-IDF values from the counts, considering the whole text corpus.

Again, we can congratulate ourselves. With this process, we are able to convert a bunch of noisy text into a concise representation of feature values.

But, as simple and powerful the bag of words approach with its extensions is, it has some drawbacks, which we should be aware of:

- **It does not cover word relations**: With the aforementioned vectorization approach, the text "Car hits wall" and "Wall hits car" will both have the same feature vector.

- **It does not capture negations correctly**: For instance, the text "I will eat ice cream" and "I will not eat ice cream" will look very similar by means of their feature vectors although they contain quite the opposite meaning. This problem, however, can be easily changed by not only counting individual words, also called "unigrams", but instead also considering bigrams (pairs of words) or trigrams (three words in a row).

- **It totally fails with misspelled words**: Although it is clear to the human beings among us readers that "database" and "databas" convey the same meaning, our approach will treat them as totally different words.

For brevity's sake, let's nevertheless stick with the current approach, which we can now use to efficiently build clusters from.

Clustering

Finally, we have our vectors, which we believe capture the posts to a sufficient degree. Not surprisingly, there are many ways to group them together. Most clustering algorithms fall into one of the two methods: flat and hierarchical clustering.

Flat clustering divides the posts into a set of clusters without relating the clusters to each other. The goal is simply to come up with a partitioning such that all posts in one cluster are most similar to each other while being dissimilar from the posts in all other clusters. Many flat clustering algorithms require the number of clusters to be specified up front.

In hierarchical clustering, the number of clusters does not have to be specified. Instead, hierarchical clustering creates a hierarchy of clusters. While similar posts are grouped into one cluster, similar clusters are again grouped into one *uber-cluster*. This is done recursively, until only one cluster is left that contains everything. In this hierarchy, one can then choose the desired number of clusters after the fact. However, this comes at the cost of lower efficiency.

SciKit provides a wide range of clustering approaches in the `sklearn.cluster` package. You can get a quick overview of advantages and drawbacks of each of them at `http://scikit-learn.org/dev/modules/clustering.html`.

In the following sections, we will use the flat clustering method K-means and play a bit with the desired number of clusters.

K-means

k-means is the most widely used flat clustering algorithm. After initializing it with the desired number of clusters, `num_clusters`, it maintains that number of so-called cluster centroids. Initially, it will pick any `num_clusters` posts and set the centroids to their feature vector. Then it will go through all other posts and assign them the nearest centroid as their current cluster. Following this, it will move each centroid into the middle of all the vectors of that particular class. This changes, of course, the cluster assignment. Some posts are now nearer to another cluster. So it will update the assignments for those changed posts. This is done as long as the centroids move considerably. After some iterations, the movements will fall below a threshold and we consider clustering to be converged.

Let's play this through with a toy example of posts containing only two words. Each point in the following chart represents one document:

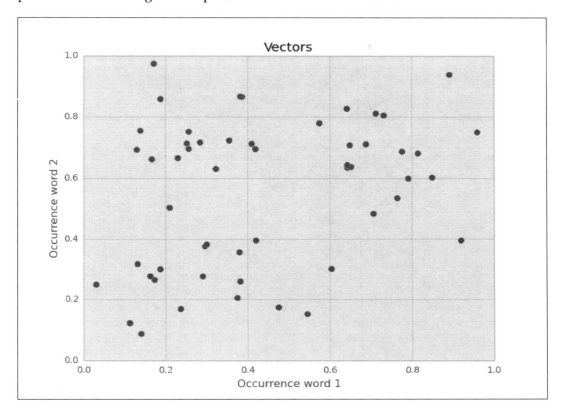

After running one iteration of K-means, that is, taking any two vectors as starting points, assigning the labels to the rest and updating the cluster centers to now be the center point of all points in that cluster, we get the following clustering:

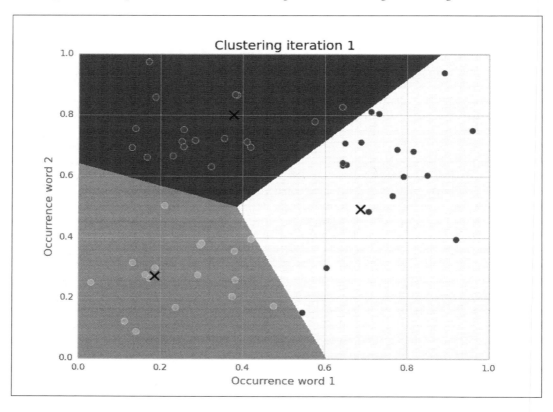

Because the cluster centers moved, we have to reassign the cluster labels and recalculate the cluster centers. After iteration 2, we get the following clustering:

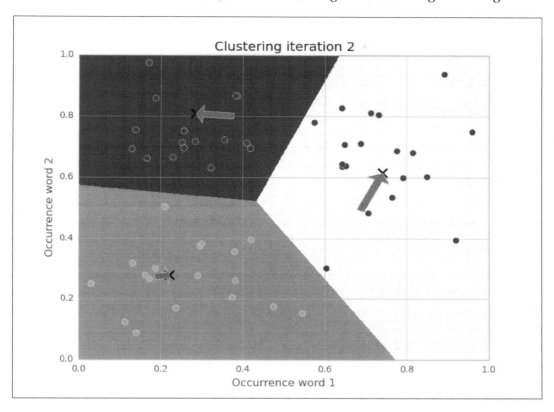

The arrows show the movements of the cluster centers. After five iterations in this example, the cluster centers don't move noticeably any more (SciKit's tolerance threshold is 0.0001 by default).

After the clustering has settled, we just need to note down the cluster centers and their identity. Each new document that comes in, we then have to vectorize and compare against all cluster centers. The cluster center with the smallest distance to our new post vector belongs to the cluster we will assign to the new post.

Getting test data to evaluate our ideas on

In order to test clustering, let's move away from the toy text examples and find a dataset that resembles the data we are expecting in the future so that we can test our approach. For our purpose, we need documents about technical topics that are already grouped together so that we can check whether our algorithm works as expected when we apply it later to the posts we hope to receive.

One standard dataset in machine learning is the `20newsgroup` dataset, which contains 18,826 posts from 20 different newsgroups. Among the groups' topics are technical ones such as `comp.sys.mac.hardware` or `sci.crypt`, as well as more politics- and religion-related ones such as `talk.politics.guns` or `soc.religion.christian`. We will restrict ourselves to the technical groups. If we assume each newsgroup as one cluster, we can nicely test whether our approach of finding related posts works.

The dataset can be downloaded from `http://people.csail.mit.edu/jrennie/20Newsgroups`. Much more comfortable, however, is to download it from MLComp at `http://mlcomp.org/datasets/379` (free registration required). SciKit already contains custom loaders for that dataset and rewards you with very convenient data loading options.

The dataset comes in the form of a ZIP file `dataset-379-20news-18828_WJQIG.zip`, which we have to unzip to get the directory `379`, which contains the datasets. We also have to notify SciKit about the path containing that data directory. It contains a metadata file and three directories `test`, `train`, and `raw`. The `test` and `train` directories split the whole dataset into 60 percent of training and 40 percent of testing posts. If you go this route, then you either need to set the environment variable `MLCOMP_DATASETS_HOME` or you specify the path directly with the `mlcomp_root` parameter when loading the dataset.

`http://mlcomp.org` is a website for comparing machine learning programs on diverse datasets. It serves two purposes: finding the right dataset to tune your machine learning program, and exploring how other people use a particular dataset. For instance, you can see how well other people's algorithms performed on particular datasets and compare against them.

For convenience, the `sklearn.datasets` module also contains the `fetch_20newsgroups` function, which automatically downloads the data behind the scenes:

```
>>> import sklearn.datasets
>>> all_data = sklearn.datasets.fetch_20newsgroups(subset='all')
>>> print(len(all_data.filenames))
18846
>>> print(all_data.target_names)
['alt.atheism', 'comp.graphics', 'comp.os.ms-windows.misc',
'comp.sys.ibm.pc.hardware', 'comp.sys.mac.hardware',
'comp.windows.x', 'misc.forsale', 'rec.autos', 'rec.motorcycles',
'rec.sport.baseball', 'rec.sport.hockey', 'sci.crypt',
'sci.electronics', 'sci.med', 'sci.space', 'soc.religion.christian',
'talk.politics.guns', 'talk.politics.mideast', 'talk.politics.misc',
'talk.religion.misc']
```

We can choose between training and test sets:

```
>>> train_data = sklearn.datasets.fetch_20newsgroups(subset='train',
categories=groups)
>>> print(len(train_data.filenames))
11314
>>> test_data = sklearn.datasets.fetch_20newsgroups(subset='test')
>>> print(len(test_data.filenames))
7532
```

For simplicity's sake, we will restrict ourselves to only some newsgroups so that the overall experimentation cycle is shorter. We can achieve this with the `categories` parameter:

```
>>> groups = ['comp.graphics', 'comp.os.ms-windows.misc',
'comp.sys.ibm.pc.hardware', 'comp.sys.mac.hardware',
'comp.windows.x', 'sci.space']
>>> train_data = sklearn.datasets.fetch_20newsgroups(subset='train',
categories=groups)
>>> print(len(train_data.filenames))
3529

>>> test_data = sklearn.datasets.fetch_20newsgroups(subset='test',
categories=groups)
>>> print(len(test_data.filenames))
2349
```

Clustering posts

You would have already noticed one thing — real data is noisy. The newsgroup dataset is no exception. It even contains invalid characters that will result in UnicodeDecodeError.

We have to tell the vectorizer to ignore them:

```
>>> vectorizer = StemmedTfidfVectorizer(min_df=10, max_df=0.5,
...                 stop_words='english', decode_error='ignore')
>>> vectorized = vectorizer.fit_transform(train_data.data)
>>> num_samples, num_features = vectorized.shape
>>> print("#samples: %d, #features: %d" % (num_samples,
num_features))
#samples: 3529, #features: 4712
```

We now have a pool of 3,529 posts and extracted for each of them a feature vector of 4,712 dimensions. That is what K-means takes as input. We will fix the cluster size to 50 for this chapter and hope you are curious enough to try out different values as an exercise.

```
>>> num_clusters = 50
>>> from sklearn.cluster import KMeans
>>> km = KMeans(n_clusters=num_clusters, init='random', n_init=1,
verbose=1, random_state=3)
>>> km.fit(vectorized)
```

That's it. We provided a random state just so that you can get the same results. In real-world applications, you will not do this. After fitting, we can get the clustering information out of members of km. For every vectorized post that has been fit, there is a corresponding integer label in km.labels_:

```
>>> print(km.labels_)
[48 23 31 ...,  6  2 22]
>>> print(km.labels_.shape)
3529
```

The cluster centers can be accessed via km.cluster_centers_.

In the next section, we will see how we can assign a cluster to a newly arriving post using km.predict.

Solving our initial challenge

We will now put everything together and demonstrate our system for the following new post that we assign to the `new_post` variable:

> *"Disk drive problems. Hi, I have a problem with my hard disk.*
>
> *After 1 year it is working only sporadically now.*
>
> *I tried to format it, but now it doesn't boot any more.*
>
> *Any ideas? Thanks."*

As you learned earlier, you will first have to vectorize this post before you predict its label:

```
>>> new_post_vec = vectorizer.transform([new_post])
>>> new_post_label = km.predict(new_post_vec)[0]
```

Now that we have the clustering, we do not need to compare `new_post_vec` to all post vectors. Instead, we can focus only on the posts of the same cluster. Let's fetch their indices in the original data set:

```
>>> similar_indices = (km.labels_==new_post_label).nonzero()[0]
```

The comparison in the bracket results in a Boolean array, and `nonzero` converts that array into a smaller array containing the indices of the `True` elements.

Using `similar_indices`, we then simply have to build a list of posts together with their similarity scores:

```
>>> similar = []
>>> for i in similar_indices:
...     dist = sp.linalg.norm((new_post_vec -
vectorized[i]).toarray())
...     similar.append((dist, dataset.data[i]))
>>> similar = sorted(similar)
>>> print(len(similar))
131
```

We found 131 posts in the cluster of our post. To give the user a quick idea of what kind of similar posts are available, we can now present the most similar post (`show_at_1`), and two less similar but still related ones – all from the same cluster.

```
>>> show_at_1 = similar[0]
>>> show_at_2 = similar[int(len(similar)/10)]
>>> show_at_3 = similar[int(len(similar)/2)]
```

The following table shows the posts together with their similarity values:

Position	Similarity	Excerpt from post
1	1.038	BOOT PROBLEM with IDE controller
		Hi,
		I've got a Multi I/O card (IDE controller + serial/parallel interface) and two floppy drives (5 1/4, 3 1/2) and a Quantum ProDrive 80AT connected to it. I was able to format the hard disk, but I could not boot from it. I can boot from drive A: (which disk drive does not matter) but if I remove the disk from drive A and press the reset switch, the LED of drive A: continues to glow, and the hard disk is not accessed at all. I guess this must be a problem of either the Multi I/o card or floppy disk drive settings (jumper configuration?) Does someone have any hint what could be the reason for it. [...]
2	1.150	Booting from B drive
		I have a 5 1/4" drive as drive A. How can I make the system boot from my 3 1/2" B drive? (Optimally, the computer would be able to boot: from either A or B, checking them in order for a bootable disk. But: if I have to switch cables around and simply switch the drives so that: it can't boot 5 1/4" disks, that's OK. Also, boot_b won't do the trick for me. [...]
		[...]
3	1.280	IBM PS/1 vs TEAC FD
		Hello, I already tried our national news group without success. I tried to replace a friend s original IBM floppy disk in his PS/1-PC with a normal TEAC drive. I already identified the power supply on pins 3 (5V) and 6 (12V), shorted pin 6 (5.25"/3.5" switch) and inserted pullup resistors (2K2) on pins 8, 26, 28, 30, and 34. The computer doesn't complain about a missing FD, but the FD s light stays on all the time. The drive spins up o.k. when I insert a disk, but I can't access it. The TEAC works fine in a normal PC. Are there any points I missed? [...]
		[...]

It is interesting how the posts reflect the similarity measurement score. The first post contains all the salient words from our new post. The second also revolves around booting problems, but is about floppy disks and not hard disks. Finally, the third is neither about hard disks, nor about booting problems. Still, of all the posts, we would say that they belong to the same domain as the new post.

Another look at noise

We should not expect a perfect clustering in the sense that posts from the same newsgroup (for example, comp.graphics) are also clustered together. An example will give us a quick impression of the noise that we have to expect. For the sake of simplicity, we will focus on one of the shorter posts:

```
>>> post_group = zip(train_data.data, train_data.target)
>>> all = [(len(post[0]), post[0], train_data.target_names[post[1]])
for post in post_group]
>>> graphics = sorted([post for post in all if
post[2]=='comp.graphics'])
>>> print(graphics[5])
(245, 'From: SITUNAYA@IBM3090.BHAM.AC.UK\nSubject:
test....(sorry)\nOrganization: The University of Birmingham, United
Kingdom\nLines: 1\nNNTP-Posting-Host: ibm3090.bham.ac.uk<...snip...>',
'comp.graphics')
```

For this post, there is no real indication that it belongs to comp.graphics considering only the wording that is left after the preprocessing step:

```
>>> noise_post = graphics[5][1]
>>> analyzer = vectorizer.build_analyzer()
>>> print(list(analyzer(noise_post)))
['situnaya', 'ibm3090', 'bham', 'ac', 'uk', 'subject', 'test',
'sorri', 'organ', 'univers', 'birmingham', 'unit', 'kingdom', 'line',
'nntp', 'post', 'host', 'ibm3090', 'bham', 'ac', 'uk']
```

This is only after tokenization, lowercasing, and stop word removal. If we also subtract those words that will be later filtered out via min_df and max_df, which will be done later in fit_transform, it gets even worse:

```
>>> useful = set(analyzer(noise_post)).intersection
(vectorizer.get_feature_names())
>>> print(sorted(useful))
['ac', 'birmingham', 'host', 'kingdom', 'nntp', 'sorri', 'test',
'uk', 'unit', 'univers']
```

Even more, most of the words occur frequently in other posts as well, as we can check with the IDF scores. Remember that the higher TF-IDF, the more discriminative a term is for a given post. As IDF is a multiplicative factor here, a low value of it signals that it is not of great value in general.

```
>>> for term in sorted(useful):
...     print('IDF(%s)=%.2f'%(term,
vectorizer._tfidf.idf_[vectorizer.vocabulary_[term]]))
IDF(ac)=3.51
IDF(birmingham)=6.77
IDF(host)=1.74
IDF(kingdom)=6.68
IDF(nntp)=1.77
IDF(sorri)=4.14
IDF(test)=3.83
IDF(uk)=3.70
IDF(unit)=4.42
IDF(univers)=1.91
```

So, the terms with the highest discriminative power, `birmingham` and `kingdom`, clearly are not that computer graphics related, the same is the case with the terms with lower IDF scores. Understandably, posts from different newsgroups will be clustered together.

For our goal, however, this is no big deal, as we are only interested in cutting down the number of posts that we have to compare a new post to. After all, the particular newsgroup from where our training data came from is of no special interest.

Tweaking the parameters

So what about all the other parameters? Can we tweak them to get better results?

Sure. We can, of course, tweak the number of clusters, or play with the vectorizer's `max_features` parameter (you should try that!). Also, we can play with different cluster center initializations. Then there are more exciting alternatives to K-means itself. There are, for example, clustering approaches that let you even use different similarity measurements, such as Cosine similarity, Pearson, or Jaccard. An exciting field for you to play.

But before you go there, you will have to define what you actually mean by "better". SciKit has a complete package dedicated only to this definition. The package is called `sklearn.metrics` and also contains a full range of different metrics to measure clustering quality. Maybe that should be the first place to go now. Right into the sources of the metrics package.

Summary

That was a tough ride from pre-processing over clustering to a solution that can convert noisy text into a meaningful concise vector representation, which we can cluster. If we look at the efforts we had to do to finally being able to cluster, it was more than half of the overall task. But on the way, we learned quite a bit on text processing and how simple counting can get you very far in the noisy real-world data.

The ride has been made much smoother, though, because of SciKit and its powerful packages. And there is more to explore. In this chapter, we were scratching the surface of its capabilities. In the next chapters, we will see more of its power.

4
Topic Modeling

In the previous chapter, we grouped text documents using clustering. This is a very useful tool, but it is not always the best. Clustering results in each text belonging to exactly one cluster. This book is about machine learning and Python. Should it be grouped with other Python-related works or with machine-related works? In a physical bookstore, we will need a single place to stock the book. In an Internet store, however, the answer is *this book is about both machine learning and Python* and the book should be listed in both the sections in an online bookstore. This does not mean that the book will be listed in all the sections, of course. We will not list this book with other baking books.

In this chapter, we will learn methods that do not cluster documents into completely separate groups but allow each document to refer to several **topics**. These topics will be identified automatically from a collection of text documents. These documents may be whole books or shorter pieces of text such as a blogpost, a news story, or an e-mail.

We would also like to be able to infer the fact that these documents may have topics that are central to them, while referring to other topics only in passing. This book mentions plotting every so often, but it is not a central topic as machine learning is. This means that documents have topics that are central to them and others that are more peripheral. The subfield of machine learning that deals with these problems is called **topic modeling** and is the subject of this chapter.

Latent Dirichlet allocation

LDA and LDA — unfortunately, there are two methods in machine learning with the initials LDA: latent Dirichlet allocation, which is a topic modeling method and linear discriminant analysis, which is a classification method. They are completely unrelated, except for the fact that the initials LDA can refer to either. In certain situations, this can be confusing. The scikit-learn tool has a submodule, `sklearn.lda`, which implements linear discriminant analysis. At the moment, scikit-learn does not implement latent Dirichlet allocation.

The topic model we will look at is **latent Dirichlet allocation (LDA)**. The mathematical ideas behind LDA are fairly complex, and we will not go into the details here.

For those who are interested, and adventurous enough, Wikipedia will provide all the equations behind these algorithms: `http://en.wikipedia.org/wiki/Latent_Dirichlet_allocation`.

However, we can understand the ideas behind LDA intuitively at a high-level. LDA belongs to a class of models that are called generative models as they have a sort of fable, which explains how the data was generated. This generative story is a simplification of reality, of course, to make machine learning easier. In the LDA fable, we first create topics by assigning probability weights to words. Each topic will assign different weights to different words. For example, a Python topic will assign high probability to the word "variable" and a low probability to the word "inebriated". When we wish to generate a new document, we first choose the topics it will use and then mix words from these topics.

For example, let's say we have only three topics that books discuss:

- Machine learning
- Python
- Baking

For each topic, we have a list of words associated with it. This book will be a mixture of the first two topics, perhaps 50 percent each. The mixture does not need to be equal, it can also be a 70/30 split. When we are generating the actual text, we generate word by word; first we decide which topic this word will come from. This is a random decision based on the topic weights. Once a topic is chosen, we generate a word from that topic's list of words. To be precise, we choose a word in English with the probability given by the topic.

In this model, the order of words does not matter. This is a *bag of words* model as we have already seen in the previous chapter. It is a crude simplification of language, but it often works well enough, because just knowing which words were used in a document and their frequencies are enough to make machine learning decisions.

In the real world, we do not know what the topics are. Our task is to take a collection of text and to reverse engineer this fable in order to discover what topics are out there and simultaneously figure out which topics each document uses.

Building a topic model

Unfortunately, scikit-learn does not support latent Dirichlet allocation. Therefore, we are going to use the gensim package in Python. Gensim is developed by Radim Řehůřek who is a machine learning researcher and consultant in the United Kingdom. We must start by installing it. We can achieve this by running the following command:

```
pip install gensim
```

As input data, we are going to use a collection of news reports from the **Associated Press (AP)**. This is a standard dataset for text modeling research, which was used in some of the initial works on topic models. After downloading the data, we can load it by running the following code:

```
>>> from gensim import corpora, models
>>> corpus = corpora.BleiCorpus('./data/ap/ap.dat',
    './data/ap/vocab.txt')
```

The corpus variable holds all of the text documents and has loaded them in a format that makes for easy processing. We can now build a topic model using this object as input:

```
>>> model = models.ldamodel.LdaModel(
            corpus,
            num_topics=100,
            id2word=corpus.id2word)
```

This single constructor call will statistically infer which topics are present in the corpus. We can explore the resulting model in many ways. We can see the list of topics a document refers to using the model[doc] syntax, as shown in the following example:

```
>>> doc = corpus.docbyoffset(0)
>>> topics = model[doc]
>>> print(topics)
[(3, 0.023607255776894751),
 (13, 0.11679936618551275),
 (19, 0.075935855202707139),
....
 (92, 0.10781541687001292)]
```

The result will almost surely look different on our computer! The learning algorithm uses some random numbers and every time you learn a new topic model on the same input data, the result is different. Some of the qualitative properties of the model will be stable across different runs if your data is well behaved. For example, if you are using the topics to compare documents, as we do here, then the similarities should be robust and change only slightly. On the other hand, the order of the different topics will be completely different.

The format of the result is a list of pairs: `(topic_index, topic_weight)`. We can see that only a few topics are used for each document (in the preceding example, there is no weight for topics 0, 1, and 2; the weight for those topics is 0). The topic model is a sparse model, as although there are many possible topics; for each document, only a few of them are used. This is not strictly true as all the topics have a nonzero probability in the LDA model, but some of them have such a small probability that we can round it to zero as a good approximation.

We can explore this further by plotting a histogram of the number of topics that each document refers to:

```
>>> num_topics_used = [len(model[doc]) for doc in corpus]
>>> plt.hist(num_topics_used)
```

You will get the following plot:

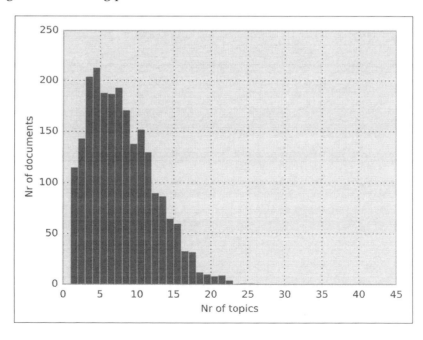

Sparsity means that while you may have large matrices and vectors, in principle, most of the values are zero (or so small that we can round them to zero as a good approximation). Therefore, only a few things are relevant at any given time.

Often problems that seem too big to solve are actually feasible because the data is sparse. For example, even though any web page can link to any other web page, the graph of links is actually very sparse as each web page will link to a very tiny fraction of all other web pages.

In the preceding graph, we can see that about 150 documents have 5 topics, while the majority deals with around 10 to 12 of them. No document talks about more than 20 different topics.

To a large extent, this is due to the value of the parameters that were used, namely, the `alpha` parameter. The exact meaning of alpha is a bit abstract, but bigger values for alpha will result in more topics per document.

Alpha needs to be a value greater than zero, but is typically set to a lesser value, usually, less than one. The smaller the value of `alpha`, the fewer topics each document will be expected to discuss. By default, gensim will set `alpha` to `1/num_topics`, but you can set it explicitly by passing it as an argument in the `LdaModel` constructor as follows:

```
>>> model = models.ldamodel.LdaModel(
        corpus,
        num_topics=100,
        id2word=corpus.id2word,
        alpha=1)
```

In this case, this is a larger alpha than the default, which should lead to more topics per document. As we can see in the combined histogram given next, gensim behaves as we expected and assigns more topics to each document:

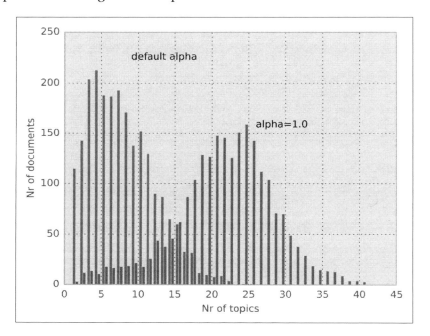

Now, we can see in the preceding histogram that many documents touch upon 20 to 25 different topics. If you set the value lower, you will observe the opposite (downloading the code from the online repository will allow you to play around with these values).

What are these topics? Technically, as we discussed earlier, they are multinomial distributions over words, which means that they assign a probability to each word in the vocabulary. Words with high probability are more associated with that topic than words with lower probability.

Our brains are not very good at reasoning with probability distributions, but we can readily make sense of a list of words. Therefore, it is typical to summarize topics by the list of the most highly weighted words.

In the following table, we display the first ten topics:

Topic no.	Topic
1	dress military soviet president new state capt carlucci states leader stance government
2	koch zambia lusaka oneparty orange kochs party i government mayor new political
3	human turkey rights abuses royal thompson threats new state wrote garden president
4	bill employees experiments levin taxation federal measure legislation senate president whistleblowers sponsor
5	ohio july drought jesus disaster percent hartford mississippi crops northern valley virginia
6	united percent billion year president world years states people i bush news
7	b hughes affidavit states united ounces squarefoot care delaying charged unrealistic bush
8	yeutter dukakis bush convention farm subsidies uruguay percent secretary general i told
9	kashmir government people srinagar india dumps city two jammukashmir group moslem pakistan
10	workers vietnamese irish wage immigrants percent bargaining last island police hutton I

Although daunting at first glance, when reading through the list of words, we can clearly see that the topics are not just random words, but instead these are logical groups. We can also see that these topics refer to older news items, from when the Soviet Union still existed and Gorbachev was its Secretary General. We can also represent the topics as word clouds, making more likely words larger. For example, this is the visualization of a topic which deals with the Middle East and politics:

We can also see that some of the words should perhaps be removed (for example, the word "I") as they are not so informative, they are stop words. When building topic modeling, it can be useful to filter out stop words, as otherwise, you might end up with a topic consisting entirely of stop words. We may also wish to preprocess the text to stems in order to normalize plurals and verb forms. This process was covered in the previous chapter and you can refer to it for details. If you are interested, you can download the code from the companion website of the book and try all these variations to draw different pictures.

 Building a word cloud like the previous one can be done with several different pieces of software. For the graphics in this chapter, we used a Python-based tool called pytagcloud. This package requires a few dependencies to install and is not central to machine learning, so we won't consider it in the main text; however, we have all of the code available in the online code repository to generate the figures in this chapter.

Comparing documents by topics

Topics can be useful on their own to build the sort of small vignettes with words that are shown in the previous screenshot. These visualizations can be used to navigate a large collection of documents. For example, a website can display the different topics as different word clouds, allowing a user to click through to the documents. In fact, they have been used in just this way to analyze large collections of documents.

However, topics are often just an intermediate tool to another end. Now that we have an estimate for each document of how much of that document comes from each topic, we can compare the documents in topic space. This simply means that instead of comparing word to word, we say that two documents are similar if they talk about the same topics.

This can be very powerful as two text documents that share few words may actually refer to the same topic! They may just refer to it using different constructions (for example, one document may read "the President of the United States" while the other will use the name "Barack Obama").

 Topic models are good on their own to build visualizations and explore data. They are also very useful as an intermediate step in many other tasks.

At this point, we can redo the exercise we performed in the last chapter and look for the most similar post to an input query, by using the topics to define similarity. Whereas, earlier we compared two documents by comparing their word vectors directly, we can now compare two documents by comparing their topic vectors.

For this, we are going to project the documents to the topic space. That is, we want to have a vector of topics that summarize the document. How to perform these types of **dimensionality reduction** in general is an important task in itself and we have a chapter entirely devoted to this task. For the moment, we just show how topic models can be used for exactly this purpose; once topics have been computed for each document, we can perform operations on its topic vector and forget about the original words. If the topics are meaningful, they will be potentially more informative than the raw words. Additionally, this may bring computational advantages, as it is much faster to compare 100 vectors of topic weights than vectors of the size of the vocabulary (which will contain thousands of terms).

Using gensim, we have seen earlier how to compute the topics corresponding to all the documents in the corpus. We will now compute these for all the documents and store it in a NumPy arrays and compute all pairwise distances:

```
>>> from gensim import matutils
>>> topics = matutils.corpus2dense(model[corpus],
    num_terms=model.num_topics)
```

Now, `topics` is a matrix of topics. We can use the `pdist` function in SciPy to compute all pairwise distances. That is, with a single function call, we compute all the values of `sum((topics[ti] - topics[tj])**2)`:

```
>>> from scipy.spatial import distance
>>> pairwise = distance.squareform(distance.pdist(topics))
```

Now, we will employ one last little trick; we will set the diagonal elements of the `distance` matrix to a high value (it just needs to be larger than the other values in the matrix):

```
>>> largest = pairwise.max()
>>> for ti in range(len(topics)):
...     pairwise[ti,ti] = largest+1
```

And we are done! For each document, we can look up the closest element easily (this is a type of nearest neighbor classifier):

```
>>> def closest_to(doc_id):
...     return pairwise[doc_id].argmin()
```

Note that this will not work if we had not set the diagonal elements to a large value: the function will always return the same element as it is the one most similar to itself (except in the weird case where two elements had exactly the same topic distribution, which is very rare unless they are exactly the same).

For example, here is one possible query document (it is the second document in our collection):

```
From: geb@cs.pitt.edu (Gordon Banks)
Subject: Re: request for information on "essential tremor" and
Indrol?


In article <1q1tbnINNnfn@life.ai.mit.edu> sundar@ai.mit.edu
writes:


Essential tremor is a progressive hereditary tremor that gets
worse
when the patient tries to use the effected member.  All limbs,
vocal
cords, and head can be involved.  Inderal is a beta-blocker and
is usually effective in diminishing the tremor.  Alcohol and
mysoline
are also effective, but alcohol is too toxic to use as a
treatment.
--
-----------------------------------------------------------------
----------
Gordon Banks  N3JXP        | "Skepticism is the chastity of the
intellect, and
geb@cadre.dsl.pitt.edu     |  it is shameful to surrender it too
soon."
   -----------------------------------------------------------------
------------
```

If we ask for the most similar document to closest_to(1), we receive the following document as a result:

```
From: geb@cs.pitt.edu (Gordon Banks)
Subject: Re: High Prolactin


In article <93088.112203JER4@psuvm.psu.edu> JER4@psuvm.psu.edu
(John E. Rodway) writes:
>Any comments on the use of the drug Parlodel for high prolactin
in the blood?
```

```
>

It can suppress secretion of prolactin.  Is useful in cases of
galactorrhea.
Some adenomas of the pituitary secret too much.


--
------------------------------------------------------------
----------
Gordon Banks  N3JXP       | "Skepticism is the chastity of the
intellect, and
geb@cadre.dsl.pitt.edu    |  it is shameful to surrender it too
soon."
```

The system returns a post by the same author discussing medications.

Modeling the whole of Wikipedia

While the initial LDA implementations can be slow, which limited their use to small document collections, modern algorithms work well with very large collections of data. Following the documentation of gensim, we are going to build a topic model for the whole of the English-language Wikipedia. This takes hours, but can be done even with just a laptop! With a cluster of machines, we can make it go much faster, but we will look at that sort of processing environment in a later chapter.

First, we download the whole Wikipedia dump from http://dumps.wikimedia.org. This is a large file (currently over 10 GB), so it may take a while, unless your Internet connection is very fast. Then, we will index it with a gensim tool:

```
python -m gensim.scripts.make_wiki \
        enwiki-latest-pages-articles.xml.bz2 wiki_en_output
```

Run the previous line on the command shell, not on the Python shell. After a few hours, the index will be saved in the same directory. At this point, we can build the final topic model. This process looks exactly like what we did for the small AP dataset. We first import a few packages:

```
>>> import logging, gensim
```

Now, we set up logging, using the standard Python logging module (which gensim uses to print out status messages). This step is not strictly necessary, but it is nice to have a little more output to know what is happening:

```
>>> logging.basicConfig(
        format='%(asctime)s : %(levelname)s : %(message)s',
        level=logging.INFO)
```

Now we load the preprocessed data:

```
>>> id2word = gensim.corpora.Dictionary.load_from_text(
            'wiki_en_output_wordids.txt')
>>> mm = gensim.corpora.MmCorpus('wiki_en_output_tfidf.mm')
```

Finally, we build the LDA model as we did earlier:

```
>>> model = gensim.models.ldamodel.LdaModel(
        corpus=mm,
        id2word=id2word,
        num_topics=100,
        update_every=1,
        chunksize=10000,
        passes=1)
```

This will again take a couple of hours. You will see the progress on your console, which can give you an indication of how long you still have to wait.

Once it is done, we can save the topic model to a file, so we don't have to redo it:

```
>>> model.save('wiki_lda.pkl')
```

If you exit your session and come back later, you can load the model again using the following command (after the appropriate imports, naturally):

```
>>> model = gensim.models.ldamodel.LdaModel.load('wiki_lda.pkl')
```

The `model` object can be used to explore the collection of documents, and build the `topics` matrix as we did earlier.

We can see that this is still a sparse model even if we have many more documents than we had earlier (over 4 million as we are writing this):

```
>>> lens = (topics > 0).sum(axis=0)
>>> print(np.mean(lens))
6.41
>>> print(np.mean(lens <= 10))
0.941
```

So, the average document mentions 6.4 topics and 94 percent of them mention 10 or fewer topics.

We can ask what the most talked about topic in Wikipedia is. We will first compute the total weight for each topic (by summing up the weights from all the documents) and then retrieve the words corresponding to the most highly weighted topic. This is performed using the following code:

```
>>> weights = topics.sum(axis=0)
>>> words = model.show_topic(weights.argmax(), 64)
```

Using the same tools as we did earlier to build up a visualization, we can see that the most talked about topic is related to music and is a very coherent topic. A full 18 percent of Wikipedia pages are partially related to this topic (5.5 percent of all the words in Wikipedia are assigned to this topic). Take a look at the following screenshot:

 These plots and numbers were obtained when the book was being written. As Wikipedia keeps changing, your results will be different. We expect that the trends will be similar, but the details may vary.

Alternatively, we can look at the least talked about topic:

```
>>> words = model.show_topic(weights.argmin(), 64)
```

The least talked about topic is harder to interpret, but many of its top words refer to airports in eastern countries. Just 1.6 percent of documents touch upon it, and it represents just 0.1 percent of the words.

Choosing the number of topics

So far in the chapter, we have used a fixed number of topics for our analyses, namely 100. This was a purely arbitrary number, we could have just as well used either 20 or 200 topics. Fortunately, for many uses, this number does not really matter. If you are going to only use the topics as an intermediate step, as we did previously when finding similar posts, the final behavior of the system is rarely very sensitive to the exact number of topics used in the model. This means that as long as you use enough topics, whether you use 100 topics or 200, the recommendations that result from the process will not be very different; 100 is often a good enough number (while 20 is too few for a general collection of text documents). The same is true of setting the alpha value. While playing around with it can change the topics, the final results are again robust against this change.

Topic modeling is often an end towards a goal. In that case, it is not always very important exactly which parameter values are used. A different number of topics or values for parameters such as `alpha` will result in systems whose end results are almost identical in their final results.

On the other hand, if you are going to explore the topics directly, or build a visualization tool that exposes them, you should probably try a few values and see which gives you the most useful or most appealing results.

Alternatively, there are a few methods that will automatically determine the number of topics for you, depending on the dataset. One popular model is called the **hierarchical Dirichlet process**. Again, the full mathematical model behind it is complex and beyond the scope of this book. However, the fable we can tell is that instead of having the topics fixed first as in the LDA generative story, the topics themselves were generated along with the data, one at a time. Whenever the writer starts a new document, they have the option of using the topics that already exist or to create a completely new one. When more topics have already been created, the probability of creating a new one, instead of reusing what exists goes down, but the possibility always exists.

This means *that the more documents we have, the more topics we will end up with*. This is one of those statements that is unintuitive at first but makes perfect sense upon reflection. We are grouping documents and the more examples we have, the more we can break them up. If we only have a few examples of news articles, then "Sports" will be a topic. However, as we have more, we start to break it up into the individual modalities: "Hockey", "Soccer", and so on. As we have even more data, we can start to tell nuances apart, articles about individual teams and even individual players. The same is true for people. In a group of many different backgrounds, with a few "computer people", you might put them together; in a slightly larger group, you will have separate gatherings for programmers and systems administrators; and in the real-world, we even have different gatherings for Python and Ruby programmers.

The **hierarchical Dirichlet process (HDP)** is available in gensim. Using it is trivial. To adapt the code we wrote for LDA, we just need to replace the call to `gensim.models.ldamodel.LdaModel` with a call to the `HdpModel` constructor as follows:

```
>>> hdp = gensim.models.hdpmodel.HdpModel(mm, id2word)
```

That's it (except that it takes a bit longer to compute — there are no free lunches). Now, we can use this model in much the same way as we used the LDA model, except that we did not need to specify the number of topics.

Summary

In this chapter, we discussed topic modeling. Topic modeling is more flexible than clustering as these methods allow each document to be partially present in more than one group. To explore these methods, we used a new package, gensim.

Topic modeling was first developed and is easier to understand in the case of text, but in the computer vision chapter we will see how some of these techniques may be applied to images as well. Topic models are very important in modern computer vision research. In fact, unlike the previous chapters, this chapter was very close to the cutting edge of research in machine learning algorithms. The original LDA algorithm was published in a scientific journal in 2003, but the method that gensim uses to be able to handle Wikipedia was only developed in 2010 and the HDP algorithm is from 2011. The research continues and you can find many variations and models with wonderful names such as *the Indian buffet process* (not to be confused with the *Chinese restaurant process*, which is a different model), or *Pachinko allocation* (Pachinko being a type of Japanese game, a cross between a slot-machine and pinball).

We have now gone through some of the major machine learning modes: classification, clustering, and topic modeling.

In the next chapter, we go back to classification, but this time, we will be exploring advanced algorithms and approaches.

5
Classification – Detecting Poor Answers

Now that we are able to extract useful features from text, we can take on the challenge of building a classifier using real data. Let's come back to our imaginary website in *Chapter 3, Clustering – Finding Related Posts*, where users can submit questions and get them answered.

A continuous challenge for owners of those Q&A sites is to maintain a decent level of quality in the posted content. Sites such as StackOverflow make considerable efforts to encourage users with diverse possibilities to score content and offer badges and bonus points in order to encourage the users to spend more energy on carving out the question or crafting a possible answer.

One particular successful incentive is the ability for the asker to flag one answer to their question as the accepted answer (again there are incentives for the asker to flag answers as such). This will result in more score points for the author of the flagged answer.

Would it not be very useful to the user to immediately see how good his answer is while he is typing it in? That means, the website would continuously evaluate his work-in-progress answer and provide feedback as to whether the answer shows some signs of a poor one. This will encourage the user to put more effort into writing the answer (providing a code example? including an image?), and thus improve the overall system.

Let's build such a mechanism in this chapter.

Sketching our roadmap

As we will build a system using real data that is very noisy, this chapter is not for the fainthearted, as we will not arrive at the golden solution of a classifier that achieves 100 percent accuracy; often, even humans disagree whether an answer was good or not (just look at some of the StackOverflow comments). Quite the contrary, we will find out that some problems like this one are so hard that we have to adjust our initial goals on the way. But on the way, we will start with the nearest neighbor approach, find out why it is not very good for the task, switch over to logistic regression, and arrive at a solution that will achieve good enough prediction quality, but on a smaller part of the answers. Finally, we will spend some time looking at how to extract the winner to deploy it on the target system.

Learning to classify classy answers

In classification, we want to find the corresponding **classes**, sometimes also called **labels**, for given data instances. To be able to achieve this, we need to answer two questions:

- How should we represent the data instances?
- Which model or structure should our classifier possess?

Tuning the instance

In its simplest form, in our case, the data instance is the text of the answer and the label would be a binary value indicating whether the asker accepted this text as an answer or not. Raw text, however, is a very inconvenient representation to process for most machine learning algorithms. They want numbers. And it will be our task to extract useful features from the raw text, which the machine learning algorithm can then use to learn the right label for it.

Tuning the classifier

Once we have found or collected enough (text, label) pairs, we can train a **classifier**. For the underlying structure of the classifier, we have a wide range of possibilities, each of them having advantages and drawbacks. Just to name some of the more prominent choices, there are logistic regression, decision trees, SVMs, and Naïve Bayes. In this chapter, we will contrast the instance-based method from the last chapter, nearest neighbor, with model-based logistic regression.

Fetching the data

Luckily for us, the team behind StackOverflow provides most of the data behind the StackExchange universe to which StackOverflow belongs under a cc-wiki license. At the time of writing this book, the latest data dump can be found at `https://archive.org/details/stackexchange`. It contains data dumps of all Q&A sites of the StackExchange family. For StackOverflow, you will find multiple files, of which we only need the `stackoverflow.com-Posts.7z` file, which is 5.2 GB.

After downloading and extracting it, we have around 26 GB of data in the format of XML, containing all questions and answers as individual `row` tags within the `root` tag posts:

```
<?xml version="1.0" encoding="utf-8"?>
<posts>
...
  <row Id="4572748" PostTypeId="2" ParentId="4568987"
CreationDate="2011-01-01T00:01:03.387" Score="4" ViewCount=""
Body="&lt;p&gt;IANAL, but &lt;a
href=&quot;http://support.apple.com/kb/HT2931&quot;
rel=&quot;nofollow&quot;&gt;this&lt;/a&gt; indicates to me that you
cannot use the loops in your
application:&lt;/p&gt;&#xA;&#xA;&lt;blockquote&gt;&#xA;
&lt;p&gt;...however, individual audio loops may&#xA;  not be
commercially or otherwise&#xA;  distributed on a standalone basis,
nor&#xA;  may they be repackaged in whole or in&#xA;  part as audio
samples, sound effects&#xA;  or music beds.&quot;&lt;/p&gt;&#xA;
&#xA;  &lt;p&gt;So don't worry, you can make&#xA;  commercial music
with GarageBand, you&#xA;  just can't distribute the loops as&#xA;
loops.&lt;/p&gt;&#xA;&lt;/blockquote&gt;&#xA;" OwnerUserId="203568"
LastActivityDate="2011-01-01T00:01:03.387" CommentCount="1" />
...
</posts>
```

Name	Type	Description
Id	Integer	This is a unique identifier.
PostTypeId	Integer	This describes the category of the post. The values interesting to us are the following: • Question • Answer Other values will be ignored.
ParentId	Integer	This is a unique identifier of the question to which this answer belongs (missing for questions).

Name	Type	Description
CreationDate	DateTime	This is the date of submission.
Score	Integer	This is the score of the post.
ViewCount	Integer or empty	This is the number of user views for this post.
Body	String	This is the complete post as encoded HTML text.
OwnerUserId	Id	This is a unique identifier of the poster. If 1, then it is a wiki question.
Title	String	This is the title of the question (missing for answers).
AcceptedAnswerId	Id	This is the ID for the accepted answer (missing for answers).
CommentCount	Integer	This is the number of comments for the post.

Slimming the data down to chewable chunks

To speed up our experimentation phase, we should not try to evaluate our classification ideas on the huge XML file. Instead, we should think of how we could trim it down so that we still keep a representable snapshot of it while being able to quickly test our ideas. If we filter the XML for row tags that have a creation date of, for example, 2012, we still end up with over 6 million posts (2,323,184 questions and 4,055,999 answers), which should be enough to pick our training data from for now. We also do not want to operate on the XML format as it will slow us down, too. The simpler the format, the better. That's why we parse the remaining XML using Python's cElementTree and write it out to a tab-separated file.

Preselection and processing of attributes

To cut down the data even more, we can certainly drop attributes that we think will not help the classifier in distinguishing between good and not-so-good answers. But we have to be cautious here. Although some features are not directly impacting the classification, they are still necessary to keep.

The PostTypeId attribute, for example, is necessary to distinguish between questions and answers. It will not be picked to serve as a feature, but we will need it to filter the data.

CreationDate could be interesting to determine the time span between posting the question and posting the individual answers, so we keep it. The Score is of course important as an indicator for the community's evaluation.

ViewCount, in contrast, is most likely of no use for our task. Even if it would help the classifier to distinguish between good and bad, we would not have this information at the time when an answer is being submitted. Drop it!

The Body attribute obviously contains the most important information. As it is encoded HTML, we will have to decode to plain text.

OwnerUserId is only useful if we take user-dependent features in to account, which we won't. Although we drop it here, we encourage you to use it to build a better classifier (maybe in connection with stackoverflow.com-Users.7z).

The Title attribute is also ignored here, although it could add some more information about the question.

CommentCount is also ignored. Similar to ViewCount, it could help the classifier with posts that are out there for a while (more comments = more ambiguous post?). It will, however, not help the classifier at the time an answer is posted.

AcceptedAnswerId is similar to Score in that it is an indicator of a post's quality. As we will access this per answer, instead of keeping this attribute, we will create the new attribute IsAccepted, which is 0 or 1 for answers and ignored for questions (ParentId=-1).

We end up with the following format:

```
Id <TAB> ParentId <TAB> IsAccepted <TAB> TimeToAnswer <TAB> Score
<TAB> Text
```

For the concrete parsing details, please refer to so_xml_to_tsv.py and choose_instance.py. Suffice to say that in order to speed up processing, we will split the data into two files: in meta.json, we store a dictionary mapping a post's Id value to its other data except Text in JSON format so that we can read it in the proper format. For example, the score of a post would reside at meta[Id]['Score']. In data.tsv, we store the Id and Text values, which we can easily read with the following method:

```python
def fetch_posts():
    for line in open("data.tsv", "r"):
        post_id, text = line.split("\t")
        yield int(post_id), text.strip()
```

Defining what is a good answer

Before we can train a classifier to distinguish between good and bad answers, we have to create the training data. So far, we only have a bunch of data. What we still have to do is define labels.

We could, of course, simply use the `IsAccepted` attribute as a label. After all, that marks the answer that answered the question. However, that is only the opinion of the asker. Naturally, the asker wants to have a quick answer and accepts the first *best* answer. If over time more answers are submitted, some of them will tend to be better than the already accepted one. The asker, however, seldom gets back to the question and changes his mind. So we end up with many questions that have accepted answers that are not scored highest.

At the other extreme, we could simply always take the best and worst scored answer per question as positive and negative examples. However, what do we do with questions that have only good answers, say, one with two and the other with four points? Should we really take an answer with, for example, two points as a negative example just because it happened to be the one with the lower score?

We should settle somewhere between these extremes. If we take all answers that are scored higher than zero as positive and all answers with zero or less points as negative, we end up with quite reasonable labels:

```
>>> all_answers = [q for q,v in meta.items() if v['ParentId']!=-1]
>>> Y = np.asarray([meta[answerId]['Score']>0 for answerId in
all_answers])
```

Creating our first classifier

Let's start with the simple and beautiful nearest neighbor method from the previous chapter. Although it is not as advanced as other methods, it is very powerful: as it is not model-based, it can *learn* nearly any data. But this beauty comes with a clear disadvantage, which we will find out very soon.

Starting with kNN

This time, we won't implement it ourselves, but rather take it from the `sklearn` toolkit. There, the classifier resides in `sklearn.neighbors`. Let's start with a simple 2-Nearest Neighbor classifier:

```
>>> from sklearn import neighbors
>>> knn = neighbors.KNeighborsClassifier(n_neighbors=2)
>>> print(knn)
```

```
KNeighborsClassifier(algorithm='auto', leaf_size=30,
metric='minkowski', n_neighbors=2, p=2, weights='uniform')
```

It provides the same interface as all other estimators in `sklearn`: we train it using `fit()`, after which we can predict the class of new data instances using `predict()`:

```
>>> knn.fit([[1],[2],[3],[4],[5],[6]], [0,0,0,1,1,1])
>>> knn.predict(1.5)
array([0])
>>> knn.predict(37)
array([1])
>>> knn.predict(3)
array([0])
```

To get the class probabilities, we can use `predict_proba()`. In this case of having two classes, `0` and `1`, it will return an array of two elements:

```
>>> knn.predict_proba(1.5)
array([[ 1.,   0.]])
>>> knn.predict_proba(37)
array([[ 0.,   1.]])
>>> knn.predict_proba(3.5)
array([[ 0.5,   0.5]])
```

Engineering the features

So, what kind of features can we provide to our classifier? What do we think will have the most discriminative power?

`TimeToAnswer` is already there in our `meta` dictionary, but it probably won't provide much value on its own. Then there is only `Text`, but in its raw form, we cannot pass it to the classifier, as the features must be in numerical form. We will have to do the dirty (and fun!) work of extracting features from it.

What we could do is check the number of HTML links in the answer as a proxy for quality. Our hypothesis would be that more hyperlinks in an answer indicate better answers and thus a higher likelihood of being up-voted. Of course, we want to only count links in normal text and not code examples:

```
import re

code_match = re.compile('<pre>(.*?)</pre>',
                        re.MULTILINE | re.DOTALL)
link_match = re.compile('<a href="http://.*?".*?>(.*?)</a>',
```

```
                              re.MULTILINE | re.DOTALL)
tag_match = re.compile('<[^>]*>',
                              re.MULTILINE | re.DOTALL)


def extract_features_from_body(s):
    link_count_in_code = 0
    # count links in code to later subtract them
    for match_str in code_match.findall(s):
        link_count_in_code += len(link_match.findall(match_str))


    return len(link_match.findall(s)) - link_count_in_code
```

 For production systems, we would not want to parse HTML content with regular expressions. Instead, we should rely on excellent libraries such as BeautifulSoup, which does a marvelous job of robustly handling all the weird things that typically occur in everyday HTML.

With this in place, we can generate one feature per answer. But before we train the classifier, let's first have a look at what we will train it with. We can get a first impression with the frequency distribution of our new feature. This can be done by plotting the percentage of how often each value occurs in the data. Have a look at the following plot:

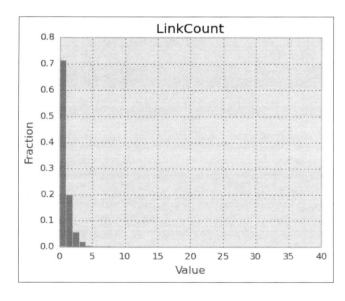

With the majority of posts having no link at all, we know now that this feature will not make a good classifier alone. Let's nevertheless try it out to get a first estimation of where we are.

Training the classifier

We have to pass the feature array together with the previously defined labels Y to the kNN learner to obtain a classifier:

```
X = np.asarray([extract_features_from_body(text) for post_id, text in
                fetch_posts() if post_id in all_answers])
knn = neighbors.KNeighborsClassifier()
knn.fit(X, Y)
```

Using the standard parameters, we just fitted a 5NN (meaning NN with k=5) to our data. Why 5NN? Well, at the current state of our knowledge about the data, we really have no clue what the right k should be. Once we have more insight, we will have a better idea of how to set k.

Measuring the classifier's performance

We have to be clear about what we want to measure. The naïve but easiest way is to simply calculate the average prediction quality over the test set. This will result in a value between 0 for predicting everything wrongly and 1 for perfect prediction. The accuracy can be obtained through knn.score().

But as we learned in the previous chapter, we will not do it just once, but apply cross-validation here using the readymade KFold class from sklearn.cross_validation. Finally, we will then average the scores on the test set of each fold and see how much it varies using standard deviation:

```
from sklearn.cross_validation import KFold
scores = []


cv = KFold(n=len(X), k=10, indices=True)


for train, test in cv:
    X_train, y_train = X[train], Y[train]
    X_test, y_test = X[test], Y[test]
    clf = neighbors.KNeighborsClassifier()
    clf.fit(X, Y)
```

```
        scores.append(clf.score(X_test, y_test))

print("Mean(scores)=%.5f\tStddev(scores)=%.5f"\
    %(np.mean(scores), np.std(scores)))
```

Here is the output:

```
Mean(scores)=0.50250    Stddev(scores)=0.055591
```

Now that is far from being usable. With only 55 percent accuracy, it is not much better than tossing a coin. Apparently, the number of links in a post is not a very good indicator for the quality of a post. So, we can say that this feature does not have much discriminative power—at least not for kNN with k=5.

Designing more features

In addition to using the number of hyperlinks as a proxy for a post's quality, the number of code lines is possibly another good one, too. At least it is a good indicator that the post's author is interested in answering the question. We can find the code embedded in the <pre>...</pre> tag. And once we have it extracted, we should count the number of words in the post while ignoring code lines:

```
def extract_features_from_body(s):
    num_code_lines = 0
    link_count_in_code = 0
    code_free_s = s

    # remove source code and count how many lines
    for match_str in code_match.findall(s):
        num_code_lines += match_str.count('\n')
        code_free_s = code_match.sub("", code_free_s)

        # Sometimes source code contains links,
        # which we don't want to count
        link_count_in_code += len(link_match.findall(match_str))

    links = link_match.findall(s)
    link_count = len(links)
    link_count -= link_count_in_code
    html_free_s = re.sub(" +", " ",
```

```
        tag_match.sub('',  code_free_s)).replace("\n", "")
link_free_s = html_free_s


# remove links from text before counting words
for link in links:
    if link.lower().startswith("http://"):
        link_free_s = link_free_s.replace(link,'')


num_text_tokens = html_free_s.count(" ")


    return num_text_tokens, num_code_lines, link_count
```

Looking at them, we notice that at least the number of words in a post shows higher variability:

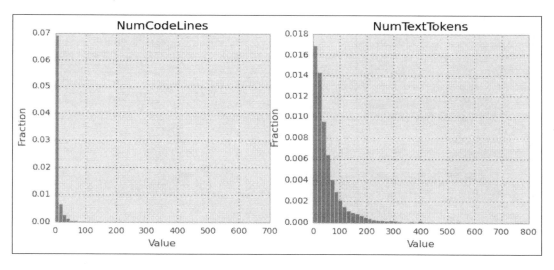

Training on the bigger feature space improves accuracy quite a bit:

```
Mean(scores)=0.59800     Stddev(scores)=0.02600
```

But still, this would mean that we would classify roughly 4 out of 10 wrong. At least we are going in the right direction. More features lead to higher accuracy, which leads us to adding more features. Therefore, let's extend the feature space by even more features:

- `AvgSentLen`: This measures the average number of words in a sentence. Maybe there is a pattern that particularly good posts don't overload the reader's brain with overly long sentences?
- `AvgWordLen`: Similar to `AvgSentLen`, this feature measures the average number of characters in the words of a post.
- `NumAllCaps`: This measures the number of words that are written in uppercase, which is considered bad style.
- `NumExclams`: This measures the number of exclamation marks.

The following charts show the value distributions for average sentence and word lengths and number of uppercase words and exclamation marks:

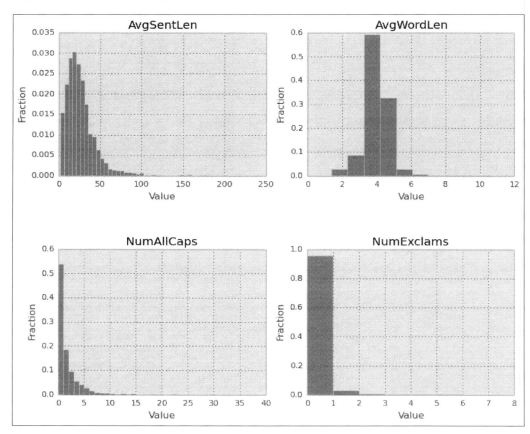

With these four additional features, we now have seven features representing the individual posts. Let's see how we progress:

```
Mean(scores)=0.61400      Stddev(scores)= 0.02154
```

Now, that's interesting. We added four more features and don't get anything in return. How can that be?

To understand this, we have to remind ourselves how kNN works. Our 5NN classifier determines the class of a new post by calculating the seven aforementioned features, LinkCount, NumTextTokens, NumCodeLines, AvgSentLen, AvgWordLen, NumAllCaps, and NumExclams, and then finds the five nearest other posts. The new post's class is then the majority of the classes of those nearest posts. The nearest posts are determined by calculating the Euclidean distance (as we did not specify it, the classifier was initialized with the default p=2, which is the parameter in the Minkowski distance). That means that all seven features are treated similarly. kNN does not really learn that, for instance, NumTextTokens is good to have but much less important than NumLinks. Let's consider the following two posts A and B that only differ in the following features and how they compare to a new post:

Post	NumLinks	NumTextTokens
A	2	20
B	0	25
new	1	23

Although we would think that links provide more value than mere text, post B would be considered more similar to the new post than post A.

Clearly, kNN has a hard time in correctly using the available data.

Deciding how to improve

To improve on this, we basically have the following options:

- **Add more data**: Maybe it is just not enough data for the learning algorithm and we should simply add more training data?
- **Play with the model complexity**: Maybe the model is not complex enough? Or maybe it is already too complex? In this case, we could decrease *k* so that it would take less nearest neighbors into account and thus be better in predicting non-smooth data. Or we could increase it to achieve the opposite.

- **Modify the feature space**: Maybe we do not have the right set of features? We could, for example, change the scale of our current features or design even more new features. Or should we rather remove some of our current features in case some features are aliasing others?

- **Change the model**: Maybe kNN is in general not a good fit for our use case such that it will never be capable of achieving good prediction performance, no matter how complex we allow it to be and how sophisticated the feature space will become?

In real life, at this point, people often try to improve the current performance by randomly picking one of the these options and trying them out in no particular order, hoping to find the golden configuration by chance. We could do the same here, but it will surely take longer than making informed decisions. Let's take the informed route, for which we need to introduce the bias-variance tradeoff.

Bias-variance and their tradeoff

In *Chapter 1*, *Getting Started with Python Machine Learning*, we tried to fit polynomials of different complexities controlled by the dimensionality parameter d to fit the data. We realized that a two-dimensional polynomial, a straight line, does not fit the example data very well, because the data was not of linear nature. No matter how elaborate our fitting procedure would have been, our two-dimensional model would see everything as a straight line. We say that it is too biased for the data at hand. It is under-fitting.

We played a bit with the dimensions and found out that the 100-dimensional polynomial is actually fitting very well to the data on which it was trained (we did not know about train-test splits at that time). However, we quickly found out that it was fitting too well. We realized that it was over-fitting so badly, that with different samples of the data points, we would have gotten totally different 100-dimensional polynomials. We say that the model has a too high variance for the given data, or that it is over-fitting.

These are the extremes between which most of our machine learning problems reside. Ideally, we want to have both, low bias and low variance. But, we are in a bad world, and have to tradeoff between them. If we improve on one, we will likely get worse on the other.

Fixing high bias

Let's now assume we suffer from high bias. In that case, adding more training data clearly does not help. Also, removing features surely will not help, as our model would have already been overly simplistic.

The only possibilities we have in this case are to get more features, make the model more complex, or change the model.

Fixing high variance

If, on the contrary, we suffer from high variance, that means that our model is too complex for the data. In this case, we can only try to get more data or decrease the complexity. This would mean to increase k so that more neighbors would be taken into account or to remove some of the features.

High bias or low bias

To find out what our problem actually is, we have to simply plot the train and test errors over the data size.

High bias is typically revealed by the test error decreasing a bit at the beginning, but then settling at a very high value with the train error approaching with a growing dataset size. High variance is recognized by a big gap between both curves.

Plotting the errors for different dataset sizes for 5NN shows a big gap between train and test errors, hinting at a high variance problem:

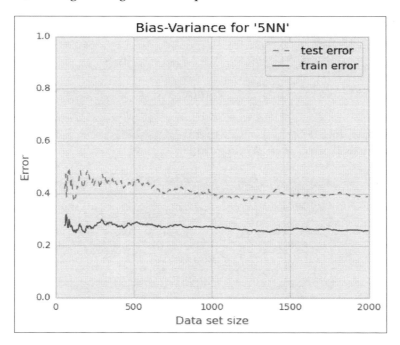

Looking at the graph, we immediately see that adding more training data will not help, as the dashed line corresponding to the test error seems to stay above 0.4. The only option we have is to decrease the complexity, either by increasing *k* or by reducing the feature space.

Reducing the feature space does not help here. We can easily confirm this by plotting the graph for a simplified feature space of only `LinkCount` and `NumTextTokens`:

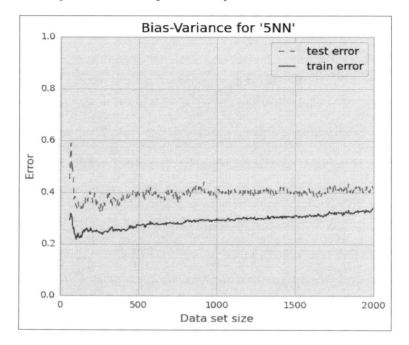

We get similar graphs for other smaller feature sets. No matter what subset of features we take, the graph would look similar.

At least reducing the model complexity by increasing *k* shows some positive impact:

k	mean(scores)	stddev(scores)
40	0.62800	0.03750
10	0.62000	0.04111
5	0.61400	0.02154

But it is not enough, and also comes at a price of lower classification runtime performance. Take, for instance, k=40, where we have a very low test error. To classify a new post, we would need to find the 40 nearest other posts to decide whether the new post is a good one or not:

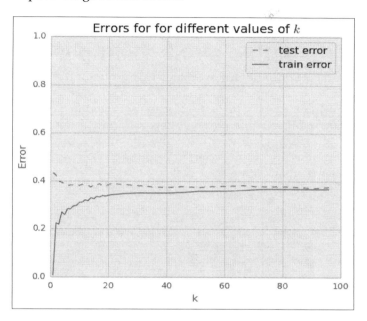

Clearly, it seems to be an issue with using nearest neighbor for our scenario. And it has another real disadvantage. Over time, we will get more and more posts into our system. As the nearest neighbor method is an instance-based approach, we will have to store all posts in our system. The more we get, the slower the prediction will be. This is different with model-based approaches, where one tries to derive a model from the data.

There we are, with enough reasons now to abandon the nearest neighbor approach to look for better places in the classification world. Of course, we will never know whether there is the one golden feature we just did not happen to think of. But for now, let's move on to another classification method that is known to work great in text-based classification scenarios.

Using logistic regression

Contrary to its name, logistic regression is a classification method. It is a very powerful one when it comes to text-based classification; it achieves this by first doing a regression on a logistic function, hence the name.

A bit of math with a small example

To get an initial understanding of the way logistic regression works, let's first take a look at the following example where we have artificial feature values X plotted with the corresponding classes, 0 or 1. As we can see, the data is noisy such that classes overlap in the feature value range between 1 and 6. Therefore, it is better to not directly model the discrete classes, but rather the probability that a feature value belongs to class 1, $P(X)$. Once we possess such a model, we could then predict class 1 if $P(X)>0.5$, and class 0 otherwise.

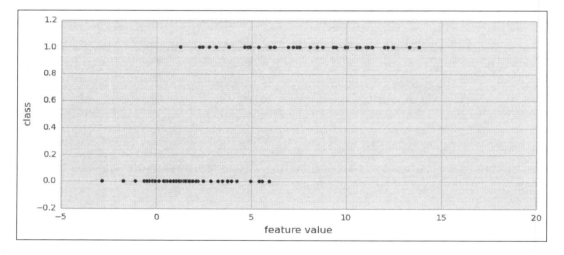

Mathematically, it is always difficult to model something that has a finite range, as is the case here with our discrete labels 0 and 1. We can, however, tweak the probabilities a bit so that they always stay between 0 and 1. And for that, we will need the odds ratio and the logarithm of it.

Let's say a feature has the probability of 0.9 that it belongs to class 1, $P(y=1) = 0.9$. The odds ratio is then $P(y=1)/P(y=0) = 0.9/0.1 = 9$. We could say that the chance is 9:1 that this feature maps to class 1. If $P(y=0.5)$, we would consequently have a 1:1 chance that the instance is of class 1. The odds ratio is bounded by 0, but goes to infinity (the left graph in the following set of graphs). If we now take the logarithm of it, we can map all probabilities between 0 and 1 to the full range from negative to positive infinity (the right graph in the following set of graphs). The nice thing is that we still maintain the relationship that higher probability leads to a higher log of odds, just not limited to 0 and 1 anymore.

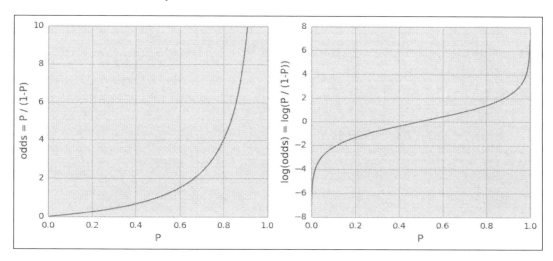

This means that we can now fit linear combinations of our features (OK, we only have one and a constant, but that will change soon) to the $\log(odds)$ values. In a sense, we replace the linear from *Chapter 1, Getting Started with Python Machine Learning,* $y_i = c_0 + c_1 x_i$ with $\log\left(\dfrac{p_i}{1-p_i}\right) = c_0 + c_1 x$ (replacing y with $\log(odds)$).

We can solve this for p_i, so that we have $p_i = \dfrac{1}{1+e^{-(c_0+c_1 x_i)}}$.

We simply have to find the right coefficients, such that the formula gives the lowest errors for all our (x_i, p_i) pairs in our data set, but that will be done by scikit-learn.

After fitting, the formula will give the probability for every new data point x that belongs to class 1:

```
>>> from sklearn.linear_model import LogisticRegression
>>> clf = LogisticRegression()
>>> print(clf)
```

```
LogisticRegression(C=1.0, class_weight=None, dual=False,
fit_intercept=True, intercept_scaling=1, penalty=l2, tol=0.0001)
>>> clf.fit(X, y)
>>> print(np.exp(clf.intercept_), np.exp(clf.coef_.ravel()))
[ 0.09437188] [ 1.80094112]
>>> def lr_model(clf, X):
...       return 1 / (1 + np.exp(-(clf.intercept_ + clf.coef_*X)))
>>> print("P(x=-1)=%.2f\tP(x=7)=%.2f"%(lr_model(clf, -1),
lr_model(clf, 7)))
P(x=-1)=0.05     P(x=7)=0.85
```

You might have noticed that scikit-learn exposes the first coefficient through the special field `intercept_`.

If we plot the fitted model, we see that it makes perfect sense given the data:

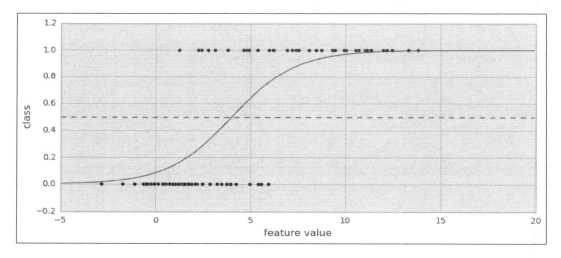

Applying logistic regression to our post classification problem

Admittedly, the example in the previous section was created to show the beauty of logistic regression. How does it perform on the real, noisy data?

Comparing it to the best nearest neighbor classifier (k=40) as a baseline, we see that it performs a bit better, but also won't change the situation a whole lot.

Method	mean(scores)	stddev(scores)
LogReg C=0.1	0.64650	0.03139
LogReg C=1.00	0.64650	0.03155
LogReg C=10.00	0.64550	0.03102
LogReg C=0.01	0.63850	0.01950
40NN	0.62800	0.03750

We have shown the accuracy for different values of the regularization parameter C. With it, we can control the model complexity, similar to the parameter k for the nearest neighbor method. Smaller values for C result in more penalization of the model complexity.

A quick look at the bias-variance chart for one of our best candidates, C=0.1, shows that our model has high bias—test and train error curves approach closely but stay at unacceptable high values. This indicates that logistic regression with the current feature space is under-fitting and cannot learn a model that captures the data correctly:

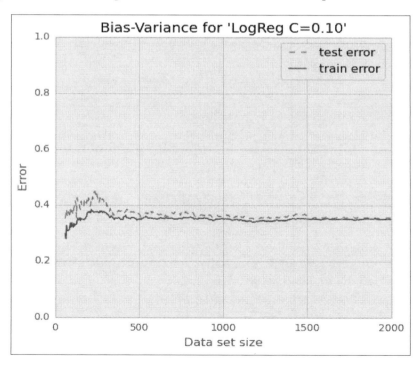

So what now? We switched the model and tuned it as much as we could with our current state of knowledge, but we still have no acceptable classifier.

More and more it seems that either the data is too noisy for this task or that our set of features is still not appropriate to discriminate the classes well enough.

Looking behind accuracy – precision and recall

Let's step back and think again about what we are trying to achieve here. Actually, we do not need a classifier that perfectly predicts good and bad answers as we measured it until now using accuracy. If we can tune the classifier to be particularly good at predicting one class, we could adapt the feedback to the user accordingly. If we, for example, had a classifier that was always right when it predicted an answer to be bad, we would give no feedback until the classifier detected the answer to be bad. On the contrary, if the classifier exceeded in predicting answers to be good, we could show helpful comments to the user at the beginning and remove them when the classifier said that the answer is a good one.

To find out in which situation we are here, we have to understand how to measure precision and recall. And to understand that, we have to look into the four distinct classification results as they are described in the following table:

		Classified as	
		Positive	Negative
In reality it is	Positive	True positive (TP)	False negative (FN)
	Negative	False positive (FP)	True negative (TN)

For instance, if the classifier predicts an instance to be positive and the instance indeed is positive in reality, this is a true positive instance. If on the other hand the classifier misclassified that instance, saying that it is negative while in reality it was positive, that instance is said to be a false negative.

What we want is to have a high success rate when we are predicting a post as either good or bad, but not necessarily both. That is, we want as much true positives as possible. This is what precision captures:

$$Precision = \frac{TP}{TP + FP}$$

If instead our goal would have been to detect as much good or bad answers as possible, we would be more interested in recall:

$$Recall = \frac{TP}{TP + FN}$$

In terms of the following graphic, precision is the fraction of the intersection of the right circle while recall is the fraction of the intersection of the left circle:

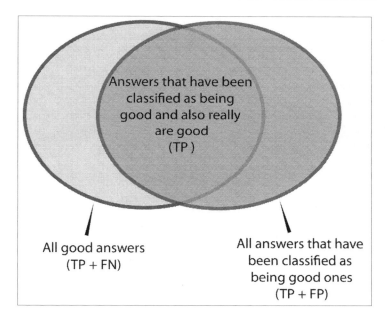

So, how can we now optimize for precision? Up to now, we have always used 0.5 as the threshold to decide whether an answer is good or not. What we can do now is count the number of TP, FP, and FN while varying that threshold between 0 and 1. With those counts, we can then plot precision over recall.

The handy function `precision_recall_curve()` from the metrics module does all the calculations for us:

```
>>> from sklearn.metrics import precision_recall_curve
>>> precision, recall, thresholds = precision_recall_curve(y_test,
    clf.predict(X_test))
```

Predicting one class with acceptable performance does not always mean that the classifier is also acceptable predicting the other class. This can be seen in the following two plots, where we plot the precision/recall curves for classifying bad (the left graph) and good (the right graph) answers:

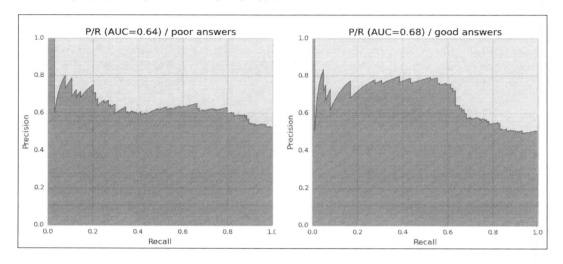

In the graphs, we have also included a much better description of a classifier's performance, the **area under curve** (**AUC**). It can be understood as the average precision of the classifier and is a great way of comparing different classifiers.

We see that we can basically forget predicting bad answers (the left plot). Precision drops to a very low recall and stays at an unacceptably low 60 percent.

Predicting good answers, however, shows that we can get above 80 percent precision at a recall of almost 40 percent. Let's find out what threshold we need for that. As we trained many classifiers on different folds (remember, we iterated over KFold() a couple of pages back), we need to retrieve the classifier that was neither too bad nor too good in order to get a realistic view. Let's call it the medium clone:

```
>>> medium = np.argsort(scores)[int(len(scores) / 2)]
>>> thresholds = np.hstack(([0],thresholds[medium]))
>>> idx80 = precisions>=0.8
>>> print("P=%.2f R=%.2f thresh=%.2f" % (precision[idx80][0],
                                recall[idx80][0], threshold[idx80]
[0]))
P=0.80 R=0.37 thresh=0.59
```

Setting the threshold at `0.59`, we see that we can still achieve a precision of 80 percent detecting good answers when we accept a low recall of 37 percent. That means that we would detect only one in three good answers as such. But from that third of good answers that we manage to detect, we would be reasonably sure that they are indeed good. For the rest, we could then politely display additional hints on how to improve answers in general.

To apply this threshold in the prediction process, we have to use `predict_proba()`, which returns per class probabilities, instead of `predict()`, which returns the class itself:

```
>>> thresh80 = threshold[idx80][0]
>>> probs_for_good = clf.predict_proba(answer_features)[:,1]
>>> answer_class = probs_for_good>thresh80
```

We can confirm that we are in the desired precision/recall range using `classification_report`:

```
>>> from sklearn.metrics import classification_report
>>> print(classification_report(y_test, clf.predict_proba [:,1]>0.63,
    target_names=['not accepted', 'accepted']))
```

	precision	recall	f1-score	support
not accepted	0.59	0.85	0.70	101
accepted	0.73	0.40	0.52	99
avg / total	0.66	0.63	0.61	200

 Note that using the threshold will not guarantee that we are always above the precision and recall values that we determined above together with its threshold.

Slimming the classifier

It is always worth looking at the actual contributions of the individual features. For logistic regression, we can directly take the learned coefficients (`clf.coef_`) to get an impression of the features' impact. The higher the coefficient of a feature, the more the feature plays a role in determining whether the post is good or not. Consequently, negative coefficients tell us that the higher values for the corresponding features indicate a stronger signal for the post to be classified as bad.

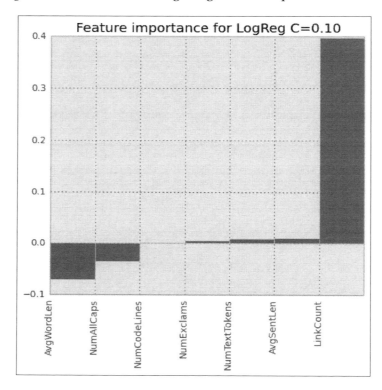

We see that `LinkCount`, `AvgWordLen`, `NumAllCaps`, and `NumExclams` have the biggest impact on the overall classification decision, while `NumImages` (a feature that we sneaked in just for demonstration purposes a second ago) and `AvgSentLen` play a rather minor role. While the feature importance overall makes sense intuitively, it is surprising that `NumImages` is basically ignored. Normally, answers containing images are always rated high. In reality, however, answers very rarely have images. So, although in principal it is a very powerful feature, it is too sparse to be of any value. We could easily drop that feature and retain the same classification performance.

Ship it!

Let's assume we want to integrate this classifier into our site. What we definitely do not want is training the classifier each time we start the classification service. Instead, we can simply serialize the classifier after training and then deserialize on that site:

```
>>> import pickle
>>> pickle.dump(clf, open("logreg.dat", "w"))
>>> clf = pickle.load(open("logreg.dat", "r"))
```

Congratulations, the classifier is now ready to be used as if it had just been trained.

Summary

We made it! For a very noisy dataset, we built a classifier that suits a part of our goal. Of course, we had to be pragmatic and adapt our initial goal to what was achievable. But on the way we learned about strengths and weaknesses of nearest neighbor and logistic regression. We learned how to extract features such as LinkCount, NumTextTokens, NumCodeLines, AvgSentLen, AvgWordLen, NumAllCaps, NumExclams, and NumImages, and how to analyze their impact on the classifier's performance.

But what is even more valuable is that we learned an informed way of how to debug bad performing classifiers. That will help us in the future to come up with usable systems much faster.

After having looked into nearest neighbor and logistic regression, in the next chapter, we will get familiar with yet another simple yet powerful classification algorithm: Naïve Bayes. Along the way, we will also learn some more convenient tools from scikit-learn.

Classification II – Sentiment Analysis

For companies, it is vital to closely monitor the public reception of key events, such as product launches or press releases. With its real-time access and easy accessibility of user-generated content on Twitter, it is now possible to do sentiment classification of tweets. Sometimes also called opinion mining, it is an active field of research, in which several companies are already selling such services. As this shows that there obviously exists a market, we have motivation to use our classification muscles built in the last chapter, to build our own home-grown sentiment classifier.

Sketching our roadmap

Sentiment analysis of tweets is particularly hard, because of Twitter's size limitation of 140 characters. This leads to a special syntax, creative abbreviations, and seldom well-formed sentences. The typical approach of analyzing sentences, aggregating their sentiment information per paragraph, and then calculating the overall sentiment of a document does not work here.

Clearly, we will not try to build a state-of-the-art sentiment classifier. Instead, we want to:

- Use this scenario as a vehicle to introduce yet another classification algorithm, **Naïve Bayes**
- Explain how **Part Of Speech** (**POS**) tagging works and how it can help us
- Show some more tricks from the scikit-learn toolbox that come in handy from time to time

Fetching the Twitter data

Naturally, we need tweets and their corresponding labels that tell whether a tweet is containing a positive, negative, or neutral sentiment. In this chapter, we will use the corpus from Niek Sanders, who has done an awesome job of manually labeling more than 5,000 tweets and has granted us permission to use it in this chapter.

To comply with Twitter's terms of services, we will not provide any data from Twitter nor show any real tweets in this chapter. Instead, we can use Sander's hand-labeled data, which contains the tweet IDs and their hand-labeled sentiment, and use his script, install.py, to fetch the corresponding Twitter data. As the script is playing nice with Twitter's servers, it will take quite some time to download all the data for more than 5,000 tweets. So it is a good idea to start it right away.

The data comes with four sentiment labels:

```
>>> X, Y = load_sanders_data()
>>> classes = np.unique(Y)
>>> for c in classes: print("#%s: %i" % (c, sum(Y==c)))
#irrelevant: 490
#negative: 487
#neutral: 1952
#positive: 433
```

Inside load_sanders_data(), we are treating irrelevant and neutral labels together as neutral and drop ping all non-English tweets, resulting in 3,362 tweets.

In case you get different counts here, it is because, in the meantime, tweets might have been deleted or set to be private. In that case, you might also get slightly different numbers and graphs than the ones shown in the upcoming sections.

Introducing the Naïve Bayes classifier

Naïve Bayes is probably one of the most elegant machine learning algorithms out there that is of practical use. And despite its name, it is not that naïve when you look at its classification performance. It proves to be quite robust to irrelevant features, which it kindly ignores. It learns fast and predicts equally so. It does not require lots of storage. So, why is it then called naïve?

The *Naïve* was added to account for one assumption that is required for Naïve Bayes to work optimally. The assumption is that the features do not impact each other. This, however, is rarely the case for real-world applications. Nevertheless, it still returns very good accuracy in practice even when the independence assumption does not hold.

Getting to know the Bayes' theorem

At its core, Naïve Bayes classification is nothing more than keeping track of which feature gives evidence to which class. The way the features are designed determines the model that is used to learn. The so-called Bernoulli model only cares about Boolean features: whether a word occurs only once or multiple times in a tweet does not matter. In contrast, the Multinomial model uses word counts as features. For the sake of simplicity, we will use the Bernoulli model to explain how to use Naïve Bayes for sentiment analysis. We will then use the Multinomial model later on to set up and tune our real-world classifiers.

Let's assume the following meanings for the variables that we will use to explain Naïve Bayes:

Variable	Meaning
C	This is the class of a tweet (positive or negative)
F_1	The word "awesome" occurs at least once in the tweet
F_2	The word "crazy" occurs at least once in the tweet

During training, we learned the Naïve Bayes model, which is the probability for a class C when we already know features F_1 and F_2. This probability is written as $P(C|F_1, F_2)$.

Since we cannot estimate $P(C|F_1, F_2)$ directly, we apply a trick, which was found out by Bayes:

$$P(A) \cdot P(B|A) = P(B) \cdot P(A|B)$$

If we substitute A with the probability of both words "awesome" and "crazy", and think of B as being our class C, we arrive at the relationship that helps us to later retrieve the probability for the data instance belonging to the specified class:

$$P(F_1, F_2) \cdot P(C|F_1, F_2) = P(C) \cdot P(F_1, F_2|C)$$

This allows us to express $P(C|F_1, F_2)$ by means of the other probabilities:

$$P(C|F_1, F_2) = \frac{P(C) \cdot P(F_1, F_2|C)}{P(F_1, F_2)}$$

We could also describe this as follows:

$$posterior = \frac{prior \cdot likelihood}{evidence}$$

The *prior* and the *evidence* are easily determined:

- $P(C)$ is the prior probability of class C without knowing about the data. We can estimate this quantity by simply calculating the fraction of all training data instances belonging to that particular class.
- $P(F_1, F_2)$ is the evidence or the probability of features F_1 and F_2.

The tricky part is the calculation of the likelihood $P(F_1, F_2|C)$. It is the value describing how likely it is to see feature values F_1 and F_2 if we know that the class of the data instance is C. To estimate this, we need to do some thinking.

Being naïve

From probability theory, we also know the following relationship:

$$P(F_1, F_2|C) = P(F_1|C) \cdot P(F_2|C, F_1)$$

This alone, however, does not help much, since we treat one difficult problem (estimating $P(F_1, F_2|C)$) with another one (estimating $P(F_2|C, F_1)$).

However, if we naïvely assume that F_1 and F_2 are independent from each other, $P(F_2|C, F_1)$ simplifies to $P(F_2|C)$ and we can write it as follows:

$$P(F_1, F_2|C) = P(F_1|C) \cdot P(F_2|C)$$

Putting everything together, we get the quite manageable formula:

$$P(C|F_1, F_2) = \frac{P(C) \cdot P(F_1|C) \cdot P(F_2|C)}{P(F_1, F_2)}$$

The interesting thing is that although it is not theoretically correct to simply tweak our assumptions when we are in the mood to do so, in this case, it proves to work astonishingly well in real-world applications.

Using Naïve Bayes to classify

Given a new tweet, the only part left is to simply calculate the probabilities:

$$P(C = \text{"pos"}|F_1, F_2) = \frac{P(C = \text{"pos"}) \cdot P(F_1|C = \text{"pos"}) \cdot P(F_2|C = \text{"pos"})}{P(F_1, F_2)}$$

$$P(C = \text{"neg"}|F_1, F_2) = \frac{P(C = \text{"neg"}) \cdot P(F_1|C = \text{"neg"}) \cdot P(F_2|C = \text{"neg"})}{P(F_1, F_2)}$$

Then choose the class c_{best} having higher probability.

As for both classes the denominator, $P(F_1, F_2)$, is the same, we can simply ignore it without changing the winner class.

Note, however, that we don't calculate any real probabilities any more. Instead, we are estimating which class is more likely, given the evidence. This is another reason why Naïve Bayes is so robust: It is not so much interested in the real probabilities, but only in the information, which class is more likely. In short, we can write:

$$c_{best} = \underset{c \in C}{\operatorname{argmax}} P(C = c) \cdot P(F_1|C = c) \cdot P(F_2|C = c)$$

This is simply telling that we are calculating the part after *argmax* for all classes of C (*pos* and *neg* in our case) and returning the class that results in the highest value.

But, for the following example, let's stick to real probabilities and do some calculations to see how Naïve Bayes works. For the sake of simplicity, we will assume that Twitter allows only for the two aforementioned words, "awesome" and "crazy", and that we had already manually classified a handful of tweets:

Tweet	Class
awesome	Positive tweet
awesome	Positive tweet
awesome crazy	Positive tweet
crazy	Positive tweet
crazy	Negative tweet
crazy	Negative tweet

In this example, we have the tweet "crazy" both in a positive and negative tweet to emulate some ambiguities you will often find in the real world (for example, "being soccer crazy" versus "a crazy idiot").

In this case, we have six total tweets, out of which four are positive and two negative, which results in the following priors:

$$P(C = "pos") = \frac{4}{6} \cong 0.67$$

$$P(C = "neg") = \frac{2}{6} \cong 0.33$$

This means, without knowing anything about the tweet itself, it would be wise to assume the tweet to be positive.

A still missing piece is the calculation of $P(F_1|C)$ and $P(F_2|C)$, which are the probabilities for the two features F_1 and F_2 conditioned in class C.

This is calculated as the number of tweets, in which we have seen the concrete feature divided by the number of tweets that have been labeled with the class of C. Let's say we want to know the probability of seeing "awesome" occurring in a tweet, knowing that its class is positive, we will have:

$$P(F_1 = 1|C = "pos") = \frac{number\ of\ positive\ tweets\ containing\ "awesome"}{number\ of\ all\ positive\ tweets} = \frac{3}{4}$$

Because out of the four positive tweets three contained the word "awesome".
Obviously, the probability for not having "awesome" in a positive tweet is its inverse:

$$P(F_1 = 0|C = \text{"pos"}) = 1 - P(F_1 = 1|C = \text{"pos"}) = 0.25$$

Similarly, for the rest (omitting the case that a word is not occurring in a tweet):

$$P(F_2 = 1|C = \text{"pos"}) = \frac{2}{4} = 0.5$$

$$P(F_1 = 1|C = \text{"neg"}) = \frac{0}{2} = 0$$

$$P(F_2 = 1|C = \text{"neg"}) = \frac{2}{2} = 1$$

For the sake of completeness, we will also compute the evidence so that we can see
real probabilities in the following example tweets. For two concrete values of F_1 and
F_2, we can calculate the evidence as follows:

$$P(F_1, F_2) = P(F_1, F_2|C = \text{"pos"}) \cdot P(C = \text{"pos"}) +$$

$$P(F_1, F_2|C = \text{"neg"}) \cdot P(C = \text{"neg"})$$

This leads to the following values:

$$P(F_1 = 1, F_2 = 1) = \frac{3}{4} \cdot \frac{2}{4} \cdot \frac{4}{6} + 0 \cdot 1 \cdot \frac{2}{6} = \frac{1}{4}$$

$$P(F_1 = 1, F_2 = 0) = \frac{3}{4} \cdot \frac{2}{4} \cdot \frac{4}{6} + 0 \cdot 0 \cdot \frac{2}{6} = \frac{1}{4}$$

$$P(F_1 = 0, F_2 = 1) = \frac{1}{4} \cdot \frac{2}{4} \cdot \frac{4}{6} + \frac{2}{2} \cdot \frac{2}{2} \cdot \frac{2}{6} = \frac{5}{12}$$

Now we have all the data to classify new tweets. The only work left is to parse the tweet and featurize it:

Tweet	F_1	F_2	Class probabilities	Classification
"awesome"	1	0	$$P(C = "pos"|F_1 = 1, F_2 = 0) = \frac{\frac{3}{4} \cdot \frac{2}{4} \cdot \frac{4}{6}}{\frac{1}{4}} = 1$$ $$P(C = "neg"|F_1 = 1, F_2 = 0) = \frac{\frac{0}{2} \cdot \frac{2}{2} \cdot \frac{2}{6}}{\frac{1}{4}} = 0$$	Positive
"crazy"	0	1	$$P(C = "pos"|F_1 = 0, F_2 = 1) = \frac{\frac{1}{4} \cdot \frac{2}{4} \cdot \frac{4}{6}}{\frac{5}{12}} = \frac{1}{5}$$ $$P(C = "neg"|F_1 = 0, F_2 = 1) = \frac{\frac{2}{2} \cdot \frac{2}{2} \cdot \frac{2}{6}}{\frac{5}{12}} = \frac{4}{5}$$	Negative
"awesome crazy"	1	1	$$P(C = "pos"|F_1 = 1, F_2 = 1) = \frac{\frac{3}{4} \cdot \frac{2}{4} \cdot \frac{4}{6}}{\frac{1}{4}} = 1$$ $$P(C = "neg"|F_1 = 1, F_2 = 1) = \frac{\frac{0}{2} \cdot \frac{2}{2} \cdot \frac{2}{6}}{\frac{1}{4}} = 0$$	Positive

So far, so good. The classification of trivial tweets seems to assign correct labels to the tweets. The question remains, however, how we should treat words that did not occur in our training corpus. After all, with the preceding formula, new words will always be assigned a probability of zero.

Accounting for unseen words and other oddities

When we calculated the probabilities earlier, we actually cheated ourselves. We were not calculating the real probabilities, but only rough approximations by means of the fractions. We assumed that the training corpus will tell us the whole truth about the real probabilities. It did not. A corpus of only six tweets obviously cannot give us all the information about every tweet that has ever been written. For example, there certainly are tweets containing the word "text" in them. It is only that we have never seen them. Apparently, our approximation is very rough and we should account for that. This is often done in practice with the so-called **add-one smoothing**.

 Add-one smoothing is sometimes also referred to as **additive smoothing** or **Laplace smoothing**. Note that Laplace smoothing has nothing to do with Laplacian smoothing, which is related to the smoothing of polygon meshes. If we do not smooth by 1 but by an adjustable parameter `alpha<0`, it is called Lidstone smoothing.

It is a very simple technique that adds one to all feature occurrences. It has the underlying assumption that even if we have not seen a given word in the whole corpus, there is still a chance that it is just that our sample of tweets happened to not include that word. So, with add-one smoothing we pretend that we have seen every occurrence once more than we actually did. That means that instead of calculating $P(F_1 = 1|C = "pos") = \frac{3}{4} = 0.75$, we now do $P(F_1 = 1|C = "pos") = \frac{3+1}{4+2} = 0.67$.

Why do we add 2 in the denominator? Because we have two features: the occurrence of "awesome" and "crazy". Since we add 1 for each feature, we have to make sure that the end result is again a probability. And indeed, we get 1 as the total probability:

$$P(F_1 = 1|C = "pos") + P(F_1 = 0|C = "pos") = \frac{3+1}{4+2} + \frac{1+1}{4+2} = 1$$

Accounting for arithmetic underflows

There is yet another road block. In reality, we work with probabilities much smaller than the ones we have dealt with in the toy example. Typically, we also have many more than only two features, which we multiply with each other. This will quickly lead to the point where the accuracy provided by NumPy does not suffice any more:

```
>>> import numpy as np
>>> np.set_printoptions(precision=20) # tell numpy to print out more
digits (default is 8)
>>> np.array([2.48E-324])
array([ 4.94065645841246544177e-324])
>>> np.array([2.47E-324])
array([ 0.])
```

So, how probable is it that we will ever hit a number like `2.47E-324`? To answer this, we just need to imagine a likelihood for the conditional probabilities of 0.0001, and then multiply 65 of them together (meaning that we have 65 low probable feature values) and you've been hit by the arithmetic underflow:

```
>>> x = 0.00001
>>> x**64 # still fine
1e-320
>>> x**65 # ouch
0.0
```

A float in Python is typically implemented using double in C. To find out whether this is the case for your platform you can check it as follows:

```
>>> import sys
>>> sys.float_info
sys.float_info(max=1.7976931348623157e+308, max_exp=1024,
max_10_exp=308, min=2.2250738585072014e-308, min_exp=-1021,
min_10_exp=-307, dig=15, mant_dig=53, epsilon=2.220446049250313e-16,
radix=2, rounds=1)
```

To mitigate this, one could switch to math libraries such as mpmath (http://code.google.com/p/mpmath/) that allow for arbitrary accuracy. However, they are not fast enough to work as a NumPy replacement.

Fortunately, there is a better way to take care of this, and it has to do with a nice relationship that we might still remember from school:

$$\log(x \cdot y) = \log(x) + \log(y)$$

If we apply it to our case, we get the following:

$$\log P(C) \cdot P(F_1|C) \cdot P(F_2|C) = \log P(C) + \log P(F_1|C) + \log P(F_2|C)$$

As the probabilities are in the interval between 0 and 1, the log of the probabilities lies in the interval $-\infty$ and 0. Don't be bothered with that. Higher numbers are still a stronger indicator for the correct class—it is only that they are negative now.

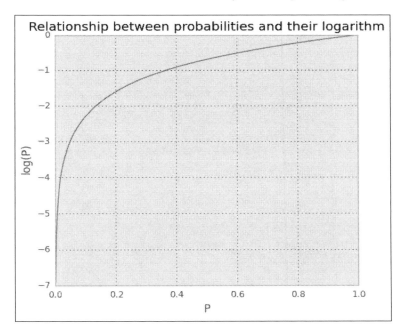

There is one caveat though: we actually don't have the log in the formula's nominator (the part above the fraction). We only have the product of the probabilities. In our case, luckily, we are not interested in the actual value of the probabilities. We simply want to know which class has the highest posterior probability. We are lucky, because if we find that $P(C = "pos"|F_1, F_2) > P(C = "neg"|F_1, F_2)$, then we will always also have $\log P(C = "pos"|F_1, F_2) > \log P(C = "neg"|F_1, F_2)$.

A quick look at the preceding graph shows that the curve is monotonically increasing, that is, it never goes down, when we go from left to right. So let's stick this into the aforementioned formula:

$$c_{best} = \text{argmax}_{c \in C}\, P(C = c) \cdot P(F_1 | C = c) \cdot P(F_2 | C = c)$$

This will finally retrieve the formula for two features that will give us the best class also for the real-world data that we will see in practice:

$$c_{best} = \underset{c \in C}{\text{argmax}}(\log P(C = c) + \log P(F_1 | C = c) + \log P(F_2 | C = c))$$

Of course, we will not be very successful with only two features, so, let's rewrite it to allow for an arbitrary number of features:

$$c_{best} = \underset{c \in C}{\text{argmax}}\left(\log P(C = c) + \sum_k \log P(F_k | C = c) \right)$$

There we are, ready to use our first classifier from the scikit-learn toolkit.

As mentioned earlier, we just learned the Bernoulli model of Naïve Bayes. Instead of having Boolean features, we can also use the number of word occurrences, also known as the Multinomial model. As this provides more information, and often also results in better performance, we will use this for our real-world data. Note, however, that the underlying formulas change a bit. However, no worries, as the general idea how Naïve Bayes works, is still the same.

Creating our first classifier and tuning it

The Naïve Bayes classifiers resides in the `sklearn.naive_bayes` package. There are different kinds of Naïve Bayes classifiers:

- `GaussianNB`: This classifier assumes the features to be normally distributed (Gaussian). One use case for it could be the classification of sex given the height and width of a person. In our case, we are given tweet texts from which we extract word counts. These are clearly not Gaussian distributed.

- `MultinomialNB`: This classifier assumes the features to be occurrence counts, which is our case going forward, since we will be using word counts in the tweets as features. In practice, this classifier also works well with TF-IDF vectors.

- `BernoulliNB`: This classifier is similar to `MultinomialNB`, but more suited when using binary word occurrences and not word counts.

As we will mainly look at the word occurrences, for our purpose the `MultinomialNB` classifier is best suited.

Solving an easy problem first

As we have seen, when we looked at our tweet data, the tweets are not only positive or negative. The majority of tweets actually do not contain any sentiment, but are neutral or irrelevant, containing, for instance, raw information (for example, "New book: Building Machine Learning … http://link"). This leads to four classes. To not complicate the task too much, let's only focus on the positive and negative tweets for now.

```
>>> # first create a Boolean list having true for tweets
>>> # that are either positive or negative
>>> pos_neg_idx = np.logical_or(Y=="positive", Y=="negative")

>>> # now use that index to filter the data and the labels
>>> X = X[pos_neg_idx]
>>> Y = Y[pos_neg_idx]

>>> # finally convert the labels themselves into Boolean
>>> Y = Y=="positive"
```

Now, we have in X the raw tweet texts and in Y the binary classification, 0 for negative and 1 for positive tweets.

We just said that we will use word occurrence counts as features. We will not use them in their raw form, though. Instead, we will use our power horse `TfidfVectorizer` to convert the raw tweet text into TF-IDF feature values, which we then use together with the labels to train our first classifier. For convenience, we will use the `Pipeline` class, which allows us to hook the vectorizer and the classifier together and provides the same interface:

```
from sklearn.feature_extraction.text import TfidfVectorizer
from sklearn.naive_bayes import MultinomialNB
```

```
from sklearn.pipeline import Pipeline

def create_ngram_model():
    tfidf_ngrams = TfidfVectorizer(ngram_range=(1, 3),
                                    analyzer="word", binary=False)
    clf = MultinomialNB()
    return Pipeline([('vect', tfidf_ngrams), ('clf', clf)])
```

The `Pipeline` instance returned by `create_ngram_model()` can now be used to fit and predict as if we had a normal classifier.

Since we do not have that much data, we should do cross-validation. This time, however, we will not use `KFold`, which partitions the data in consecutive folds, but instead, we use `ShuffleSplit`. It shuffles the data for us, but does not prevent the same data instance to be in multiple folds. For each fold, then, we keep track of the area under the Precision-Recall curve and for accuracy.

To keep our experimentation agile, let's wrap everything together in a `train_model()` function, which takes a function as a parameter that creates the classifier.

```
from sklearn.metrics import precision_recall_curve, auc
from sklearn.cross_validation import ShuffleSplit

def train_model(clf_factory, X, Y):
    # setting random_state to get deterministic behavior
    cv = ShuffleSplit(n=len(X), n_iter=10, test_size=0.3,
    random_state=0)

    scores = []
    pr_scores = []

    for train, test in cv:
        X_train, y_train = X[train], Y[train]
        X_test, y_test = X[test], Y[test]

        clf = clf_factory()
        clf.fit(X_train, y_train)

        train_score = clf.score(X_train, y_train)
        test_score = clf.score(X_test, y_test)

        scores.append(test_score)
```

```
proba = clf.predict_proba(X_test)

precision, recall, pr_thresholds =
precision_recall_curve(y_test, proba[:,1])

pr_scores.append(auc(recall, precision))

summary = (np.mean(scores), np.std(scores),
np.mean(pr_scores), np.std(pr_scores))
        print("%.3f\t%.3f\t%.3f\t%.3f" % summary)
```

Putting everything together, we can train our first model:

```
>>> X, Y = load_sanders_data()
>>> pos_neg_idx = np.logical_or(Y=="positive", Y=="negative")
>>> X = X[pos_neg_idx]
>>> Y = Y[pos_neg_idx]
>>> Y = Y=="positive"
>>> train_model(create_ngram_model, X, Y)
0.788   0.024   0.882   0.036
```

With our first try using Naïve Bayes on vectorized TF-IDF trigram features, we get an accuracy of 78.8 percent and an average P/R AUC of 88.2 percent. Looking at the P/R chart of the median (the train/test split that is performing most similar to the average), it shows a much more encouraging behavior than the plots we have seen in the previous chapter.

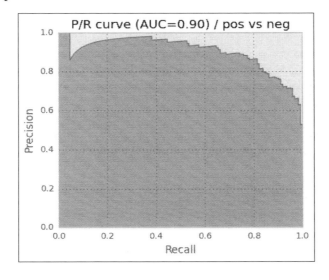

For a start, the results are quite encouraging. They get even more impressive when we realize that 100 percent accuracy is probably never achievable in a sentiment classification task. For some tweets, even humans often do not really agree on the same classification label.

Using all classes

Once again, we simplified our task a bit, since we used only positive or negative tweets. That means, we assumed a perfect classifier that upfront classified whether the tweet contains a sentiment and forwarded that to our Naïve Bayes classifier.

So, how well do we perform if we also classify whether a tweet contains any sentiment at all? To find that out, let's first write a convenience function that returns a modified class array providing a list of sentiments that we would like to interpret as positive:

```python
def tweak_labels(Y, pos_sent_list):
    pos = Y==pos_sent_list[0]
    for sent_label in pos_sent_list[1:]:
        pos |= Y==sent_label


    Y = np.zeros(Y.shape[0])
    Y[pos] = 1
    Y = Y.astype(int)


return Y
```

Note that we are talking about two different positives now. The sentiment of a tweet can be positive, which is to be distinguished from the class of the training data. If, for example, we want to find out how good we can separate tweets having sentiment from neutral ones, we could do:

```python
>>> Y = tweak_labels(Y, ["positive", "negative"])
```

In Y we have now 1 (positive class) for all tweets that are either positive or negative and 0 (negative class) for neutral and irrelevant ones.

```python
>>> train_model(create_ngram_model, X, Y, plot=True)
0.750    0.012    0.659    0.023
```

Have a look at the following plot:

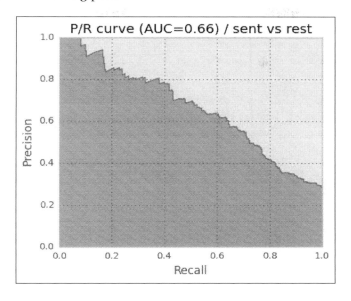

As expected, P/R AUC drops considerably, being only 66 percent now. The accuracy is still high, but that is only due to the fact that we have a highly imbalanced dataset. Out of 3,362 total tweets, only 920 are either positive or negative, which is about 27 percent. This means, if we create a classifier that always classifies a tweet as not containing any sentiment, we will already have an accuracy of 73 percent. This is another case to always look at precision and recall if the training and test data is unbalanced.

So, how will the Naïve Bayes classifier perform on classifying positive tweets versus the rest and negative tweets versus the rest? One word: bad.

```
== Pos vs. rest ==
0.873   0.009   0.305   0.026
== Neg vs. rest ==
0.861   0.006   0.497   0.026
```

Pretty unusable if you ask me. Looking at the P/R curves in the following plots, we will also find no usable precision/recall trade-off, as we were able to do in the last chapter:

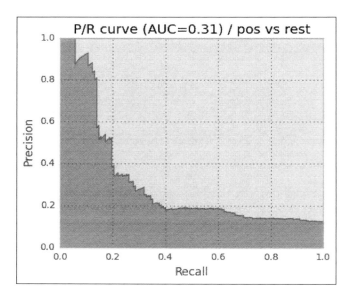

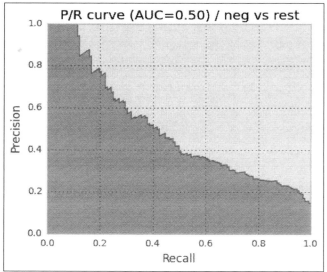

Tuning the classifier's parameters

Certainly, we have not explored the current setup enough and should investigate more. There are roughly two areas, where we can play with the knobs: TfidfVectorizer and MultinomialNB. As we have no real intuition in which area we should explore, let's try to distribute the parameters' values.

We will see the TfidfVectorizer parameter first:

- Using different settings for NGrams:
    - unigrams (1,1)
    - unigrams and bigrams (1,2)
    - unigrams, bigrams, and trigrams (1,3)
- Playing with min_df: 1 or 2
- Exploring the impact of IDF within TF-IDF using use_idf and smooth_idf: False or True
- Whether to remove stop words or not, by setting stop_words to english or None
- Whether to use the logarithm of the word counts (sublinear_tf)
- Whether to track word counts or simply track whether words occur or not, by setting binary to True or False

Now we will see the MultinomialNB classifier:

- Which smoothing method to use by setting alpha:
    - Add-one or Laplace smoothing: 1
    - Lidstone smoothing: 0.01, 0.05, 0.1, or 0.5
    - No smoothing: 0

A simple approach could be to train a classifier for all those reasonable exploration values, while keeping the other parameters constant and check the classifier's results. As we do not know whether those parameters affect each other, doing it right will require that we train a classifier for every possible combination of all parameter values. Obviously, this is too tedious for us.

Because this kind of parameter exploration occurs frequently in machine learning tasks, scikit-learn has a dedicated class for it, called GridSearchCV. It takes an estimator (instance with a classifier-like interface), which will be the Pipeline instance in our case, and a dictionary of parameters with their potential values.

`GridSearchCV` expects the dictionary's keys to obey a certain format so that it is able to set the parameters of the correct estimator. The format is as follows:

```
<estimator>__<subestimator>__...__<param_name>
```

For example, if we want to specify the desired values to explore for the `min_df` parameter of `TfidfVectorizer` (named `vect` in the `Pipeline` description), we would have to say:

`param_grid={"vect__ngram_range"=[(1, 1), (1, 2), (1, 3)]}`

This will tell `GridSearchCV` to try out unigrams to trigrams as parameter values for the `ngram_range` parameter of `TfidfVectorizer`.

Then, it trains the estimator with all possible parameter value combinations. Here, we make sure that it trains on random samples of the training data using `ShuffleSplit`, which generates an iterator of random train/test splits. Finally, it provides the best estimator in the form of the member variable, `best_estimator_`.

As we want to compare the returned best classifier with our current best one, we need to evaluate it in the same way. Therefore, we can pass the `ShuffleSplit` instance using the `cv` parameter (therefore, `CV` in `GridSearchCV`).

The last missing piece is to define how `GridSearchCV` should determine the best estimator. This can be done by providing the desired score function to (surprise!) the `score_func` parameter. We can either write one ourselves, or pick one from the `sklearn.metrics` package. We should certainly not take `metric.accuracy` because of our class imbalance (we have a lot less tweets containing sentiment than neutral ones). Instead, we want to have good precision and recall on both classes, tweets with sentiment and tweets without positive or negative opinions. One metric that combines both precision and recall is the so-called **F-measure**, which is implemented as `metrics.f1_score`:

$$F = \frac{2 \cdot precision \cdot recall}{precision + recall}$$

After putting everything together, we get the following code:

```
from sklearn.grid_search import GridSearchCV
from sklearn.metrics import f1_score

def grid_search_model(clf_factory, X, Y):
    cv = ShuffleSplit(
```

```
        n=len(X), n_iter=10, test_size=0.3,random_state=0)


    param_grid = dict(vect__ngram_range=[(1, 1), (1, 2), (1, 3)],
        vect__min_df=[1, 2],
        vect__stop_words=[None, "english"],
        vect__smooth_idf=[False, True],
        vect__use_idf=[False, True],
        vect__sublinear_tf=[False, True],
        vect__binary=[False, True],
        clf__alpha=[0, 0.01, 0.05, 0.1, 0.5, 1],
        )


    grid_search = GridSearchCV(clf_factory(),
        param_grid=param_grid,
        cv=cv,
        score_func=f1_score,
        verbose=10)
    grid_search.fit(X, Y)


    return grid_search.best_estimator_
```

We have to be patient while executing this:

```
clf = grid_search_model(create_ngram_model, X, Y)
print(clf)
```

Since we have just requested a parameter, sweep over $3 \cdot 2 \cdot 2 \cdot 2 \cdot 2 \cdot 2 \cdot 2 \cdot 6 = 1152$ parameter combinations, each being trained on 10 folds:

```
... waiting some hours   ...
Pipeline(clf=MultinomialNB(
alpha=0.01, class_weight=None, fit_prior=True),
clf__alpha=0.01,
clf__class_weight=None,
clf__fit_prior=True,
vect=TfidfVectorizer(
analyzer=word, binary=False,
   charset=utf-8, charset_error=strict,
dtype=<type 'long'>,input=content,
```

```
lowercase=True, max_df=1.0,
max_features=None, max_n=None,
min_df=1, min_n=None, ngram_range=(1, 2),
norm=l2, preprocessor=None, smooth_idf=False,
stop_words=None,strip_accents=None,
sublinear_tf=True,token_pattern=(?u)\b\w\w+\b,
token_processor=None, tokenizer=None,
use_idf=False, vocabulary=None),
vect__analyzer=word, vect__binary=False,
vect__charset=utf-8,
vect__charset_error=strict,
vect__dtype=<type 'long'>,
vect__input=content, vect__lowercase=True,
vect__max_df=1.0,vect__max_features=None,
vect__max_n=None, vect__min_df=1,
vect__min_n=None, vect__ngram_range=(1, 2),
vect__norm=l2, vect__preprocessor=None,
vect__smooth_idf=False, vect__stop_words=None,
vect__strip_accents=None, vect__sublinear_tf=True,
vect__token_pattern=(?u)\b\w\w+\b,
vect__token_processor=None, vect__tokenizer=None,
vect__use_idf=False, vect__vocabulary=None)
0.795   0.007   0.702   0.028
```

The best estimator indeed improves the P/R AUC by nearly 3.3 percent to now 70.2, with the settings shown in the previous code.

Also, the devastating results for positive tweets against the rest and negative tweets against the rest improve if we configure the vectorizer and classifier with those parameters we have just found out:

```
== Pos vs. rest ==
0.889    0.010    0.509    0.041
== Neg vs. rest ==
0.886    0.007    0.615    0.035
```

Have a look at the following plots:

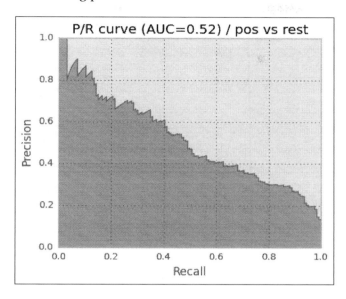

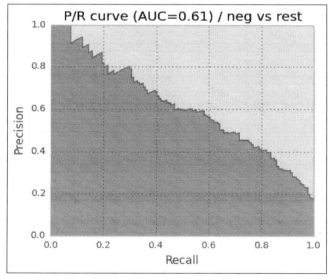

Indeed, the P/R curves look much better (note that the plots are from the medium of the fold classifiers, thus, slightly diverging AUC values). Nevertheless, we probably still wouldn't use those classifiers. Time for something completely different...

Cleaning tweets

New constraints lead to new forms. Twitter is no exception in this regard. Because the text has to fit into 140 characters, people naturally develop new language shortcuts to say the same in less characters. So far, we have ignored all the diverse emoticons and abbreviations. Let's see how much we can improve by taking that into account. For this endeavor, we will have to provide our own `preprocessor()` to `TfidfVectorizer`.

First, we define a range of frequent emoticons and their replacements in a dictionary. Although we can find more distinct replacements, we go with obvious positive or negative words to help the classifier:

```
emo_repl = {
    # positive emoticons
    "&lt;3": " good ",
    ":d": " good ", # :D in lower case
    ":dd": " good ", # :DD in lower case
    "8)": " good ",
    ":-)": " good ",
    ":)": " good ",
    ";)": " good ",
    "(-:": " good ",
    "(:": " good ",

    # negative emoticons:
    ":/": " bad ",
    ":&gt;": " sad ",
    ":')": " sad ",
    ":-(": " bad ",
    ":(": " bad ",
    ":S": " bad ",
    ":-S": " bad ",
    }


# make sure that e.g. :dd is replaced before :d
emo_repl_order = [k for (k_len,k) in reversed(sorted([(len(k),k) for k in
emo_repl.keys()]))]
```

Then, we define abbreviations as regular expressions together with their expansions (\b marks the word boundary):

```
re_repl = {
r"\br\b": "are",
r"\bu\b": "you",
r"\bhaha\b": "ha",
r"\bhahaha\b": "ha",
r"\bdon't\b": "do not",
r"\bdoesn't\b": "does not",
r"\bdidn't\b": "did not",
r"\bhasn't\b": "has not",
r"\bhaven't\b": "have not",
r"\bhadn't\b": "had not",
r"\bwon't\b": "will not",
r"\bwouldn't\b": "would not",
r"\bcan't\b": "can not",
r"\bcannot\b": "can not",
    }


def create_ngram_model(params=None):
    def preprocessor(tweet):
        tweet = tweet.lower()
        for k in emo_repl_order:
            tweet = tweet.replace(k, emo_repl[k])
        for r, repl in re_repl.items():
            tweet = re.sub(r, repl, tweet)

        return tweet

    tfidf_ngrams = TfidfVectorizer(preprocessor=preprocessor,
analyzer="word")
    # ...
```

Certainly, there are many more abbreviations that can be used here. But already with this limited set, we get an improvement for sentiment versus not sentiment of half a point, being now 70.7 percent:

```
== Pos vs. neg ==
0.808    0.024    0.885    0.029
== Pos/neg vs. irrelevant/neutral ==
0.793    0.010    0.685    0.024
== Pos vs. rest ==
0.890    0.011    0.517    0.041
== Neg vs. rest ==
0.886    0.006    0.624    0.033
```

Taking the word types into account

So far, our hope was that simply using the words independent of each other with the bag-of-words approach would suffice. Just from our intuition, however, neutral tweets probably contain a higher fraction of nouns, while positive or negative tweets are more colorful, requiring more adjectives and verbs. What if we use this linguistic information of the tweets as well? If we could find out how many words in a tweet were nouns, verbs, adjectives, and so on, the classifier could probably take that into account as well.

Determining the word types

This is what part-of-speech tagging, or POS tagging, is all about. A POS tagger parses a full sentence with the goal to arrange it into a dependence tree, where each node corresponds to a word and the parent-child relationship determines which word it depends on. With this tree, it can then make more informed decisions, for example, whether the word "book" is a noun ("This is a good book.") or a verb ("Could you please book the flight?").

You might have already guessed that NLTK will play its role in this area as well. And indeed, it comes readily packaged with all sorts of parsers and taggers. The POS tagger we will use, `nltk.pos_tag()`, is actually a full blown classifier trained using manually annotated sentences from the Penn Treebank Project (http://www.cis.upenn.edu/~treebank). It takes as input a list of word tokens and outputs a list of tuples, where each element contains the part of the original sentence and its part-of-speech tag.

```
>>> import nltk
>>> nltk.pos_tag(nltk.word_tokenize("This is a good book."))
```

```
[('This', 'DT'), ('is', 'VBZ'), ('a', 'DT'), ('good', 'JJ'), ('book',
'NN'), ('.', '.')]
>>> nltk.pos_tag(nltk.word_tokenize("Could you please book the
flight?"))
[('Could', 'MD'), ('you', 'PRP'), ('please', 'VB'), ('book', 'NN'),
('the', 'DT'), ('flight', 'NN'), ('?', '.')]
```

The POS tag abbreviations are taken from the Penn Treebank (adapted from http://www.anc.org/OANC/penn.html):

POS tag	Description	Example
CC	coordinating conjunction	or
CD	cardinal number	2, second
DT	determiner	the
EX	existential there	*there* are
FW	foreign word	kindergarten
IN	preposition/subordinating conjunction	on, of, like
JJ	adjective	cool
JJR	adjective, comparative	cooler
JJS	adjective, superlative	coolest
LS	list marker	1)
MD	modal	could, will
NN	noun, singular or mass	book
NNS	noun plural	books
NNP	proper noun, singular	Sean
NNPS	proper noun, plural	Vikings
PDT	predeterminer	both the boys
POS	possessive ending	friend's
PRP	personal pronoun	I, he, it
PRP$	possessive pronoun	my, his
RB	adverb	however, usually, naturally, here, good
RBR	adverb, comparative	better
RBS	adverb, superlative	best
RP	particle	give *up*
TO	to	*to* go, *to* him
UH	interjection	uhhuhhuhh
VB	verb, base form	take

POS tag	Description	Example
VBD	verb, past tense	took
VBG	verb, gerund/present participle	taking
VBN	verb, past participle	taken
VBP	verb, sing. present, non-3d	take
VBZ	verb, 3rd person sing. present	takes
WDT	wh-determiner	which
WP	wh-pronoun	who, what
WP$	possessive wh-pronoun	whose
WRB	wh-adverb	where, when

With these tags, it is pretty easy to filter the desired tags from the output of `pos_tag()`. We simply have to count all words whose tags start with NN for nouns, VB for verbs, JJ for adjectives, and RB for adverbs.

Successfully cheating using SentiWordNet

While linguistic information, as mentioned in the preceding section, will most likely help us, there is something better we can do to harvest it: SentiWordNet (`http://sentiwordnet.isti.cnr.it`). Simply put, it is a 13 MB file that assigns most of the English words a positive and negative value. More complicated put, for every synonym set, it records both the positive and negative sentiment values. Some examples are as follows:

POS	ID	PosScore	NegScore	SynsetTerms	Description
a	00311354	0.25	0.125	studious#1	Marked by care and effort; "made a studious attempt to fix the television set"
a	00311663	0	0.5	careless#1	Marked by lack of attention or consideration or forethought or thoroughness; not careful...
n	03563710	0	0	implant#1	A prosthesis placed permanently in tissue
v	00362128	0	0	kink#2 curve#5 curl#1	Form a curl, curve, or kink; "the cigar smoke curled up at the ceiling"

With the information in the **POS** column, we will be able to distinguish between the noun "book" and the verb "book". PosScore and NegScore together will help us to determine the neutrality of the word, which is 1-PosScore-NegScore. SynsetTerms lists all words in the set that are synonyms. We can safely ignore the **ID** and **Description** columns for our purposes.

The synset terms have a number appended, because some occur multiple times in different synsets. For example, "fantasize" conveys two quite different meanings, which also leads to different scores:

POS	ID	PosScore	NegScore	SynsetTerms	Description
v	01636859	0.375	0	fantasize#2 fantasise#2	Portray in the mind; "he is fantasizing the ideal wife"
v	01637368	0	0.125	fantasy#1 fantasize#1 fantasise#1	Indulge in fantasies; "he is fantasizing when he says he plans to start his own company"

To find out which of the synsets to take, we will need to really understand the meaning of the tweets, which is beyond the scope of this chapter. The field of research that is focusing on this challenge is called word-sense-disambiguation. For our task, we take the easy route and simply average the scores over all the synsets, in which a term is found. For "fantasize", PosScore will be 0.1875 and NegScore will be 0.0625.

The following function, load_sent_word_net(), does all that for us and returns a dictionary where the keys are strings of the form *word type/word*, for example, n/implant, and the values are the positive and negative scores:

```
import csv, collections


def load_sent_word_net():
    # making our life easier by using a dictionary that
    # automatically creates an empty list whenever we access
    # a not yet existing key
    sent_scores = collections.defaultdict(list)


    with open(os.path.join(DATA_DIR, SentiWordNet_3.0.0_20130122.txt"),
"r") as csvfile:
        reader = csv.reader(csvfile, delimiter='\t',
quotechar='"')
```

```
    for line in reader:
        if line[0].startswith("#"):
            continue
        if len(line)==1:
            continue

        POS, ID, PosScore, NegScore, SynsetTerms, Gloss = line
        if len(POS)==0 or len(ID)==0:
            continue
        for term in SynsetTerms.split(" "):
            # drop number at the end of every term
            term = term.split("#")[0]
            term = term.replace("-", " ").replace("_", " ")
            key = "%s/%s"%(POS, term.split("#")[0])
            sent_scores[key].append((float(PosScore),
float(NegScore)))

    for key, value in sent_scores.items():
        sent_scores[key] = np.mean(value, axis=0)

    return sent_scores
```

Our first estimator

Now, we have everything in place to create our own first vectorizer. The most convenient way to do it is to inherit it from BaseEstimator. It requires us to implement the following three methods:

- get_feature_names(): This returns a list of strings of the features that we will return in transform().

- fit(document, y=None): As we are not implementing a classifier, we can ignore this one and simply return self.

- transform(documents): This returns numpy.array(), containing an array of shape (len(documents), len(get_feature_names)). This means, for every document in documents, it has to return a value for every feature name in get_feature_names().

Here is the implementation:

```python
sent_word_net = load_sent_word_net()


class LinguisticVectorizer(BaseEstimator):
    def get_feature_names(self):
        return np.array(['sent_neut', 'sent_pos', 'sent_neg',
            'nouns', 'adjectives', 'verbs', 'adverbs',
            'allcaps', 'exclamation', 'question', 'hashtag',
            'mentioning'])

    # we don't fit here but need to return the reference
    # so that it can be used like fit(d).transform(d)
    def fit(self, documents, y=None):
        return self

    def _get_sentiments(self, d):
        sent = tuple(d.split())
        tagged = nltk.pos_tag(sent)

        pos_vals = []
        neg_vals = []

        nouns = 0.
        adjectives = 0.
        verbs = 0.
        adverbs = 0.

        for w,t in tagged:
            p, n = 0,0
            sent_pos_type = None
            if t.startswith("NN"):
                sent_pos_type = "n"
                nouns += 1
            elif t.startswith("JJ"):
                sent_pos_type = "a"
                adjectives += 1
```

```python
        elif t.startswith("VB"):
            sent_pos_type = "v"
            verbs += 1
        elif t.startswith("RB"):
            sent_pos_type = "r"
            adverbs += 1

        if sent_pos_type is not None:
            sent_word = "%s/%s" % (sent_pos_type, w)

            if sent_word in sent_word_net:
                p,n = sent_word_net[sent_word]

        pos_vals.append(p)
        neg_vals.append(n)

    l = len(sent)
    avg_pos_val = np.mean(pos_vals)
    avg_neg_val = np.mean(neg_vals)
    return [1-avg_pos_val-avg_neg_val, avg_pos_val, avg_neg_val,
        nouns/l, adjectives/l, verbs/l, adverbs/l]



def transform(self, documents):
    obj_val, pos_val, neg_val, nouns, adjectives, \
verbs, adverbs = np.array([self._get_sentiments(d) \
for d in documents]).T

    allcaps = []
    exclamation = []
    question = []
    hashtag = []
    mentioning = []

    for d in documents:
        allcaps.append(np.sum([t.isupper() \
```

```
        for t in d.split() if len(t)>2]))


    exclamation.append(d.count("!"))
    question.append(d.count("?"))
    hashtag.append(d.count("#"))
    mentioning.append(d.count("@"))


    result = np.array([obj_val, pos_val, neg_val, nouns, adjectives,
verbs, adverbs, allcaps, exclamation, question,
hashtag, mentioning]).T


    return result
```

Putting everything together

Nevertheless, using these linguistic features in isolation without the words themselves will not take us very far. Therefore, we have to combine the TfidfVectorizer parameter with the linguistic features. This can be done with scikit-learn's FeatureUnion class. It is initialized in the same manner as Pipeline; however, instead of evaluating the estimators in a sequence each passing the output of the previous one to the next one, FeatureUnion does it in parallel and joins the output vectors afterwards.

```
def create_union_model(params=None):
    def preprocessor(tweet):
        tweet = tweet.lower()

        for k in emo_repl_order:
            tweet = tweet.replace(k, emo_repl[k])
        for r, repl in re_repl.items():
            tweet = re.sub(r, repl, tweet)

        return tweet.replace("-", " ").replace("_", " ")

    tfidf_ngrams = TfidfVectorizer(preprocessor=preprocessor,
analyzer="word")
    ling_stats = LinguisticVectorizer()
    all_features = FeatureUnion([('ling', ling_stats), ('tfidf',
tfidf_ngrams)])
```

```
clf = MultinomialNB()
pipeline = Pipeline([('all', all_features), ('clf', clf)])

if params:
    pipeline.set_params(**params)

return pipeline
```

Training and testing on the combined featurizers, gives another 0.4 percent improvement on average P/R AUC for positive versus negative:

```
== Pos vs. neg ==
0.810    0.023    0.890    0.025
== Pos/neg vs. irrelevant/neutral ==
0.791    0.007    0.691    0.022
== Pos vs. rest ==
0.890    0.011    0.529    0.035
== Neg vs. rest ==
0.883    0.007    0.617    0.033
time spent: 214.12578797340393
```

With these results, we probably do not want to use the positive versus rest and negative versus rest classifiers, but instead use first the classifier determining whether the tweet contains sentiment at all (pos/neg versus irrelevant/neutral) and then, in case it does, use the positive versus negative classifier to determine the actual sentiment.

Summary

Congratulations for sticking with us until the end! Together we have learned how Naïve Bayes works and why it is not that naïve at all. Especially, for training sets, where we don't have enough data to learn all the niches in the class probability space, Naïve Bayes does a great job of generalizing. We learned how to apply it to tweets and that cleaning the rough tweets' texts helps a lot. Finally, we realized that a bit of "cheating" (only after we have done our fair share of work) is okay. Especially when it gives another improvement of the classifier's performance, as we have experienced with the use of SentiWordNet.

In the next chapter, we will look at regressions.

7
Regression

You probably learned about regression in your high school mathematics class. The specific method you learned was probably what is called **ordinary least squares (OLS)** regression. This 200-year-old technique is computationally fast and can be used for many real-world problems. This chapter will start by reviewing it and showing you how it is available in scikit-learn.

For some problems, however, this method is insufficient. This is particularly true when we have many features, and it completely fails when we have more features than datapoints. For those cases, we need more advanced methods. These methods are very modern, with major developments happening in the last decade. They go by names such as Lasso, Ridge, or ElasticNets. We will go into these in detail. They are also available in scikit-learn.

Predicting house prices with regression

Let's start with a simple problem, predicting house prices in Boston; a problem for which we can use a publicly available dataset. We are given several demographic and geographical attributes, such as the crime rate or the pupil-teacher ratio in the neighborhood. The goal is to predict the median value of a house in a particular area. As usual, we have some training data, where the answer is known to us.

This is one of the built-in datasets that scikit-learn comes with, so it is very easy to load the data into memory:

```
>>> from sklearn.datasets import load_boston
>>> boston = load_boston()
```

The `boston` object contains several attributes; in particular, `boston.data` contains the input data and `boston.target` contains the price of houses.

We will start with a simple one-dimensional regression, trying to regress the price on a single attribute, the average number of rooms per dwelling in the neighborhood, which is stored at position 5 (you can consult `boston.DESCR` and `boston.feature_names` for detailed information on the data):

```
>>> from matplotlib import pyplot as plt
>>> plt.scatter(boston.data[:,5], boston.target, color='r')
```

The `boston.target` attribute contains the average house price (our target variable). We can use the standard least squares regression you probably first saw in high-school. Our first attempt looks like this:

```
>>> from sklearn.linear_model import LinearRegression
>>> lr = LinearRegression()
```

We import `LinearRegression` from the `sklearn.linear_model` module and construct a `LinearRegression` object. This object will behave analogously to the classifier objects from scikit-learn that we used earlier.

```
>>> x = boston.data[:,5]
>>> y = boston.target
>>> x = np.transpose(np.atleast_2d(x))
>>> lr.fit(x, y)
>>> y_predicted = lr.predict(x)
```

The only nonobvious line in this code block is the call to `np.atleast_2d`, which converts x from a one-dimensional to a two-dimensional array. This conversion is necessary as the `fit` method expects a two-dimensional array as its first argument. Finally, for the dimensions to work out correctly, we need to transpose this array.

Note that we are calling methods named `fit` and predict on the `LinearRegression` object, just as we did with classifier objects, even though we are now performing regression. This regularity in the API is one of the nicer features of scikit-learn.

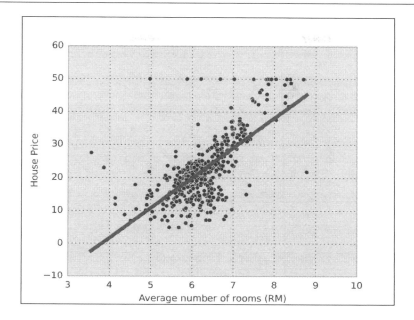

The preceding graph shows all the points (as dots) and our fit (the solid line). We can see that visually it looks good, except for a few outliers.

Ideally, though, we would like to measure how good of a fit this is quantitatively. This will be critical in order to be able to compare alternative methods. To do so, we can measure how close our prediction is to the true values. For this task, we can use the `mean_squared_error` function from the `sklearn.metrics` module:

```
>>> from sklearn.metrics import mean_squared_error
```

This function takes two arguments, the true value and the predictions, as follows:

```
>>> mse = mean_squared_error(y, lr.predict(x))
>>> print("Mean squared error (of training data): {:.3}".format(mse))
Mean squared error (of training data): 58.4
```

This value can sometimes be hard to interpret, and it's better to take the square root, to obtain the **root mean square error (RMSE)**:

```
>>> rmse = np.sqrt(mse)
>>> print("RMSE (of training data): {:.3}".format(rmse))
RMSE (of training data): 6.6
```

One advantage of using RMSE is that we can quickly obtain a very rough estimate of the error by multiplying it by two. In our case, we can expect the estimated price to be different from the real price by, at most, 13 thousand dollars.

Root mean squared error and prediction

Root mean squared error corresponds approximately to an estimate of the standard deviation. Since most data is at most two standard deviations from the mean, we can double our RMSE to obtain a rough confident interval. This is only completely valid if the errors are normally distributed, but it is often roughly correct even if they are not.

A number such as 6.6 is still hard to immediately intuit. Is this a good prediction? One possible way to answer this question is to compare it with the most simple baseline, the constant model. If we knew nothing of the input, the best we could do is predict that the output will always be the average value of y. We can then compare the mean-squared error of this model with the mean-squared error of the null model. This idea is formalized in the **coefficient of determination**, which is defined as follows:

$$1 - \frac{\sum_i (y_i - \hat{y}_i)^2}{\sum_i (y_i - \bar{y})^2} \approx 1 - \frac{\text{MSE}}{\text{VAR}(y)}$$

In this formula, y_i represents the value of the element with index i, while $\bar{y}_i$ is the estimate for the same element obtained by the regression model. Finally, $\bar{y}$ is the mean value of y, which represents the *null model* that always returns the same value. This is roughly the same as first computing the ratio of the mean squared error with the variance of the output and, finally, considering one minus this ratio. This way, a perfect model obtains a score of one, while the null model obtains a score of zero. Note that it is possible to obtain a negative score, which means that the model is so poor that one is better off using the mean as a prediction.

The coefficient of determination can be obtained using `r2_score` of the `sklearn.metrics` module:

```
>>> from sklearn.metrics import r2_score
>>> r2 = r2_score(y, lr.predict(x))
>>> print("R2 (on training data): {:.2}".format(r2))
R2 (on training data): 0.31
```

This measure is also called the R² score. If you are using linear regression and evaluating the error on the training data, then it does correspond to the square of the correlation coefficient, R. However, this measure is more general, and as we discussed, may even return a negative value.

An alternative way to compute the coefficient of determination is to use the `score` method of the `LinearRegression` object:

```
>>> r2 = lr.score(x,y)
```

Multidimensional regression

So far, we have only used a single variable for prediction, the number of rooms per dwelling. We will now use all the data we have to fit a model, using multidimensional regression. We now try to predict a single output (the average house price) based on multiple inputs.

The code looks very much like before. In fact, it's even simpler as we can now pass the value of `boston.data` directly to the `fit` method:

```
>>> x = boston.data
>>> y = boston.target
>>> lr.fit(x, y)
```

Using all the input variables, the root mean squared error is only 4.7, which corresponds to a coefficient of determination of 0.74. This is better than what we had before, which indicates that the extra variables did help. We can no longer easily display the regression line as we did, because we have a 14-dimensional regression hyperplane instead of a single line.

We can, however, plot the prediction versus the actual value. The code is as follows:

```
>>> p = lr.predict(x)
>>> plt.scatter(p, y)
>>> plt.xlabel('Predicted price')
>>> plt.ylabel('Actual price')
>>> plt.plot([y.min(), y.max()], [[y.min()], [y.max()]])
```

The last line plots a diagonal line that corresponds to perfect agreement. This aids with visualization. The results are shown in the following plot, where the solid line shows the diagonal (where all the points would lie if there was perfect agreement between the prediction and the underlying value):

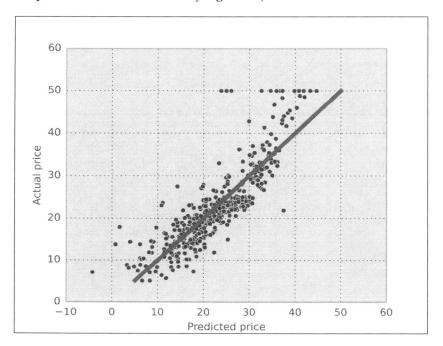

Cross-validation for regression

If you remember when we first introduced classification, we stressed the importance of cross-validation for checking the quality of our predictions. In regression, this is not always done. In fact, we discussed only the training error in this chapter so far. This is a mistake if you want to confidently infer the generalization ability. Since ordinary least squares is a very simple model, this is often not a very serious mistake. In other words, the amount of overfitting is slight. However, we should still test this empirically, which we can easily do with scikit-learn.

We will use the Kfold class to build a 5 fold cross-validation loop and test the generalization ability of linear regression:

```
>>> from sklearn.cross_validation import Kfold
>>> kf = KFold(len(x), n_folds=5)
>>> p = np.zeros_like(y)
>>> for train,test in kf:
```

```
...     lr.fit(x[train], y[train])
...     p[test] = lr.predict(x[test])
>>> rmse_cv = np.sqrt(mean_squared_error(p, y))
>>> print('RMSE on 5-fold CV: {:.2}'.format(rmse_cv))
RMSE on 5-fold CV: 5.6
```

With cross-validation, we obtain a more conservative estimate (that is, the error is larger): 5.6. As in the case of classification, the cross-validation estimate is a better estimate of how well we could generalize to predict on unseen data.

Ordinary least squares is fast at learning time and returns a simple model, which is fast at prediction time. For these reasons, it should often be the first model that you try in a regression problem. However, we are now going to see more advanced methods and why they are sometimes preferable.

Penalized or regularized regression

This section introduces penalized regression, also called **regularized regression**, an important class of regression models.

In ordinary regression, the returned fit is the best fit on the training data. This can lead to over-fitting. Penalizing means that we add a penalty for over-confidence in the parameter values. Thus, we accept a slightly worse fit in order to have a simpler model.

Another way to think about it is to consider that the default is that there is no relationship between the input variables and the output prediction. When we have data, we change this opinion, but adding a penalty means that we require more data to convince us that this is a strong relationship.

Penalized regression is about tradeoffs

Penalized regression is another example of the bias-variance tradeoff. When using a penalty, we get a worse fit in the training data, as we are adding bias. On the other hand, we reduce the variance and tend to avoid over-fitting. Therefore, the overall result might generalize better to unseen (test) data.

L1 and L2 penalties

We now explore these ideas in detail. Readers who do not care about some of the mathematical aspects should feel free to skip directly to the next section on how to use regularized regression in scikit-learn.

The problem, in general, is that we are given a matrix X of training data (rows are observations and each column is a different feature), and a vector y of output values. The goal is to obtain a vector of weights, which we will call b^*. The ordinary least squares regression is given by the following formula:

$$\vec{b}^* = \arg\min_{\vec{b}} \|\vec{y} - X\vec{b}\|^2$$

That is, we find vector b that minimizes the squared distance to the target y. In these equations, we ignore the issue of setting an intercept by assuming that the training data has been preprocessed so that the mean of y is zero.

Adding a penalty or a regularization means that we do not simply consider the best fit on the training data, but also how vector $\vec{b}$ is composed. There are two types of penalties that are typically used for regression: L1 and L2 penalties. An L1 penalty means that we penalize the regression by the sum of the absolute values of the coefficients, while an L2 penalty penalizes by the sum of squares.

When we add an L1 penalty, instead of the preceding equation, we instead optimize the following:

$$\vec{b}^* = \arg\min_{\vec{b}} \|\vec{y} - X\vec{b}\|^2 + \alpha \sum_i |b_i|$$

Here, we are trying to simultaneously make the error small, but also make the values of the coefficients small (in absolute terms). Using an L2 penalty, means that we use the following formula:

$$\vec{b}^* = \arg\min_{\vec{b}} \|\vec{y} - X\vec{b}\|^2 + \alpha \sum_i b_i^2$$

The difference is rather subtle: we now penalize by the square of the coefficient rather than their absolute value. However, the difference in the results is dramatic.

Ridge, Lasso, and ElasticNets

These penalized models often go by rather interesting names. The L1 penalized model is often called the **Lasso**, while an L2 penalized one is known as **Ridge Regression**. When using both, we call this an **ElasticNet** model.

Both the Lasso and the Ridge result in smaller coefficients than unpenalized regression (smaller in absolute value, ignoring the sign). However, the Lasso has the additional property that it results in many coefficients being set to exactly zero! This means that the final model does not even use some of its input features, the model is **sparse**. This is often a very desirable property as the model performs both feature selection and **regression** in a single step.

You will notice that whenever we add a penalty, we also add a weight *a*, which governs how much penalization we want. When *a* is close to zero, we are very close to unpenalized regression (in fact, if you set *a* to zero, you will simply perform OLS), and when *a* is large, we have a model that is very different from the unpenalized one.

The Ridge model is older as the Lasso is hard to compute with pen and paper. However, with modern computers, we can use the Lasso as easily as Ridge, or even combine them to form ElasticNets. An ElasticNet has two penalties, one for the absolute value and the other for the squares and it solves the following equation:

$$\vec{b}^* = \arg\min_{\vec{b}} \|\vec{y} - X\vec{b}\|^2 + \alpha_1 \sum_i |b_i| + \alpha_2 \sum_i b_i^2$$

This formula is a combination of the two previous ones, with two parameters, a_1 and a_2. Later in this chapter, we will discuss how to choose a good value for parameters.

Using Lasso or ElasticNet in scikit-learn

Let's adapt the preceding example to use ElasticNets. Using scikit-learn, it is very easy to swap in the ElasticNet regressor for the least squares one that we had before:

```
>>> from sklearn.linear_model import ElasticNet
>>> en = ElasticNet(alpha=0.5)
```

Now, we use `en`, whereas earlier we had used `lr`. This is the only change that is needed. The results are exactly what we would have expected. The training error increases to 5.0 (it was 4.6 before), but the cross-validation error decreases to 5.4 (it was 5.6 before). We trade a larger error on the training data in order to gain better generalization. We could have tried an L1 penalty using the `Lasso` class or L2 using the `Ridge` class with the same code.

Visualizing the Lasso path

Using scikit-learn, we can easily visualize what happens as the value of the regularization parameter (alpha) changes. We will again use the Boston data, but now we will use the `Lasso` regression object:

```
>>> las = Lasso(normalize=1)
>>> alphas = np.logspace(-5, 2, 1000)
>>> alphas, coefs, _ = las.path(x, y, alphas=alphas)
```

For each value in alphas, the `path` method on the `Lasso` object returns the coefficients that solve the lasso problem with that parameter value. Because the result changes smoothly with alpha, this can be computed very efficiently.

A typical way to visualize this path is to plot the value of the coefficients as alpha decreases. You can do so as follows:

```
>>> fig,ax = plt.subplots()
>>> ax.plot(alphas, coefs.T)
>>> # Set log scale
>>> ax.set_xscale('log')
>>> # Make alpha decrease from left to right
>>> ax.set_xlim(alphas.max(), alphas.min())
```

This results in the following plot (we left out the trivial code that adds axis labels and the title):

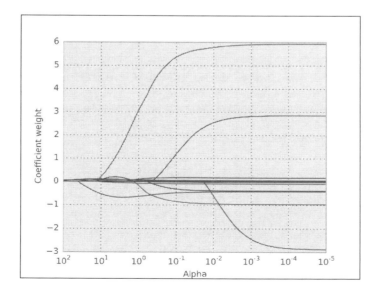

In this plot, the x axis shows decreasing amounts of regularization from left to right (alpha is decreasing). Each line shows how a different coefficient varies as alpha changes. The plot shows that when using very strong regularization (left side, very high alpha), the best solution is to have all values be exactly zero. As the regularization becomes weaker, one by one, the values of the different coefficients first shoot up, then stabilize. At some point, they all plateau as we are probably already close to the unpenalized solution.

P-greater-than-N scenarios

The title of this section is a bit of inside jargon, which you will learn now. Starting in the 1990s, first in the biomedical domain, and then on the Web, problems started to appear where P was greater than N. What this means is that the number of features, P, was greater than the number of examples, N (these letters were the conventional statistical shorthand for these concepts). These became known as *P greater than N* problems.

For example, if your input is a set of written documents, a simple way to approach it is to consider each possible word in the dictionary as a feature and regress on those (we will later work on one such problem ourselves). In the English language, you have over 20,000 words (this is if you perform some stemming and only consider common words; it is more than ten times that if you skip this preprocessing step). If you only have a few hundred or a few thousand examples, you will have more features than examples.

In this case, as the number of features is greater than the number of examples, it is possible to have a perfect fit on the training data. This is a mathematical fact, which is independent of your data. You are, in effect, solving a system of linear equations with fewer equations than variables. You can find a set of regression coefficients with zero training error (in fact, you can find more than one perfect solution, infinitely many).

However, and this is a major problem, *zero training error does not mean that your solution will generalize well*. In fact, it may generalize very poorly. Whereas earlier regularization could give you a little extra boost, it is now absolutely required for a meaningful result.

An example based on text documents

We will now turn to an example that comes from a study performed at Carnegie Mellon University by Prof. Noah Smith's research group. The study was based on mining the so-called 10-K reports that companies file with the **Securities and Exchange Commission** (SEC) in the United States. This filing is mandated by law for all publicly traded companies. The goal of their study was to predict, based on this piece of public information, what the future volatility of the company's stock will be. In the training data, we are actually using historical data for which we already know what happened.

There are 16,087 examples available. The features, which have already been preprocessed for us, correspond to different words, 150,360 in total. Thus, we have many more features than examples, almost ten times as much. In the introduction, it was stated that ordinary least regression fails in these cases and we will now see why by attempting to blindly apply it.

The dataset is available in SVMLight format from multiple sources, including the book's companion website. This is a format that scikit-learn can read. SVMLight is, as the name says, a support vector machine implementation, which is also available through scikit-learn; right now, we are only interested in the file format:

```
>>> from sklearn.datasets import load_svmlight_file
>>> data,target = load_svmlight_file('E2006.train')
```

In the preceding code, data is a sparse matrix (that is, most of its entries are zeros and, therefore, only the nonzero entries are saved in memory), while the target is a simple one-dimensional vector. We can start by looking at some attributes of the target:

```
>>> print('Min target value: {}'.format(target.min()))
Min target value: -7.89957807347
>>> print('Max target value: {}'.format(target.max()))
Max target value: -0.51940952694
>>> print('Mean target value: {}'.format(target.mean()))
Mean target value: -3.51405313669
>>> print('Std. dev. target: {}'.format(target.std()))
Std. dev. target: 0.632278353911
```

So, we can see that the data lies between -7.9 and -0.5. Now that we have a feel for the data, we can check what happens when we use OLS to predict. Note that we can use exactly the same classes and methods as we did earlier:

```
>>> from sklearn.linear_model import LinearRegression
>>> lr = LinearRegression()
>>> lr.fit(data,target)
>>> pred = lr.predict(data)
>>> rmse_train = np.sqrt(mean_squared_error(target, pred))
>>> print('RMSE on training: {:.2}'.format(rmse_train))
RMSE on training: 0.0025
>>> print('R2 on training: {:.2}'.format(r2_score(target, pred)))
R2 on training: 1.0
```

The root mean squared error is not exactly zero because of rounding errors, but it is very close. The coefficient of determination is `1.0`. That is, the linear model is reporting a perfect prediction on its training data.

When we use cross-validation (the code is very similar to what we used earlier in the Boston example), we get something very different: RMSE of 0.75, which corresponds to a negative coefficient of determination of -0.42. This means that if we always "predict" the mean value of -3.5, we do better than when using the regression model!

> **Training and generalization error**
>
> When the number of features is greater than the number of examples, you always get zero training errors with OLS, except perhaps for issues due to rounding off. However, this is rarely a sign that your model will do well in terms of generalization. In fact, you may get zero training error and have a completely useless model.

The natural solution is to use regularization to counteract the overfitting. We can try the same cross-validation loop with an ElasticNet learner, having set the penalty parameter to `0.1`:

```
>>> from sklearn.linear_model import ElasticNet
>>> met = ElasticNet(alpha=0.1)

>>> kf = KFold(len(target), n_folds=5)
>>> pred = np.zeros_like(target)
>>> for train, test in kf:
...     met.fit(data[train], target[train])
```

```
...        pred[test] = met.predict(data[test])

>>> # Compute RMSE
>>> rmse = np.sqrt(mean_squared_error(target, pred))
>>> print('[EN 0.1] RMSE on testing (5 fold): {:.2}'.format(rmse))
[EN 0.1] RMSE on testing (5 fold): 0.4

>>> # Compute Coefficient of determination
>>> r2 = r2_score(target, pred)
>>> print('[EN 0.1] R2 on testing (5 fold): {:.2}'.format(r2))
[EN 0.1] R2 on testing (5 fold): 0.61
```

Now, we get `0.4` RMSE and an R2 of `0.61`, much better than just predicting the mean. There is one problem with this solution, though, which is the choice of alpha. When using the default value (`1.0`), the result is very different (and worse).

In this case, we cheated as the author had previously tried a few values to see which ones would give a good result. This is not effective and can lead to over estimates of confidence (we are looking at the test data to decide which parameter values to use and which we should never use). The next section explains how to do it properly and how this is supported by scikit-learn.

Setting hyperparameters in a principled way

In the preceding example, we set the penalty parameter to `0.1`. We could just as well have set it to 0.7 or 23.9. Naturally, the results vary each time. If we pick an overly large value, we get underfitting. In the extreme case, the learning system will just return every coefficient equal to zero. If we pick a value that is too small, we are very close to OLS, which overfits and generalizes poorly (as we saw earlier).

How do we choose a good value? This is a general problem in machine learning: setting parameters for our learning methods. A generic solution is to use cross-validation. We pick a set of possible values, and then use cross-validation to choose which one is best. This performs more computation (five times more if we use five folds), but is always applicable and unbiased.

We must be careful, though. In order to obtain an estimate of generalization, we have to use **two-levels of cross-validation**: one level is to estimate the generalization, while the second level is to get good parameters. That is, we split the data in, for example, five folds. We start by holding out the first fold and will learn on the other four. Now, we split these again into 5 folds in order to choose the parameters. Once we have set our parameters, we test on the first fold. Now, we repeat this four other times:

The preceding figure shows how you break up a single training fold into subfolds. We would need to repeat it for all the other folds. In this case, we are looking at five outer folds and five inner folds, but there is no reason to use the same number of outer and inner folds, you can use any number you want as long as you keep the folds separate.

This leads to a lot of computation, but it is necessary in order to do things correctly. The problem is that if you use a piece of data to make any decisions about your model (including which parameters to set), you have contaminated it and you can no longer use it to test the generalization ability of your model. This is a subtle point and it may not be immediately obvious. In fact, it is still the case that many users of machine learning get this wrong and overestimate how well their systems are doing, because they do not perform cross-validation correctly!

Fortunately, scikit-learn makes it very easy to do the right thing; it provides classes named `LassoCV`, `RidgeCV`, and `ElasticNetCV`, all of which encapsulate an inner cross-validation loop to optimize for the necessary parameter. The code is almost exactly like the previous one, except that we do not need to specify any value for alpha:

```
>>> from sklearn.linear_model import ElasticNetCV
>>> met = ElasticNetCV()
>>> kf = KFold(len(target), n_folds=5)
>>> p = np.zeros_like(target)
>>> for train,test in kf:
```

```
...       met.fit(data[train],target[train])
...       p[test] = met.predict(data[test])
>>> r2_cv = r2_score(target, p)
>>> print("R2 ElasticNetCV: {:.2}".format(r2_cv))
R2 ElasticNetCV: 0.65
```

This results in a lot of computation, so you may want to get some coffee while you are waiting (depending on how fast your computer is). You might get better performance by taking advantage of multiple processors. This is a built-in feature of scikit-learn, which can be accessed quite trivially by using the n_jobs parameter to the ElasticNetCV constructor. To use four CPUs, make use of the following code:

```
>>> met = ElasticNetCV(n_jobs=4)
```

Set the n_jobs parameter to -1 to use all the available CPUs:

```
>>> met = ElasticNetCV(n_jobs=-1)
```

You may have wondered why, if ElasticNets have two penalties, the L1 and the L2 penalty, we only need to set a single value for alpha. In fact, the two values are specified by separately specifying alpha and the l1_ratio variable (that is spelled *ell-1-underscore-ratio*). Then, α_1 and α_2 are set as follows (where ρ stands for l1_ratio):

$$\alpha_1 = \rho\alpha$$

$$\alpha_2 = (1 - \rho)\alpha$$

In an intuitive sense, alpha sets the overall amount of regularization while l1_ratio sets the tradeoff between the different types of regularization, L1 and L2.

We can request that the ElasticNetCV object tests different values of l1_ratio, as is shown in the following code:

```
>>> l1_ratio=[.01, .05, .25, .5, .75, .95, .99]
>>> met = ElasticNetCV(
              l1_ratio=l1_ratio,
              n_jobs=-1)
```

This set of l1_ratio values is recommended in the documentation. It will test models that are almost like Ridge (when l1_ratio is 0.01 or 0.05) as well as models that are almost like Lasso (when l1_ratio is 0.95 or 0.99). Thus, we explore a full range of different options.

Because of its flexibility and the ability to use multiple CPUs, `ElasticNetCV` is an excellent default solution for regression problems when you don't have any particular reason to prefer one type of model over the rest.

Putting all this together, we can now visualize the prediction versus real fit on this large dataset:

```
>>> l1_ratio = [.01, .05, .25, .5, .75, .95, .99]
>>> met = ElasticNetCV(
                l1_ratio=l1_ratio,
                n_jobs=-1)
>>> p = np.zeros_like(target)
>>> for train,test in kf:
...     met.fit(data[train],target[train])
...     p[test] = met.predict(data[test])
>>> plt.scatter(p, y)
>>> # Add diagonal line for reference
>>> # (represents perfect agreement)
>>> plt.plot([p.min(), p.max()], [p.min(), p.max()])
```

This results in the following plot:

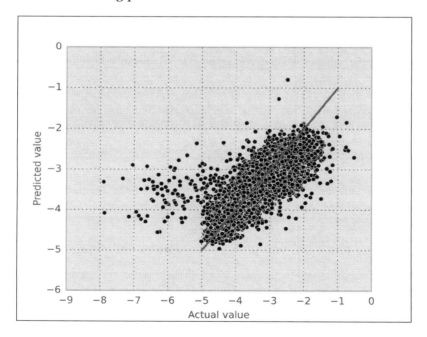

We can see that the predictions do not match very well on the bottom end of the value range. This is perhaps because there are so many fewer elements on this end of the target range (which also implies that this affects only a small minority of datapoints).

One last note: the approach of using an inner cross-validation loop to set a parameter is also available in scikit-learn using a grid search. In fact, we already used it in the previous chapter.

Summary

In this chapter, we started with the oldest trick in the book, ordinary least squares regression. Although centuries old, it is still often the best solution for regression. However, we also saw more modern approaches that avoid overfitting and can give us better results especially when we have a large number of features. We used Ridge, Lasso, and ElasticNets; these are the state-of-the-art methods for regression.

We saw, once again, the danger of relying on training error to estimate generalization: it can be an overly optimistic estimate to the point where our model has zero training error, but we know that it is completely useless. When thinking through these issues, we were led into two-level cross-validation, an important point that many in the field still have not completely internalized.

Throughout this chapter, we were able to rely on scikit-learn to support all the operations we wanted to perform, including an easy way to achieve correct cross-validation. ElasticNets with an inner cross-validation loop for parameter optimization (as implemented in scikit-learn by `ElasticNetCV`) should probably become your default method for regression.

One reason to use an alternative is when you are interested in a sparse solution. In this case, a pure Lasso solution is more appropriate as it will set many coefficients to zero. It will also allow you to discover from the data a small number of variables, which are important to the output. Knowing the identity of these may be interesting in and of itself, in addition to having a good regression model.

In the next chapter, we will look at recommendations, another machine learning problem. Our first approach will be to use regression to predict consumer product ratings. We will then see alternative models to generate recommendations.

8
Recommendations

Recommendations have become one of the staples of online services and commerce. This type of automated system can provide each user with a personalized list of suggestions (be it a list of products to purchase, features to use, or new connections). In this chapter, we will see the basic ways in which automated recommendation generation systems work. The field of recommendation based on consumer inputs is often called collaborative filtering, as the users collaborate through the system to find the best items for each other.

In the first part of this chapter, we will see how we can use past product ratings from consumers to predict new ratings. We start with a few ideas that are helpful and then combine all of them. When combining, we use regression to learn the best way in they can be combined. This will also allow us to explore a generic concept in machine learning: ensemble learning.

In the second part of this chapter, we will take a look at a different way of learning recommendations: basket analysis. Unlike the case in which we have numeric ratings, in the basket analysis setting, all we have is information about the shopping baskets, that is, what items were bought together. The goal is to learn about recommendations. You have probably already seen features of the form "people who bought X also bought Y" in online shopping. We will develop a similar feature of our own.

Rating predictions and recommendations

If you have used any online shopping system in the last 10 years, you have probably seen these recommendations. Some are like Amazon's "costumers who bought X also bought Y". These will be dealt with later in the chapter in the *Basket analysis* section. Other recommendations are based on predicting the rating of a product, such as a movie.

The problem of learning recommendations based on past product ratings was made famous by the Netflix Prize, a million-dollar machine learning public challenge by Netflix. Netflix (well-known in the USA and UK and in a process of international expansion) is a movie rental company. Traditionally, you would receive DVDs in the mail; more recently, Netflix has focused on the online streaming of movies and TV shows. From the start, one of the distinguishing features of the service was that it gives users the option to rate the films they have seen. Netflix then uses these ratings to recommend other films to its customers. In this machine learning problem, you not only have the information about which films the user saw but also about how the user rated them.

In 2006, Netflix made a large number of customer ratings of films in its database available for a public challenge. The goal was to improve on their in-house algorithm for rating prediction. Whoever would be able to beat it by 10 percent or more would win 1 million dollars. In 2009, an international team named BellKor's Pragmatic Chaos was able to beat this mark and take the prize. They did so just 20 minutes before another team, The Ensemble, and passed the 10 percent mark as well—an exciting photo finish for a competition that lasted several years.

Machine learning in the real world

Much has been written about the Netflix Prize, and you may learn a lot by reading up on it. The techniques that won were a mixture of advanced machine learning and a lot of work put into preprocessing the data. For example, some users like to rate everything very highly, while others are always more negative; if you do not account for this in preprocessing, your model will suffer. Other normalizations were also necessary for a good result: how old is the film and how many ratings did it receive. Good algorithms are a good thing, but you always need to "get your hands dirty" and tune your methods to the properties of the data you have in front of you. Preprocessing and normalizing the data is often the most time-consuming part of the machine learning process. However, this is also the place where one can have the biggest impact on the final performance of the system.

The first thing to note about the Netflix Prize is how hard it was. Roughly speaking, the internal system that Netflix used was about 10 percent better than no recommendations (that is, assigning each movie just the average value for all users). The goal was to obtain just another 10 percent improvement on this. In total, the winning system was roughly just 20 percent better than no personalization. Yet, it took a tremendous amount of time and effort to achieve this goal. And even though 20 percent does not seem like much, the result is a system that is useful in practice.

Unfortunately, for legal reasons, this dataset is no longer available. Although the data was anonymous, there were concerns that it might be possible to discover who the clients were and reveal private details of movie rentals. However, we can use an academic dataset with similar characteristics. This data comes from GroupLens, a research laboratory at the University of Minnesota.

How can we solve a Netflix style ratings prediction question? We will see two different approaches, neighborhood approaches and regression approaches. We will also see how to combine these to obtain a single prediction.

Splitting into training and testing

At a high level, splitting the dataset into training and testing data in order to obtain a principled estimate of the system's performance is performed as in previous chapters: we take a certain fraction of our data points (we will use 10 percent) and reserve them for testing; the rest will be used for training. However, because the data is structured differently in this context, the code is different. The first step is to load the data from disk, for which we use the following function:

```python
def load():
    import numpy as np
    from scipy import sparse

    data = np.loadtxt('data/ml-100k/u.data')
    ij = data[:, :2]
    ij -= 1  # original data is in 1-based system
    values = data[:, 2]
    reviews = sparse.csc_matrix((values, ij.T)).astype(float)
    return reviews.toarray()
```

Note that zero entries in this matrix represent missing ratings.

```python
>>> reviews = load()
>>> U,M = np.where(reviews)
```

We now use the standard random module to choose indices to test:

```python
>>> import random
>>> test_idxs = np.array(random.sample(range(len(U)), len(U)//10))
```

Now, we build the `train` matrix, which is like `reviews`, but with the testing entries set to zero:

```
>>> train = reviews.copy()
>>> train[U[test_idxs], M[test_idxs]] = 0
```

Finally, the `test` matrix contains just the testing values:

```
>>> test = np.zeros_like(reviews)
>>> test[U[test_idxs], M[test_idxs]] = reviews[U[test_idxs],
                                              M[test_idxs]]
```

From now on, we will work on taking the training data, and try to predict all the missing entries in the dataset. That is, we will write code that assigns each (user, movie) pair a recommendation.

Normalizing the training data

As we discussed, it is best to normalize the data to remove obvious movie or user-specific effects. We will just use one very simple type of normalization, which we used before: conversion to z-scores.

Unfortunately, we cannot simply use scikit-learn's normalization objects as we have to deal with the missing values in our data (that is, not all movies were rated by all users). Thus, we want to normalize by the mean and standard deviation of the values that are, in fact, present.

We will write our own class, which ignores missing values. This class will follow the scikit-learn preprocessing API:

```
class NormalizePositive(object):
```

We want to choose the axis of normalization. By default, we normalize along the first axis, but sometimes it will be useful to normalize along the second one. This follows the convention of many other NumPy-related functions:

```
    def __init__(self, axis=0):
        self.axis = axis
```

The most important method is the fit method. In our implementation, we compute the mean and standard deviation of the values that are not zero. Recall that zeros indicate "missing values":

```
    def fit(self, features, y=None):
```

If the axis is 1, we operate on the transposed array as follows:

```
    if self.axis == 1:
        features = features.T
    #  count features that are greater than zero in axis 0:
    binary = (features > 0)
    count0 = binary.sum(axis=0)

    # to avoid division by zero, set zero counts to one:
    count0[count0 == 0] = 1.

    # computing the mean is easy:
    self.mean = features.sum(axis=0)/count0

    # only consider differences where binary is True:
    diff = (features - self.mean) * binary
    diff **= 2
    # regularize the estimate of std by adding 0.1
    self.std = np.sqrt(0.1 + diff.sum(axis=0)/count0)
    return self
```

We add 0.1 to the direct estimate of the standard deviation to avoid underestimating the value of the standard deviation when there are only a few samples, all of which may be exactly the same. The exact value used does not matter much for the final result, but we need to avoid division by zero.

The `transform` method needs to take care of maintaining the binary structure as follows:

```
def transform(self, features):
    if self.axis == 1:
        features = features.T
    binary = (features > 0)
    features = features - self.mean
    features /= self.std
    features *= binary
    if self.axis == 1:
        features = features.T
    return features
```

Notice how we took care of transposing the input matrix when the axis is 1 and then transformed it back so that the return value has the same shape as the input. The `inverse_transform` method performs the inverse operation to transform as shown here:

```
def inverse_transform(self, features, copy=True):
    if copy:
        features = features.copy()
    if self.axis == 1:
        features = features.T
    features *= self.std
    features += self.mean
    if self.axis == 1:
        features = features.T
    return features
```

Finally, we add the `fit_transform` method which, as the name indicates, combines both the `fit` and `transform` operations:

```
def fit_transform(self, features):
    return self.fit(features).transform(features)
```

The methods that we defined (`fit`, `transform`, `transform_inverse`, and `fit_transform`) were the same as the objects defined in the `sklearn.preprocessing` module. In the following sections, we will first normalize the inputs, generate normalized predictions, and finally apply the inverse transformation to obtain the final predictions.

A neighborhood approach to recommendations

The neighborhood concept can be implemented in two ways: user neighbors or movie neighbors. User neighborhoods are based on a very simple concept: to know how a user will rate a movie, find the users most similar to them, and look at their ratings. We will only consider user neighbors for the moment. At the end of this section, we will discuss how the code can be adapted to compute movie neighbors.

One of the interesting techniques that we will now explore is to just see which movies each user has rated, even without taking a look at what rating was given. Even with a binary matrix where we have an entry equal to 1 when a user rates a movie, and 0 when they did not, we can make useful predictions. In hindsight, this makes perfect sense; we do not completely randomly choose movies to watch, but instead pick those where we already have an expectation of liking them. We also do not make random choices of which movies to rate, but perhaps only rate those we feel most strongly about (naturally, there are exceptions, but on average this is probably true).

We can visualize the values of the matrix as an image, where each rating is depicted as a little square. Black represents the absence of a rating and the gray levels represent the rating value.

The code to visualize the data is very simple (you can adapt it to show a larger fraction of the matrix than is possible to show in this book), as shown in the following:

```
>>> from matplotlib import pyplot as plt
>>> # Build an instance of the object we defined above
>>> norm = NormalizePositive(axis=1)
>>> binary = (train > 0)
>>> train = norm.fit_transform(train)
>>> # plot just 200x200 area for space reasons
>>> plt.imshow(binary[:200, :200], interpolation='nearest')
```

The following screenshot is the output of this code:

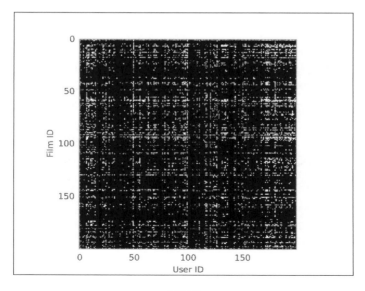

We can see that the matrix is sparse — most of the squares are black. We can also see that some users rate a lot more movies than others and that some movies are the target of many more ratings than others.

We are now going to use this binary matrix to make predictions of movie ratings. The general algorithm will be (in pseudo code) as follows:

1. For each user, rank every other user in terms of closeness. For this step, we will use the binary matrix and use correlation as the measure of closeness (interpreting the binary matrix as zeros and ones allows us to perform this computation).

2. When we need to estimate a rating for a (user, movie) pair, we look at all the users who have rated that movie and split them into two: the most similar half and the most dissimilar half. We then use the average of the most similar half as the prediction.

We can use the `scipy.spatial.distance.pdist` function to obtain the distance between all the users as a matrix. This function returns the correlation distance, which transforms the correlation value by inverting it so that larger numbers mean less similar. Mathematically, the correlation distance is $lift(X \rightarrow Y) = \dfrac{\hat{P}(Y \mid X)}{\hat{P}(Y)}$, where $1-r$ is the correlation value. The code is as follows:

```
>>> from scipy.spatial import distance
>>> # compute all pair-wise distances:
>>> dists = distance.pdist(binary, 'correlation')
>>> # Convert to square form, so that dists[i,j]
>>> # is distance between binary[i] and binary[j]:
>>> dists = distance.squareform(dists)
```

We can use this matrix to select the nearest neighbors of each user. These are the users that most resemble it.

```
>>> neighbors = dists.argsort(axis=1)
```

Now, we iterate over all users to estimate predictions for all inputs:

```
>>> # We are going to fill this matrix with results
>>> filled = train.copy()
>>> for u in range(filled.shape[0]):
...       # n_u is neighbors of user
...       n_u = neighbors[u, 1:]
```

```
...        # t_u is training data

...        for m in range(filled.shape[1]):
...            # get relevant reviews in order!
...            revs = [train[neigh, m]
...                        for neigh in n_u
...                            if binary    [neigh, m]]
...            if len(revs):
...                # n is the number of reviews for this movie
...                n = len(revs)
...                # consider half of the reviews plus one
...                n //= 2
...                n += 1
...                revs = revs[:n]
...                filled[u,m] = np.mean(revs )
```

The tricky part in the preceding snippet is indexing by the right values to select the neighbors who have rated the movie. Then, we choose the half that is closest to the user (in the `rev[:n]` line) and average those. Because some films have many reviews and others very few, it is hard to find a single number of users for all cases. Choosing half of the available data is a more generic approach.

To obtain the final result, we need to un-normalize the predictions as follows:

```
>>> predicted = norm.inverse_transform(filled)
```

We can use the same metrics we learned about in the previous chapter:

```
>>> from sklearn import metrics
>>> r2 = metrics.r2_score(test[test > 0], predicted[test > 0])
>>> print('R2 score (binary neighbors): {:.1%}'.format(r2))
R2 score (binary neighbors): 29.5%
```

The preceding code computes the result for user neighbors, but we can use it to compute the movie neighbors by simply transposing the input matrix. In fact, the code computes neighbors of whatever are the rows of its input matrix.

So we can rerun the following code, by just inserting the following line at the top:

```
>>> reviews = reviews.T
>>> # use same code as before …
>>> r2 = metrics.r2_score(test[test > 0], predicted[test > 0])
>>> print('R2 score (binary movie neighbors): {:.1%}'.format(r2))
R2 score (binary movie neighbors): 29.8%
```

Thus we can see that the results are not that different.

In this book's code repository, the neighborhood code has been wrapped into a simple function, which makes it easier to reuse.

A regression approach to recommendations

An alternative to neighborhoods is to formulate recommendations as a regression problem and apply the methods that we learned in the previous chapter.

We also consider why this problem is not a good fit for a classification formulation. We could certainly attempt to learn a five-class model, using one class for each possible movie rating. There are two problems with this approach:

- The different possible errors are not at all the same. For example, mistaking a 5-star movie for a 4-star one is not as serious a mistake as mistaking a 5-star movie for a 1-star one.

- Intermediate values make sense. Even if our inputs are only integer values, it is perfectly meaningful to say that the prediction is 4.3. We can see that this is a different prediction than 3.5, even if they both round to 4.

These two factors together mean that classification is not a good fit to the problem. The regression framework is a better fit.

For a basic approach, we again have two choices: we can build movie-specific or user-specific models. In our case, we are going to first build user-specific models. This means that, for each user, we take the movies that the user has rated as our target variable. The inputs are the ratings of other users. We hypothesize that this will give a high value to users who are similar to our user (or a negative value to users who like the same movies that our user dislikes).

Setting up the `train` and `test` matrices is as before (including running the normalization steps). Therefore, we jump directly to the learning step. First, we instantiate a regressor as follows:

```
>>> reg = ElasticNetCV(alphas=[
                0.0125, 0.025, 0.05, .125, .25, .5, 1., 2., 4.])
```

We build a data matrix, which will contain a rating for every (user, movie) pair. We initialize it as a copy of the training data:

```
>>> filled = train.copy()
```

Now, we iterate over all the users, and each time learn a regression model based only on the data that that user has given us:

```
>>> for u in range(train.shape[0]):
...        curtrain = np.delete(train, u, axis=0)
...        # binary records whether this rating is present
...        bu = binary[u]
...        # fit the current user based on everybody else
...        reg.fit(curtrain[:,bu].T, train[u, bu])
...        # Fill in all the missing ratings
...        filled[u, ~bu] = reg.predict(curtrain[:,~bu].T)
```

Evaluating the method can be done exactly as before:

```
>>> predicted = norm.inverse_transform(filled)
>>> r2 = metrics.r2_score(test[test > 0], predicted[test > 0])
>>> print('R2 score (user regression): {:.1%}'.format(r2))
R2 score (user regression): 32.3%
```

As before, we can adapt this code to perform movie regression by using the transposed matrix.

Combining multiple methods

We now combine the aforementioned methods in a single prediction. This seems intuitively a good idea, but how can we do this in practice? Perhaps, the first thought that comes to mind is that we can average the predictions. This might give decent results, but there is no reason to think that all estimated predictions should be treated the same. It might be that one is better than others.

We can try a weighted average, multiplying each prediction by a given weight before summing it all up. How do we find the best weights, though? We learn them from the data, of course!

Ensemble learning

We are using a general technique in machine learning, which is not only applicable in regression: **ensemble learning**. We learn an ensemble (that is, a set) of predictors. Then, we to combine them to obtain a single output. What is interesting is that we can see each prediction as being a new feature, and we are now just combining features based on training data, which is what we have been doing all along. Note that we are doing so for regression here, but the same reasoning is applicable to classification: you learn several classifiers, then a master classifier, which takes the output of all of them and gives a final prediction. Different forms of ensemble learning differ on how you combine the base predictors.

In order to combine the methods, we will use a technique called **stacked learning**. The idea is you learn a set of predictors, then you use the output of these predictors as features for another predictor. You can even have several layers, where each layer learns by using the output of the previous layer as features for its prediction. Have a look at the following diagram:

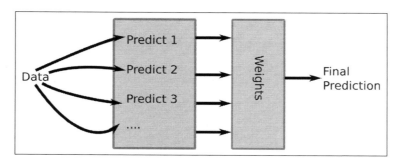

In order to fit this combination model, we will split the training data into two. Alternatively, we could have used cross-validation (the original stacked learning model worked like this). However, in this case, we have enough data to obtain good estimates by leaving some aside.

As when fitting hyperparameters, though, we need two layers of training/testing splits: a first, higher-level split, and then, inside the training split, a second split to be able to fit the stacked learner, as show in the following:

```
>>> train,test = load_ml100k.get_train_test(random_state=12)
>>> # Now split the training again into two subgroups
>>> tr_train,tr_test = load_ml100k.get_train_test(train,
    random_state=34)
>>> # Call all the methods we previously defined:
>>> # these have been implemented as functions:
>>> tr_predicted0 = regression.predict(tr_train)
>>> tr_predicted1 = regression.predict(tr_train.T).T
>>> tr_predicted2 = corrneighbours.predict(tr_train)
>>> tr_predicted3 = corrneighbours.predict(tr_train.T).T
>>> tr_predicted4 = norm.predict(tr_train)
>>> tr_predicted5 = norm.predict(tr_train.T).T


>>> # Now assemble these predictions into a single array:
>>> stack_tr = np.array([
...      tr_predicted0[tr_test > 0],
...      tr_predicted1[tr_test > 0],
...      tr_predicted2[tr_test > 0],
...      tr_predicted3[tr_test > 0],
...      tr_predicted4[tr_test > 0],
...      tr_predicted5[tr_test > 0],
...      ]).T


>>> # Fit a simple linear regression
>>> lr = linear_model.LinearRegression()
>>> lr.fit(stack_tr, tr_test[tr_test > 0])
```

Now, we apply the whole process to the testing split and evaluate:

```
>>> stack_te = np.array([
...      tr_predicted0.ravel(),
...      tr_predicted1.ravel(),
...      tr_predicted2.ravel(),
...      tr_predicted3.ravel(),
...      tr_predicted4.ravel(),
...      tr_predicted5.ravel(),
...      ]).T
>>> predicted = lr.predict(stack_te).reshape(train.shape)
```

Evaluation is as before:

```
>>> r2 = metrics.r2_score(test[test > 0], predicted[test > 0])
>>> print('R2 stacked: {:.2%}'.format(r2))
R2 stacked: 33.15%
```

The result of stacked learning is better than what any single method had achieved. It is quite typical that combining methods is a simple way to obtain a small performance boost, but that the results are not earth shattering.

By having a flexible way to combine multiple methods, we can simply try any idea we wish by adding it into the mix of learners and letting the system fold it into the prediction. We can, for example, replace the neighborhood criterion in the nearest neighbor code.

However, we do have to be careful to not overfit our dataset. In fact, if we randomly try too many things, some of them will work well on this dataset, but will not generalize. Even though we are splitting our data, we are not rigorously cross-validating our design decisions. In order to have a good estimate, and if data is plentiful, you should leave a portion of the data untouched until you have a final model that is about to go into production. Then, testing your model on this held out data gives you an unbiased prediction of how well you should expect it to work in the real world.

Basket analysis

The methods we have discussed so far work well when you have numeric ratings of how much a user liked a product. This type of information is not always available, as it requires active behavior on the part of consumers.

Basket analysis is an alternative mode of learning recommendations. In this mode, our data consists only of what items were bought together; it does not contain any information on whether individual items were enjoyed or not. Even if users sometimes buy items they regret, on average, knowing their purchases gives you enough information to build good recommendations. It is often easier to get this data rather than rating data, as many users will not provide ratings, while the basket data is generated as a side effect of shopping. The following screenshot shows you a snippet of Amazon.com's web page for Tolstoy's classic book *War and Peace*, which demonstrates a common way to use these results:

This mode of learning is not only applicable to actual shopping baskets, naturally. It is applicable in any setting where you have groups of objects together and need to recommend another. For example, recommending additional recipients to a user writing an e-mail is done by Gmail and could be implemented using similar techniques (we do not know what Gmail uses internally; perhaps, they combine multiple techniques, as we did earlier). Or, we could use these methods to develop an app to recommend web pages to visit based on your browsing history. Even if we are handling purchases, it may make sense to group all purchases by a customer into a single basket, independently of whether the items were bought together or on separate transactions. This depends on the business context, but keep in mind that the techniques are flexible and can be useful in many settings.

Beer and diapers. One of the stories that is often mentioned in the context of basket analysis is the *diapers and beer* story. It says that when supermarkets first started to look at their data, they found that diapers were often bought together with beer. Supposedly, it was the father who would go out to the supermarket to buy diapers and then would pick up some beer as well. There has been much discussion of whether this is true or just an urban myth. In this case, it seems that it is true. In the early 1990s, Osco Drug did discover that in the early evening, beer and diapers were bought together, and it did surprise the managers who had, until then, never considered these two products to be similar. What is not true is that this led the store to move the beer display closer to the diaper section. Also, we have no idea whether it was really that fathers were buying beer and diapers together more than mothers (or grandparents).

Obtaining useful predictions

It is not just "customers who bought X also bought Y" even though that is how many online retailers phrase it (see the Amazon.com screenshot given earlier); a real system cannot work like this. Why not? Because such a system would get fooled by very frequently bought items and would simply recommend that which is popular without any personalization.

For example, at a supermarket, many customers buy bread every time they shop or close to it (for the sake of argument, let us say that 50 percent of visits include bread). So, if you focus on any particular item, say dishwasher soap and look at what is frequently bought with dishwasher soap, you might find that bread is frequently bought with soap. In fact, just by random chance, 50 percent of the times someone buys dishwasher soap, they buy bread. However, bread is frequently bought with anything else just because everybody buys bread very often.

What we are really looking for is "customers who bought X, are statistically more likely to buy Y than the average customer who has not bought X". If you buy dishwasher soap, you are likely to buy bread, but not more so than the baseline. Similarly, a bookstore that simply recommended bestsellers no matter which books you had already bought would not be doing a good job of personalizing recommendations.

Analyzing supermarket shopping baskets

As an example, we will look at a dataset consisting of anonymous transactions at a supermarket in Belgium. This dataset was made available by Tom Brijs at Hasselt University. Due to privacy concerns, the data has been anonymized, so we only have a number for each product and a basket is a set of numbers. The data file is available from several online sources (including this book's companion website).

We begin by loading the dataset and looking at some statistics (this is always a good idea):

```
>>> from collections import defaultdict
>>> from itertools import chain

>>> # File is downloaded as a compressed file
>>> import gzip
>>> # file format is a line per transaction
>>> # of the form '12 34 342 5...'
>>> dataset = [[int(tok) for tok in line.strip().split()]
...             for line in gzip.open('retail.dat.gz')]
>>> # It is more convenient to work with sets
>>> dataset = [set(d) for d in dataset]
>>> # count how often each product was purchased:
>>> counts = defaultdict(int)
>>> for elem in chain(*dataset):
...         counts[elem] += 1
```

We can see the resulting counts summarized in the following table:

# of times bought	# of products
Just once	2,224
2 or 3	2,438
4 to 7	2,508
8 to 15	2,251
16 to 31	2,182
32 to 63	1,940
64 to 127	1,523
128 to 511	1,225
512 or more	179

There are many products that have only been bought a few times. For example, 33 percent of products were bought four or fewer times. However, this represents only 1 percent of purchases. This phenomenon that many products are only purchased a small number of times is sometimes labeled *the long tail* and has only become more prominent as the Internet made it cheaper to stock and sell niche items. In order to be able to provide recommendations for these products, we would need a lot more data.

There are a few open source implementations of basket analysis algorithms out there, but none that are well integrated with scikit-learn or any of the other packages we have been using. Therefore, we are going to implement one classic algorithm ourselves. This algorithm is called the Apriori algorithm, and it is a bit old (it was published in 1994 by Rakesh Agrawal and Ramakrishnan Srikant), but it still works (algorithms, of course, never stop working, they just get superceded by better ideas).

Formally, the Apriori algorithm takes a collection of sets (that is, your shopping baskets) and returns sets that are very frequent as subsets (that is, items that together are part of many shopping baskets).

The algorithm works using a bottom-up approach: starting with the smallest candidates (those composed of one single element), it builds up, adding one element at a time. Formally, the algorithm takes a set of baskets and the minimum input that should be considered (a parameter we will call minsupport). The first step is to consider all baskets with just one element with minimal support. Then, these are combined in all possible ways to build up two-element baskets. These are filtered in order to keep only those that have minimal support. Then, all possible three-element baskets are considered and those with minimal support are kept, and so on. The trick of Apriori is that when building a larger basket, *it only needs to consider those that are built up of smaller sets.*

The following diagram presents a schematic view of the algorithm:

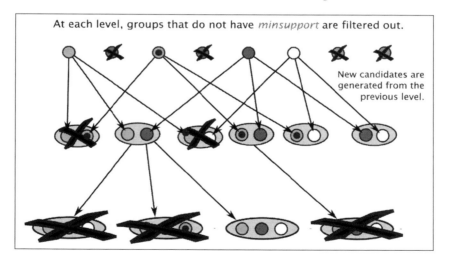

We shall now implement this algorithm in code. We need to define the minimum support we are looking for:

```
>>> minsupport = 80
```

Support is the number of times a set of products was purchased together. The goal of Apriori is to find itemsets with high support. Logically, any itemset with more than minimal support can only be composed of items which themselves have at least minimal support:

```
>>> valid = set(k for k,v in counts.items()
...             if (v >= minsupport))
```

Our initial itemsets are singletons (sets with a single element). In particular, all singletons that have at least minimal support are frequent itemsets:

```
>>>  itemsets = [frozenset([v]) for v in valid]
```

Now, our loop is given as follows:

```
>>> freqsets = []
>>> for i in range(16):
...     nextsets = []
...     tested = set()
...     for it in itemsets:
...         for v in valid:
...             if v not in it:
...                 # Create a new candidate set by adding v to it
...                 c = (it | frozenset([v]))
...                 # check If we have tested it already
...                 if c in tested:
...                     continue
...                 tested.add(c)
...
...                 # Count support by looping over dataset
...                 # This step is slow.
...                 # Check `apriori.py` for a better implementation.
...                 support_c = sum(1 for d in dataset if
                    d.issuperset(c))
...                 if support_c > minsupport:
...                     nextsets.append(c)
...     freqsets.extend(nextsets)
...     itemsets = nextsets
```

```
...         if not len(itemsets):
...             break
>>> print("Finished!")
Finished!
```

This works correctly, but it is slow. A better implementation has more infrastructure to avoid having to loop over all the datasets to get the count (`support_c`). In particular, we keep track of which shopping baskets have which frequent itemsets. This accelerates the loop but makes the code harder to follow. Therefore we will not show it here. As usual, you can find both the implementations on this book's companion website. The code there is also wrapped into a function that can be applied to other datasets.

The Apriori algorithm returns frequent itemsets, that is, baskets that are present above a certain threshold (given by the `minsupport` variable in the code).

Association rule mining

Frequent itemsets are not very useful by themselves. The next step is to build **association rules**. Because of this final goal, the whole field of basket analysis is sometimes called association rule mining.

An association rule is a statement of the type "If X, then Y", for example, "if a customer bought War and Peace, then they will buy Anna Karenina". Note that the rule is not deterministic (not all customers who buy X will buy Y), but it is rather cumbersome to always spell it out: "if a customer bought X, he is more likely than baseline to buy Y"; thus, we say "if X, then Y", but we mean it in a probabilistic sense.

Interestingly, both the antecedent and the conclusion may contain multiple objects: costumers who bought X, Y, and Z also bought A, B, and C. Multiple antecedents may allow you to make more specific predictions than are possible from a single item.

You can get from a frequent set to a rule by just trying all the possible combinations of X implies Y. It is easy to generate many of these rules. However, you only want to have valuable rules. Therefore, we need to measure the value of a rule. A commonly used measure is called the **lift**. The lift is the ratio between the probability obtained by applying the rule and the baseline, as in the following formula:

$$lift(X \to Y) = \frac{\hat{P}(Y \mid X)}{\hat{P}(Y)}$$

In the preceding formula, P(Y) is the fraction of all the transactions that include Y, while P(Y | X) is the fraction of transactions that include Y, given that they also include X. Using the lift helps avoid the problem of recommending bestsellers; for a bestseller, both P(Y) and P(Y | X) will be large. Therefore, the lift will be close to one and the rule will be deemed irrelevant. In practice, we wish to have values of lift of at least 10, perhaps even 100.

Refer to the following code:

```
>>> minlift = 5.0
>>> nr_transactions = float(len(dataset))
>>> for itemset in freqsets:
...         for item in itemset:
...             consequent = frozenset([item])
...             antecedent = itemset-consequent
...             base = 0.0
...             # acount: antecedent count
...             acount = 0.0
...
...             # ccount : consequent count
...             ccount = 0.0
...             for d in dataset:
...               if item in d: base += 1
...               if d.issuperset(itemset): ccount += 1
...               if d.issuperset(antecedent): acount += 1
...             base /= nr_transactions
...             p_y_given_x = ccount/acount
...             lift = p_y_given_x / base
...             if lift > minlift:
...                 print('Rule {0} -> {1} has lift {2}'
...                     .format(antecedent, consequent,lift))
```

Some of the results are shown in the following table. The counts are the number of transactions which include the **consequent alone** (that is, the base rate at which that product is bought), **all the items in the antecedent**, and **all the items in the antecedent and the consequent**.

Antecedent	Consequent	Consequent count	Antecedent count	Antecedent & consequent count	Lift
1,378, 1,379, 1,380	1,269	279 (0.3 percent)	80	57	225
48, 41, 976	117	1026 (1.1 percent)	122	51	35
48, 41, 1,6011	16,010	1316 (1.5 percent)	165	159	64

We can see, for example, that there were 80 transactions in which 1,378, 1,379, and 1,380 were bought together. Of these, 57 also included 1,269, so the estimated conditional probability is $57/80 \approx 71$ percent. Compared to the fact that only 0.3 percent of all transactions included 1,269, this gives us a lift of 255.

The need to have a decent number of transactions in these counts in order to be able to make relatively solid inferences is why we must first select frequent itemsets. If we were to generate rules from an infrequent itemset, the counts would be very small; due to this, the relative values would be meaningless (or subject to very large error bars).

Note that there are many more association rules discovered from this dataset: the algorithm discovers 1,030 rules (requiring support for the baskets of at least 80 and a minimum lift of 5). This is still a small dataset when compared to what is now possible with the web. With datasets containing millions of transactions, you can expect to generate many thousands of rules, even millions.

However, for each customer or each product, only a few rules will be relevant at any given time. So each costumer only receives a small number of recommendations.

More advanced basket analysis

There are now other algorithms for basket analysis that run faster than Apriori. The code we saw earlier was simple and it was good enough for us, as we only had circa 100 thousand transactions. If we had many millions, it might be worthwhile to use a faster algorithm. Note, though, that learning association rules can often be done offline, where efficiency is not as great a concern.

There are also methods to work with temporal information, leading to rules that take into account the order in which you have made your purchases. Consider, as an example, that someone buying supplies for a large party may come back for trash bags. Thus, it may make sense to propose trash bags on the first visit. However, it would not make sense to propose party supplies to everyone who buys a trash bag.

Summary

In this chapter, we started by using regression for rating predictions. We saw a couple of different ways in which to do so, and then combined them all in a single prediction by learning a set of weights. This technique, ensemble learning, in particular stacked learning, is a general technique that can be used in many situations, not just for regression. It allows you to combine different ideas even if their internal mechanics are completely different; you can combine their final outputs.

In the second half of the chapter, we switched gears and looked at another mode of producing recommendations: shopping basket analysis or association rule mining. In this mode, we try to discover (probabilistic) association rules of the "customers who bought X are likely to be interested in Y" form. This takes advantage of the data that is generated from sales alone without requiring users to numerically rate items. This is not available in scikit-learn at this moment, so we wrote our own code.

Association rule mining needs to be careful to not simply recommend bestsellers to every user (otherwise, what is the point of personalization?). In order to do this, we learned about measuring the value of rules in relation to the baseline, using a measure called the lift of a rule.

At this point in the book, we have seen the major modes of machine learning: classification. In the next two chapters, we will look at techniques used for two specific kinds of data, music and images. Our first goal will be to build a music genre classifier.

Classification – Music Genre Classification

9

So far, we have had the luxury that every training data instance could easily be described by a vector of feature values. In the Iris dataset, for example, the flowers are represented by vectors containing values for length and width of certain aspects of a flower. In the text-based examples, we could transform the text into a bag of word representations and manually craft our own features that captured certain aspects of the texts.

It will be different in this chapter, when we try to classify songs by their genre. Or, how would we, for instance, represent a three-minute-long song? Should we take the individual bits of its MP3 representation? Probably not, since treating it like a text and creating something like a "bag of sound bites" would certainly be way too complex. Somehow, we will, nevertheless, have to convert a song into a series of values that describe it sufficiently.

Sketching our roadmap

This chapter will show how we can come up with a decent classifier in a domain that is outside our comfort zone. For one, we will have to use sound-based features, which are much more complex than the text-based ones we have used before. And then we will learn how to deal with multiple classes, whereas we have only encountered binary classification problems up to now. In addition, we will get to know new ways of measuring classification performance.

Let us assume a scenario in which, for some reason, we find a bunch of randomly named MP3 files on our hard disk, which are assumed to contain music. Our task is to sort them according to the music genre into different folders such as jazz, classical, country, pop, rock, and metal.

Fetching the music data

We will use the GTZAN dataset, which is frequently used to benchmark music genre classification tasks. It is organized into 10 distinct genres, of which we will use only 6 for the sake of simplicity: Classical, Jazz, Country, Pop, Rock, and Metal. The dataset contains the first 30 seconds of 100 songs per genre. We can download the dataset from `http://opihi.cs.uvic.ca/sound/genres.tar.gz`.

> The tracks are recorded at 22,050 Hz (22,050 readings per second) mono in the WAV format.

Converting into a WAV format

Sure enough, if we would want to test our classifier later on our private MP3 collection, we would not be able to extract much meaning. This is because MP3 is a lossy music compression format that cuts out parts that the human ear cannot perceive. This is nice for storing because with MP3 you can fit 10 times as many songs on your device. For our endeavor, however, it is not so nice. For classification, we will have an easier game with WAV files, because they can be directly read by the `scipy.io.wavfile` package. We would, therefore, have to convert our MP3 files in case we want to use them with our classifier.

> In case you don't have a conversion tool nearby, you might want to check out SoX at `http://sox.sourceforge.net`. It claims to be the Swiss Army Knife of sound processing, and we agree with this bold claim.

One advantage of having all our music files in the WAV format is that it is directly readable by the SciPy toolkit:

```
>>> sample_rate, X = scipy.io.wavfile.read(wave_filename)
```

X now contains the samples and `sample_rate` is the rate at which they were taken. Let us use that information to peek into some music files to get a first impression of what the data looks like.

Looking at music

A very convenient way to get a quick impression of what the songs of the diverse genres "look" like is to draw a spectrogram for a set of songs of a genre. A spectrogram is a visual representation of the frequencies that occur in a song. It shows the intensity for the frequencies at the y axis in the specified time intervals at the x axis. That is, the darker the color, the stronger the frequency is in the particular time window of the song.

Matplotlib provides the convenient function `specgram()` that performs most of the under-the-hood calculation and plotting for us:

```
>>> import scipy
>>> from matplotlib.pyplot import specgram
>>> sample_rate, X = scipy.io.wavfile.read(wave_filename)
>>> print sample_rate, X.shape
22050, (661794,)
>>> specgram(X, Fs=sample_rate, xextent=(0,30))
```

The WAV file we just read in was sampled at a rate of 22,050 Hz and contains 661,794 samples.

If we now plot the spectrogram for these first 30 seconds for diverse WAV files, we can see that there are commonalities between songs of the same genre, as shown in the following image:

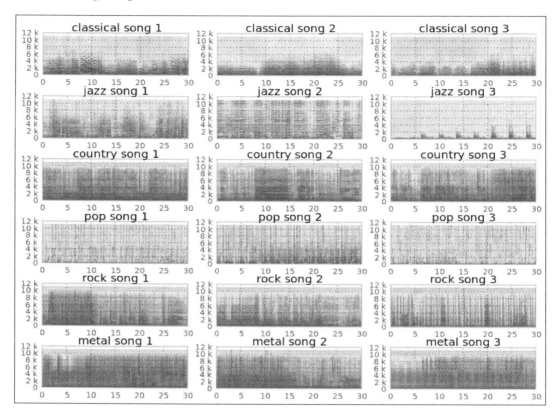

Just glancing at the image, we immediately see the difference in the spectrum between, for example, metal and classical songs. While metal songs have high intensity over most of the frequency spectrum all the time (they're energetic!), classical songs show a more diverse pattern over time.

It should be possible to train a classifier that discriminates at least between Metal and Classical songs with high enough accuracy. Other genre pairs like Country and Rock could pose a bigger challenge, though. This looks like a real challenge to us, since we need to discriminate not only between two classes, but between six. We need to be able to discriminate between all of them reasonably well.

Decomposing music into sine wave components

Our plan is to extract individual frequency intensities from the raw sample readings (stored in x earlier) and feed them into a classifier. These frequency intensities can be extracted by applying the so-called **fast Fourier transform** (**FFT**). As the theory behind FFT is outside the scope of this chapter, let us just look at an example to get an intuition of what it accomplishes. Later on, we will treat it as a black box feature extractor.

For example, let us generate two WAV files, `sine_a.wav` and `sine_b.wav`, that contain the sound of 400 Hz and 3,000 Hz sine waves respectively. The aforementioned "Swiss Army Knife", SoX, is one way to achieve this:

```
$ sox --null -r 22050 sine_a.wav synth 0.2 sine 400
$ sox --null -r 22050 sine_b.wav synth 0.2 sine 3000
```

In the following charts, we have plotted their first 0.008 seconds. Below we can see the FFT of the sine waves. Not surprisingly, we see a spike at 400 Hz and 3,000 Hz below the corresponding sine waves.

Now, let us mix them both, giving the 400 Hz sound half the volume of the 3,000 Hz one:

```
$ sox --combine mix --volume 1 sine_b.wav --volume 0.5 sine_a.wav
sine_mix.wav
```

We see two spikes in the FFT plot of the combined sound, of which the 3,000 Hz spike is almost double the size of the 400 Hz.

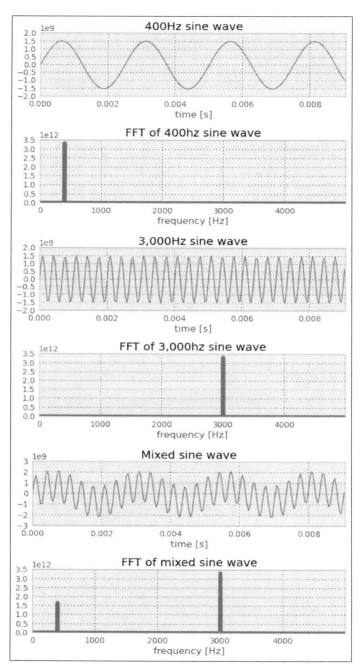

For real music, we quickly see that the FFT doesn't look as beautiful as in the preceding toy example:

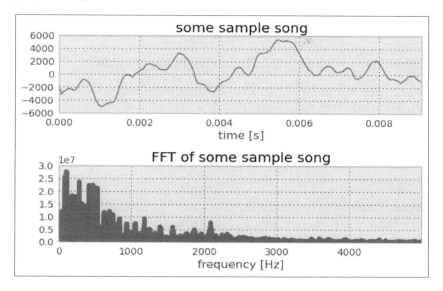

Using FFT to build our first classifier

Nevertheless, we can now create some kind of musical fingerprint of a song using FFT. If we do that for a couple of songs and manually assign their corresponding genres as labels, we have the training data that we can feed into our first classifier.

Increasing experimentation agility

Before we dive into the classifier training, let us first spend some thoughts on experimentation agility. Although we have the word "fast" in FFT, it is much slower than the creation of the features in our text-based chapters. And because we are still in an experimentation phase, we might want to think about how we could speed up the whole feature creation process.

Of course, the creation of the FFT per file will be the same each time we are running the classifier. We could, therefore, cache it and read the cached FFT representation instead of the complete WAV file. We do this with the `create_fft()` function, which, in turn, uses `scipy.fft()` to create the FFT. For the sake of simplicity (and speed!), let us fix the number of FFT components to the first 1,000 in this example. With our current knowledge, we do not know whether these are the most important ones with regard to music genre classification — only that they show the highest intensities in the preceding FFT example. If we would later want to use more or fewer FFT components, we would of course have to recreate the FFT representations for each sound file.

```
import os
import scipy


def create_fft(fn):
    sample_rate, X = scipy.io.wavfile.read(fn)
    fft_features = abs(scipy.fft(X)[:1000])
    base_fn, ext = os.path.splitext(fn)
    data_fn = base_fn + ".fft"
    scipy.save(data_fn, fft_features)
```

We save the data using NumPy's `save()` function, which always appends `.npy` to the filename. We only have to do this once for every WAV file needed for training or predicting.

The corresponding FFT reading function is `read_fft()`:

```
import glob


def read_fft(genre_list, base_dir=GENRE_DIR):
    X = []
    y = []

    for label, genre in enumerate(genre_list):
        genre_dir = os.path.join(base_dir, genre, "*.fft.npy")
        file_list = glob.glob(genre_dir)

        for fn in file_list:
```

```
fft_features = scipy.load(fn)

X.append(fft_features[:1000])
y.append(label)

return np.array(X), np.array(y)
```

In our scrambled music directory, we expect the following music genres:

```
genre_list = ["classical", "jazz", "country", "pop", "rock", "metal"]
```

Training the classifier

Let us use the logistic regression classifier, which has already served us well in the *Chapter 6, Classification II - Sentiment Analysis*. The added difficulty is that we are now faced with a multiclass classification problem, whereas up to now we had to discriminate only between two classes.

Just to mention one aspect that is surprising is the evaluation of accuracy rates when first switching from binary to multiclass classification. In binary classification problems, we have learned that an accuracy of 50 percent is the worst case, as it could have been achieved by mere random guessing. In multiclass settings, 50 percent can already be very good. With our six genres, for instance, random guessing would result in only 16.7 percent (equal class sizes assumed).

Using a confusion matrix to measure accuracy in multiclass problems

With multiclass problems, we should not only be interested in how well we manage to correctly classify the genres. In addition, we should also look into which genres we actually confuse with each other. This can be done with the so-called confusion matrix, as shown in the following:

```
>>> from sklearn.metrics import confusion_matrix
>>> cm = confusion_matrix(y_test, y_pred)
>>> print(cm)
[[26  1  2  0  0  2]
 [ 4  7  5  0  5  3]
 [ 1  2 14  2  8  3]
 [ 5  4  7  3  7  5]
 [ 0  0 10  2 10 12]
 [ 1  0  4  0 13 12]]
```

This prints the distribution of labels that the classifier predicted for the test set for every genre. The diagonal represents the correct classifications. Since we have six genres, we have a six-by-six matrix. The first row in the matrix says that for 31 Classical songs (sum of first row), it predicted 26 to belong to the genre Classical, 1 to be a Jazz song, 2 to belong to the Country genre, and 2 to be Metal songs. The diagonal shows the correct classifications. In the first row, we see that out of (26+1+2+2)=31 songs, 26 have been correctly classified as classical and 5 were misclassifications. This is actually not that bad. The second row is more sobering: only 7 out of 24 Jazz songs have been correctly classified—that is, only 29 percent.

Of course, we follow the train/test split setup from the previous chapters, so that we actually have to record the confusion matrices per cross-validation fold. We have to average and normalize later on, so that we have a range between 0 (total failure) and 1 (everything classified correctly).

A graphical visualization is often much easier to read than NumPy arrays. The `matshow()` function of matplotlib is our friend:

```
from matplotlib import pylab


def plot_confusion_matrix(cm, genre_list, name, title):
    pylab.clf()
    pylab.matshow(cm, fignum=False, cmap='Blues',
                  vmin=0, vmax=1.0)


    ax = pylab.axes()    ax.set_xticks(range(len(genre_list)))
    ax.set_xticklabels(genre_list)
    ax.xaxis.set_ticks_position("bottom")
    ax.set_yticks(range(len(genre_list)))
    ax.set_yticklabels(genre_list)


    pylab.title(title)
    pylab.colorbar()
    pylab.grid(False)
    pylab.xlabel('Predicted class')
    pylab.ylabel('True class')
    pylab.grid(False)


    pylab.show()
```

When you create a confusion matrix, be sure to choose a color map (the `cmap` parameter of `matshow()`) with an appropriate color ordering so that it is immediately visible what a lighter or darker color means. Especially discouraged for these kinds of graphs are rainbow color maps, such as matplotlib's default `jet` or even the `Paired` color map.

The final graph looks like the following:

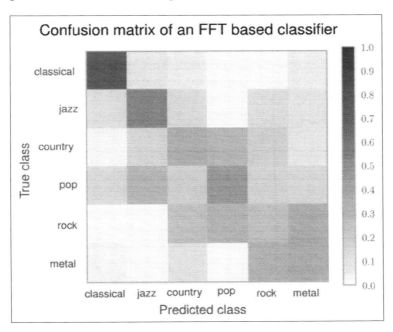

For a perfect classifier, we would have expected a diagonal of dark squares from the left-upper corner to the right lower one, and light colors for the remaining area. In the preceding graph, we immediately see that our FFT-based classifier is far away from being perfect. It only predicts Classical songs correctly (dark square). For Rock, for instance, it preferred the label Metal most of the time.

Obviously, using FFT points in the right direction (the Classical genre was not that bad), but is not enough to get a decent classifier. Surely, we can play with the number of FFT components (fixed to 1,000). But before we dive into parameter tuning, we should do our research. There we find that FFT is indeed not a bad feature for genre classification—it is just not refined enough. Shortly, we will see how we can boost our classification performance by using a processed version of it.

Before we do that, however, we will learn another method of measuring classification performance.

An alternative way to measure classifier performance using receiver-operator characteristics

We already learned that measuring accuracy is not enough to truly evaluate a classifier. Instead, we relied on **precision-recall (P/R)** curves to get a deeper understanding of how our classifiers perform.

There is a sister of P/R curves, called **receiver-operator-characteristics (ROC)**, which measures similar aspects of the classifier's performance, but provides another view of the classification performance. The key difference is that P/R curves are more suitable for tasks where the positive class is much more interesting than the negative one, or where the number of positive examples is much less than the number of negative ones. Information retrieval and fraud detection are typical application areas. On the other hand, ROC curves provide a better picture on how well the classifier behaves in general.

To better understand the differences, let us consider the performance of the previously trained classifier in classifying country songs correctly, as shown in the following graph:

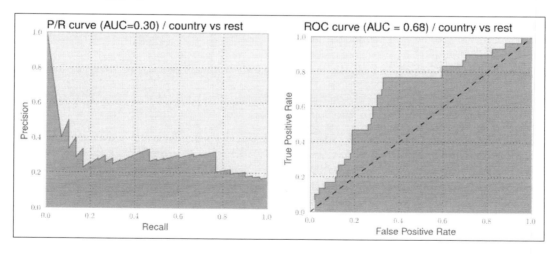

On the left, we see the P/R curve. For an ideal classifier, we would have the curve going from the top left directly to the top right and then to the bottom right, resulting in an area under curve (AUC) of 1.0.

The right graph depicts the corresponding ROC curve. It plots the True Positive Rate over the False Positive Rate. There, an ideal classifier would have a curve going from the lower left to the top left, and then to the top right. A random classifier would be a straight line from the lower left to the upper right, as shown by the dashed line, having an AUC of 0.5. Therefore, we cannot compare an AUC of a P/R curve with that of an ROC curve.

Independent of the curve, when comparing two different classifiers on the same dataset, we are always safe to assume that a higher AUC of a P/R curve for one classifier also means a higher AUC of the corresponding ROC curve and vice versa. Thus, we never bother to generate both. More on this can be found in the very insightful paper *The Relationship Between Precision-Recall and ROC Curves* by Davis and Goadrich (ICML, 2006).

The following table summarizes the differences between P/R and ROC curves:

	x axis	y axis
P/R	$Recall = \dfrac{TP}{TP + FN}$	$Precision = \dfrac{TP}{TP + FP}$
ROC	$FPR = \dfrac{FP}{FP + TN}$	$TPR = \dfrac{TP}{TP + FN}$

Looking at the definitions of both curves' x and y axis, we see that the True Positive Rate in the ROC curve's y axis is the same as Recall of the P/R graph's x axis.

The False Positive Rate measures the fraction of true negative examples that were falsely identified as positive ones, giving a 0 in a perfect case (no false positives) and 1 otherwise. Contrast this to the precision, where we track exactly the opposite, namely the fraction of true positive examples that we correctly classified as such.

Going forward, let us use ROC curves to measure our classifiers' performance to get a better feeling for it. The only challenge for our multiclass problem is that both ROC and P/R curves assume a binary classification problem. For our purpose, let us, therefore, create one chart per genre that shows how the classifier performed a one versus rest classification:

```
from sklearn.metrics import roc_curve


y_pred = clf.predict(X_test)


for label in labels:
    y_label_test = scipy.asarray(y_test==label, dtype=int)
    proba = clf.predict_proba(X_test)
    proba_label = proba[:,label]

    # calculate false and true positive rates as well as the
    # ROC thresholds
    fpr, tpr, roc_thres = roc_curve(y_label_test, proba_label)

    # plot tpr over fpr ...
```

The outcomes are the following six ROC plots. As we have already found out, our first version of a classifier only performs well on Classical songs. Looking at the individual ROC curves, however, tells us that we are really underperforming for most of the other genres. Only Jazz and Country provide some hope. The remaining genres are clearly not usable.

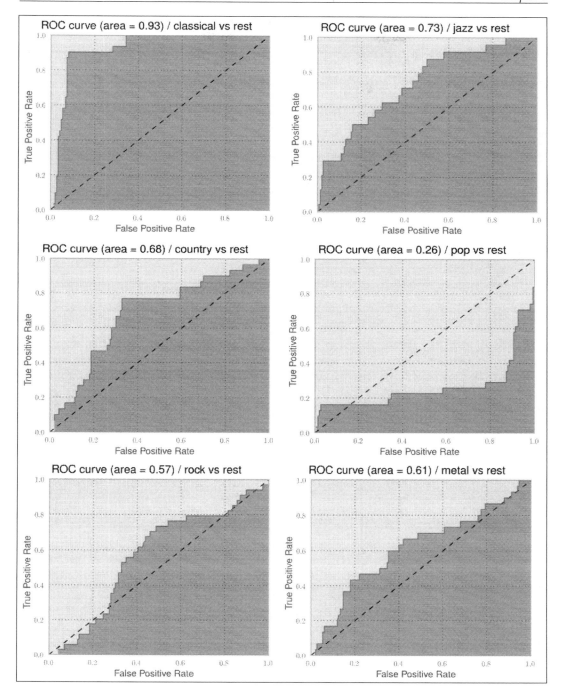

Improving classification performance with Mel Frequency Cepstral Coefficients

We already learned that FFT is pointing in the right direction, but in itself it will not be enough to finally arrive at a classifier that successfully manages to organize our scrambled directory of songs of diverse music genres into individual genre directories. We need a somewhat more advanced version of it.

At this point, it is always wise to acknowledge that we have to do more research. Other people might have had similar challenges in the past and already have found out new ways that might also help us. And, indeed, there is even a yearly conference dedicated to only music genre classification, organized by the **International Society for Music Information Retrieval (ISMIR)**. Apparently, **Automatic Music Genre Classification (AMGC)** is an established subfield of Music Information Retrieval. Glancing over some of the AMGC papers, we see that there is a bunch of work targeting automatic genre classification that might help us.

One technique that seems to be successfully applied in many of those works is called Mel Frequency Cepstral Coefficients. The **Mel Frequency Cepstrum (MFC)** encodes the power spectrum of a sound, which is the power of each frequency the sound contains. It is calculated as the Fourier transform of the logarithm of the signal's spectrum. If that sounds too complicated, simply remember that the name "cepstrum" originates from "spectrum" having the first four characters reversed. MFC has been successfully used in speech and speaker recognition. Let's see whether it also works in our case.

We are in a lucky situation in that someone else already needed exactly this and published an implementation of it as the Talkbox SciKit. We can install it from https://pypi.python.org/pypi/scikits.talkbox. Afterward, we can call the mfcc() function, which calculates the MFC coefficients, as follows:

```
>>> from scikits.talkbox.features import mfcc
>>> sample_rate, X = scipy.io.wavfile.read(fn)
>>> ceps, mspec, spec = mfcc(X)
>>> print(ceps.shape)
(4135, 13)
```

The data we would want to feed into our classifier is stored in `ceps`, which contains 13 coefficients (default value for the `nceps` parameter of `mfcc()`) for each of the 4,135 frames for the song with the filename `fn`. Taking all of the data would overwhelm our classifier. What we could do, instead, is to do an averaging per coefficient over all the frames. Assuming that the start and end of each song are possibly less genre specific than the middle part of it, we also ignore the first and last 10 percent:

```
x = np.mean(ceps[int(num_ceps*0.1):int(num_ceps*0.9)], axis=0)
```

Sure enough, the benchmark dataset we will be using contains only the first 30 seconds of each song, so that we would not need to cut off the last 10 percent. We do it, nevertheless, so that our code works on other datasets as well, which are most likely not truncated.

Similar to our work with FFT, we certainly would also want to cache the once generated MFCC features and read them instead of recreating them each time we train our classifier.

This leads to the following code:

```
def write_ceps(ceps, fn):
    base_fn, ext = os.path.splitext(fn)
    data_fn = base_fn + ".ceps"
    np.save(data_fn, ceps)
    print("Written to %s" % data_fn)


def create_ceps(fn):
    sample_rate, X = scipy.io.wavfile.read(fn)
    ceps, mspec, spec = mfcc(X)
    write_ceps(ceps, fn)


def read_ceps(genre_list, base_dir=GENRE_DIR):
    X, y = [], []
    for label, genre in enumerate(genre_list):
        for fn in glob.glob(os.path.join(
                          base_dir, genre, "*.ceps.npy")):
            ceps = np.load(fn)
            num_ceps = len(ceps)
            X.append(np.mean(
                    ceps[int(num_ceps*0.1):int(num_ceps*0.9)], axis=0))
            y.append(label)

    return np.array(X), np.array(y)
```

We get the following promising results with a classifier that uses only 13 features per song:

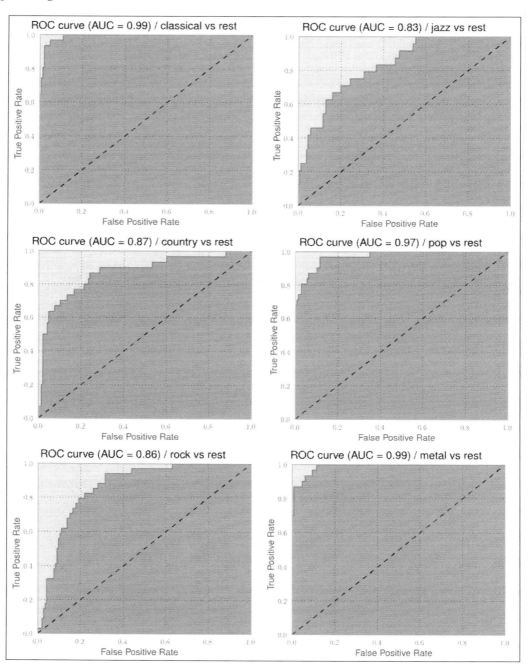

The classification performances for all genres have improved. Classical and Metal are even at almost 1.0 AUC. And indeed, also the confusion matrix in the following plot looks much better now. We can clearly see the diagonal showing that the classifier manages to classify the genres correctly in most of the cases. This classifier is actually quite usable to solve our initial task.

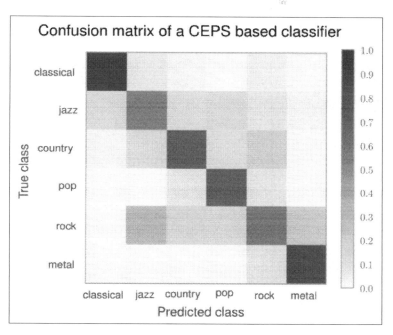

If we would want to improve on this, this confusion matrix tells us quickly what to focus on: the non-white spots on the non-diagonal places. For instance, we have a darker spot where we mislabel Rock songs as being Jazz with considerable probability. To fix this, we would probably need to dive deeper into the songs and extract things such as drum patterns and similar genre specific characteristics. And then—while glancing over the ISMIR papers—we also have read about the so-called **Auditory Filterbank Temporal Envelope (AFTE)** features, which seem to outperform MFCC features in certain situations. Maybe we should have a look at them as well?

The nice thing is that, only equipped with ROC curves and confusion matrices, we are free to pull in other experts' knowledge in terms of feature extractors without requiring ourselves to fully understand their inner workings. Our measurement tools will always tell us, when the direction is right and when to change it. Of course, being a machine learner who is eager to learn, we will always have the dim feeling that there is an exciting algorithm buried somewhere in a black box of our feature extractors, which is just waiting for us to be understood.

Summary

In this chapter, we totally stepped out of our comfort zone when we built a music genre classifier. Not having a deep understanding of music theory, at first we failed to train a classifier that predicts the music genre of songs with reasonable accuracy using FFT. But, then, we created a classifier that showed really usable performance using MFC features.

In both the cases, we used features that we understood only enough to know how and where to put them into our classifier setup. The one failed, the other succeeded. The difference between them is that in the second case we relied on features that were created by experts in the field.

And that is totally OK. If we are mainly interested in the result, we sometimes simply have to take shortcuts — we just have to make sure to take these shortcuts from experts in the specific domains. And because we had learned how to correctly measure the performance in this new multiclass classification problem, we took these shortcuts with confidence.

In the next chapter, we will look at how to apply techniques you have learned in the rest of this book to this specific type of data. We will learn how to use the mahotas computer vision package to preprocess images using traditional image processing functions.

10
Computer Vision

Image analysis and computer vision have always been important in industrial and scientific applications. With the popularization of cell phones with powerful cameras and Internet connections, images now are increasingly generated by consumers. Therefore, there are opportunities to make use of computer vision to provide a better user experience in new contexts.

In this chapter, we will look at how to apply techniques you have learned in the rest of this book to this specific type of data. In particular, we will learn how to use the mahotas computer vision package to extract features from images. These features can be used as input to the same classification methods we studied in other chapters. We will apply these techniques to publicly available datasets of photographs. We will also see how the same features can be used on another problem, that is, the problem of finding similar looking images.

Finally, at the end of this chapter, we will learn about using local features. These are relatively new methods (the first of these methods to achieve state-of-the-art performance, the **scale-invariant feature transform** (**SIFT**), was introduced in 1999) and achieve very good results in many tasks.

Introducing image processing

From the point of view of the computer, an image is a large rectangular array of pixel values. Our goal is to process this image and to arrive at a decision for our application.

The first step will be to load the image from disk, where it is typically stored in an image-specific format such as PNG or JPEG, the former being a lossless compression format, and the latter a lossy compression one that is optimized for visual assessment of photographs. Then, we may wish to perform preprocessing on the images (for example, normalizing them for illumination variations).

We will have a classification problem as a driver for this chapter. We want to be able to learn a support vector machine (or other) classifier that can be trained from images. Therefore, we will use an intermediate representation, extracting numeric features from the images before applying machine learning.

Loading and displaying images

In order to manipulate images, we will use a package called mahotas. You can obtain mahotas from `https://pypi.python.org/pypi/mahotas` and read its manual at `http://mahotas.readthedocs.org`. Mahotas is an open source package (MIT license, so it can be used in any project) that was developed by one of the authors of this book. Fortunately, it is based on NumPy. The NumPy knowledge you have acquired so far can be used for image processing. There are other image packages, such as scikit-image (skimage), the ndimage (n-dimensional image) module in SciPy, and the Python bindings for OpenCV. All of these work natively with NumPy arrays, so you can even mix and match functionality from different packages to build a combined pipeline.

We start by importing mahotas, with the `mh` abbreviation, which we will use throughout this chapter, as follows:

```
>>> import mahotas as mh
```

Now, we can load an image file using `imread` as follows:

```
>>> image = mh.imread('scene00.jpg')
```

The `scene00.jpg` file (this file is contained in the dataset available on this book's companion code repository) is a color image of height `h` and width `w`; the image will be an array of shape `(h, w, 3)`. The first dimension is the height, the second is the width, and the third is red/green/blue. Other systems put the width in the first dimension, but this is the convention that is used by all NumPy-based packages. The type of the array will typically be `np.uint8` (an unsigned 8-bit integer). These are the images that your camera takes or that your monitor can fully display.

Some specialized equipment, used in scientific and technical applications, can take images with higher bit resolution (that is, with more sensitivity to small variations in brightness). Twelve or sixteen bits are common in this type of equipment. Mahotas can deal with all these types, including floating point images. In many computations, even if the original data is composed of unsigned integers, it is advantageous to convert to floating point numbers in order to simplify handling of rounding and overflow issues.

Mahotas can use a variety of different input/output backends. Unfortunately, none of them can load all image formats that exist (there are hundreds, with several variations of each). However, loading PNG and JPEG images is supported by all of them. We will focus on these common formats and refer you to the mahotas documentation on how to read uncommon formats.

We can display the image on screen using matplotlib, the plotting library we have already used several times, as follows:

```
>>> from matplotlib import pyplot as plt
>>> plt.imshow(image)
>>> plt.show()
```

As shown in the following, this code shows the image using the convention that the first dimension is the height and the second the width. It correctly handles color images as well. When using Python for numerical computation, we benefit from the whole ecosystem working well together: mahotas works with NumPy arrays, which can be displayed with matplotlib; later we will compute features from images to use with scikit-learn.

Thresholding

Thresholding is a very simple operation: we transform all pixel values above a certain threshold to `1` and all those below it to `0` (or by using Booleans, transform it to `True` and `False`). The important question in thresholding is to select a good value to use as the threshold limit. Mahotas implements a few methods for choosing a threshold value from the image. One is called **Otsu**, after its inventor. The first necessary step is to convert the image to grayscale, with `rgb2gray` in the `mahotas.colors` submodule.

Instead of `rgb2gray`, we could also have just the mean value of the red, green, and blue channels, by callings `image.mean(2)`. The result, however, would not be the same, as `rgb2gray` uses different weights for the different colors to give a subjectively more pleasing result. Our eyes are not equally sensitive to the three basic colors.

```
>>> image = mh.colors.rgb2grey(image, dtype=np.uint8)
>>> plt.imshow(image) # Display the image
```

By default, matplotlib will display this single-channel image as a false color image, using red for high values and blue for low values. For natural images, a grayscale is more appropriate. You can select it with:

```
>>> plt.gray()
```

Now the image is shown in gray scale. Note that only the way in which the pixel values are interpreted and shown has changed and the image data is untouched. We can continue our processing by computing the threshold value:

```
>>> thresh = mh.thresholding.otsu(image)
>>> print('Otsu threshold is {}.'.format(thresh))
Otsu threshold is 138.
>>> plt.imshow(image > thresh)
```

When applied to the previous screenshot, this method finds the threshold to be 138, which separates the ground from the sky above, as shown in the following image:

Gaussian blurring

Blurring your image may seem odd, but it often serves to reduce noise, which helps with further processing. With mahotas, it is just a function call:

```
>>> im16 = mh.gaussian_filter(image, 16)
```

Notice that we did not convert the grayscale image to unsigned integers: we just made use of the floating point result as it is. The second argument to the `gaussian_filter` function is the size of the filter (the standard deviation of the filter). Larger values result in more blurring, as shown in the following screenshot:

We can use the screenshot on the left and threshold with Otsu (using the same previous code). Now, the boundaries are smoother, without the jagged edges, as shown in the following screenshot:

Putting the center in focus

The final example shows how to mix NumPy operators with a tiny bit of filtering to get an interesting result. We start with the Lena image and split it into the color channels:

```
>>> im = mh.demos.load('lena')
```

This is an image of a young woman that has been often for image processing demos. It is shown in the following screenshot:

To split the red, green, and blue channels, we use the following code:

```
>>> r,g,b = im.transpose(2,0,1)
```

Now, we filter the three channels separately and build a composite image out of it with mh.as_rgb. This function takes three two-dimensional arrays, performs contrast stretching to make each be an 8-bit integer array, and then stacks them, returning a color RGB image:

```
>>> r12 = mh.gaussian_filter(r, 12.)
>>> g12 = mh.gaussian_filter(g, 12.)
>>> b12 = mh.gaussian_filter(b, 12.)
>>> im12 = mh.as_rgb(r12, g12, b12)
```

Now, we blend the two images from the center away to the edges. First, we need to build a weights array W, which will contain at each pixel a normalized value, which is its distance to the center:

```
>>> h, w = r.shape # height and width
>>> Y, X = np.mgrid[:h, :w]
```

We used the `np.mgrid` object, which returns arrays of size `(h, w)`, with values corresponding to the *y* and *x* coordinates, respectively. The next steps are as follows:

```
>>> Y = Y - h/2. # center at h/2
>>> Y = Y / Y.max() # normalize to -1 .. +1


>>> X = X - w/2.
>>> X = X / X.max()
```

We now use a Gaussian function to give the center region a high value:

```
>>> C = np.exp(-2.*(X**2+ Y**2))


>>> # Normalize again to 0..1
>>> C = C - C.min()
>>> C = C / C.ptp()
>>> C = C[:,:,None] # This adds a dummy third dimension to C
```

Notice how all of these manipulations are performed using NumPy arrays and not some mahotas-specific methodology. Finally, we can combine the two images to have the center be in sharp focus and the edges softer:

```
>>> ringed = mh.stretch(im*C + (1-C)*im12)
```

Basic image classification

We will start with a small dataset that was collected especially for this book. It has three classes: buildings, natural scenes (landscapes), and pictures of texts. There are 30 images in each category, and they were all taken using a cell phone camera with minimal composition. The images are similar to those that would be uploaded to a modern website by users with no photography training. This dataset is available from this book's website or the GitHub code repository. Later in this chapter, we will look at a harder dataset with more images and more categories.

When classifying images, we start with a large rectangular array of numbers (pixel values). Nowadays, millions of pixels are common. We could try to feed all these numbers as features into the learning algorithm. This is not a very good idea. This is because the relationship of each pixel (or even each small group of pixels) to the final result is very indirect. Also, having millions of pixels, but only as a small number of example images, results in a very hard statistical learning problem. This is an extreme form of the P greater than N type of problem we discussed in *Chapter 7, Regression*. Instead, a good approach is to compute features from the image and use those features for classification.

Having said that, I will point out that, in fact, there are a few methods that do work directly from the pixel values. They have feature computation submodules inside them. They may even attempt to learn good features automatically. These methods are the topic of current research. They typically work best with very large datasets (millions of images).

We previously used an example of the scene class. The following are examples of the text and building classes:

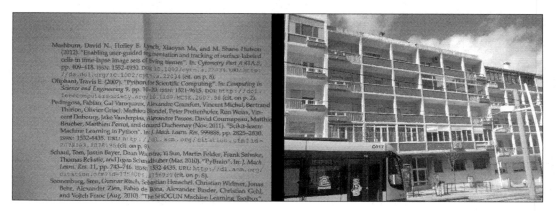

Computing features from images

With mahotas, it is very easy to compute features from images. There is a submodule named `mahotas.features`, where feature computation functions are available.

A commonly used set of texture features is the Haralick. As with many methods in image processing, the name is due to its inventor. These features are texture-based: they distinguish between images that are smooth from those that are patterned, and between different patterns. With mahotas, it is very easy to compute them as follows:

```
>>> haralick_features = mh.features.haralick(image)
>>> haralick_features_mean = np.mean(haralick_features, axis=0)
>>> haralick_features_all = np.ravel(haralick_features)
```

The `mh.features.haralick` function returns a 4x13 array. The first dimension refers to four possible directions in which to compute the features (vertical, horizontal, diagonal, and the anti-diagonal). If we are not interested in the direction specifically, we can use the average over all the directions (shown in the earlier code as `haralick_features_mean`). Otherwise, we can use all the features separately (using `haralick_features_all`). This decision should be informed by the properties of the dataset. In our case, we reason that the horizontal and vertical directions should be kept separately. Therefore, we will use `haralick_features_all`.

There are a few other feature sets implemented in mahotas. Linear binary patterns are another texture-based feature set, which is very robust against illumination changes. There are other types of features, including local features, which we will discuss later in this chapter.

With these features, we use a standard classification method such as logistic regression as follows:

```
>>> from glob import glob
>>> images = glob('SimpleImageDataset/*.jpg')
>>> features = []
>>> labels = []
>>> for im in images:
...     labels.append(im[:-len('00.jpg')])
...     im = mh.imread(im)
...     im = mh.colors.rgb2gray(im, dtype=np.uint8)
...     features.append(mh.features.haralick(im).ravel())


>>> features = np.array(features)
>>> labels = np.array(labels)
```

The three classes have very different textures. Buildings have sharp edges and big blocks where the color is similar (the pixel values are rarely exactly the same, but the variation is slight). Text is made of many sharp dark-light transitions, with small black areas in a sea of white. Natural scenes have smoother variations with fractal-like transitions. Therefore, a classifier based on texture is expected to do well.

As a classifier, we are going to use a logistic regression classifier with preprocessing of the features as follows:

```
>>> from sklearn.pipeline import Pipeline
>>> from sklearn.preprocessing import StandardScaler
>>> from sklearn.linear_model import LogisticRegression
>>> clf = Pipeline([('preproc', StandardScaler()),
                    ('classifier', LogisticRegression())])
```

Since our dataset is small, we can use leave-one-out regression as follows:

```
>>> from sklearn import cross_validation
>>> cv = cross_validation.LeaveOneOut(len(images))
>>> scores = cross_validation.cross_val_score(
...     clf, features, labels, cv=cv)
>>> print('Accuracy: {:.1%}'.format(scores.mean()))
Accuracy: 81.1%
```

Eighty-one percent is not bad for the three classes (random guessing would correspond to 33 percent). We can do better, however, by writing our own features.

Writing your own features

A feature is nothing magical. It is simply a number that we computed from an image. There are several feature sets already defined in the literature. These often have the added advantage that they have been designed and studied to be invariant to many unimportant factors. For example, linear binary patterns are completely invariant to multiplying all pixel values by a number or adding a constant to all these values. This makes this feature set robust against illumination changes of images.

However, it is also possible that your particular use case would benefit from a few specially designed features.

A simple type of feature that is not shipped with mahotas is a color histogram. Fortunately, this feature is easy to implement. A color histogram partitions the color space into a set of bins, and then counts how many pixels fall into each of the bins.

The images are in RGB format, that is, each pixel has three values: R for red, G for green, and B for blue. Since each of these components is an 8-bit value, the total is 17 million different colors. We are going to reduce this number to only 64 colors by grouping colors into bins. We will write a function to encapsulate this algorithm as follows:

```
def chist(im):
```

To bin the colors, we first divide the image by 64, rounding down the pixel values as follows:

```
im = im // 64
```

This makes the pixel values range from 0 to 3, which gives a total of 64 different colors.

Separate the red, green, and blue channels as follows:

```
r,g,b = im.transpose((2,0,1))
pixels = 1 * r + 4 * b + 16 * g
hist = np.bincount(pixels.ravel(), minlength=64)
hist = hist.astype(float)
```

Convert to log scale, as seen in the following code snippet. This is not strictly necessary, but makes for better features. We use np.log1p, which computes *log(h+1)*. This ensures that zero values are kept as zero values (mathematically, the logarithm of zero is not defined, and NumPy prints a warning if you attempt to compute it).

```
hist = np.log1p(hist)
return hist
```

We can adapt the previous processing code to use the function we wrote very easily:

```
>>> features = []
>>> for im in images:
...     image = mh.imread(im)
...     features.append(chist(im))
```

Using the same cross-validation code we used earlier, we obtain 90 percent accuracy. The best results, however, come from combining all the features, which we can implement as follows:

```
>>> features = []
>>> for im in images:
...     imcolor = mh.imread(im)
...     im = mh.colors.rgb2gray(imcolor, dtype=np.uint8)
```

```
...      features.append(np.concatenate([
...              mh.features.haralick(im).ravel(),
...              chist(imcolor),
...          ]))
```

By using all of these features, we get 95.6 percent accuracy, as shown in the following code snippet:

```
>>> scores = cross_validation.cross_val_score(
...      clf, features, labels, cv=cv)
>>> print('Accuracy: {:.1%}'.format(scores.mean()))
Accuracy: 95.6%
```

This is a perfect illustration of the principle that good algorithms are the easy part. You can always use an implementation of state-of-the-art classification from scikit-learn. The real secret and added value often comes in feature design and engineering. This is where knowledge of your dataset is valuable.

Using features to find similar images

The basic concept of representing an image by a relatively small number of features can be used for more than just classification. For example, we can also use it to find similar images to a given query image (as we did before with text documents).

We will compute the same features as before, with one important difference: we will ignore the bordering area of the picture. The reason is that due to the amateur nature of the compositions, the edges of the picture often contain irrelevant elements. When the features are computed over the whole image, these elements are taken into account. By simply ignoring them, we get slightly better features. In the supervised example, it is not as important, as the learning algorithm will then learn which features are more informative and weigh them accordingly. When working in an unsupervised fashion, we need to be more careful to ensure that our features are capturing important elements of the data. This is implemented in the loop as follows:

```
>>> features = []
>>> for im in images:
...      imcolor = mh.imread(im)
...      # ignore everything in the 200 pixels closest to the borders
...      imcolor = imcolor[200:-200, 200:-200]
...      im = mh.colors.rgb2gray(imcolor, dtype=np.uint8)
...      features.append(np.concatenate([
```

```
...            mh.features.haralick(im).ravel(),
...            chist(imcolor),
...        ]))
```

We now normalize the features and compute the distance matrix as follows:

```
>>> sc = StandardScaler()
>>> features = sc.fit_transform(features)
>>> from scipy.spatial import distance
>>> dists = distance.squareform(distance.pdist(features))
```

We will plot just a subset of the data (every 10th element) so that the query will be on top and the returned "nearest neighbor" at the bottom, as shown in the following:

```
>>> fig, axes = plt.subplots(2, 9)
>>> for ci,i in enumerate(range(0,90,10)):
...        left = images[i]
...        dists_left = dists[i]
...        right = dists_left.argsort()
...        # right[0] is same as left[i], so pick next closest
...        right = right[1]
...        right = images[right]
...        left = mh.imread(left)
...        right = mh.imread(right)
...        axes[0, ci].imshow(left)
...        axes[1, ci].imshow(right)
```

The result is shown in the following screenshot:

It is clear that the system is not perfect, but can find images that are at least visually similar to the queries. In all but one case, the image found comes from the same class as the query.

Classifying a harder dataset

The previous dataset was an easy dataset for classification using texture features. In fact, many of the problems that are interesting from a business point of view are relatively easy. However, sometimes we may be faced with a tougher problem and need better and more modern techniques to get good results.

We will now test a public dataset, which has the same structure: several photographs split into a small number of classes. The classes are animals, cars, transportation, and natural scenes.

When compared to the three class problem we discussed previously, these classes are harder to tell apart. Natural scenes, buildings, and texts have very different textures. In this dataset, however, texture and color are not as clear marker, of the image class. The following is one example from the animal class:

And here is another example from the car class:

Both objects are against natural backgrounds, and with large smooth areas inside the objects. This is a harder problem than the simple dataset, so we will need to use more advanced methods. The first improvement will be to use a slightly more powerful classifier. The logistic regression that scikit-learn provides is a penalized form of logistic regression, which contains an adjustable parameter, C. By default, C = 1.0, but this may not be optimal. We can use grid search to find a good value for this parameter as follows:

```
>>> from sklearn.grid_search import GridSearchCV
>>> C_range = 10.0 ** np.arange(-4, 3)
>>> grid = GridSearchCV(LogisticRegression(), param_grid={'C' : C_range})
>>> clf = Pipeline([('preproc', StandardScaler()),
...                  ('classifier', grid)])
```

The data is not organized in a random order inside the dataset: similar images are close together. Thus, we use a cross-validation schedule that considers the data shuffled so that each fold has a more representative training set, as shown in the following:

```
>>> cv = cross_validation.KFold(len(features), 5,
...                             shuffle=True, random_state=123)
>>> scores = cross_validation.cross_val_score(
...     clf, features, labels, cv=cv)
>>> print('Accuracy: {:.1%}'.format(scores.mean()))
Accuracy: 72.1%
```

This is not so bad for four classes, but we will now see if we can do better by using a different set of features. In fact, we will see that we need to combine these features with other methods to get the best possible results.

Local feature representations

A relatively recent development in the computer vision world has been the development of local-feature based methods. Local features are computed on a small region of the image, unlike the previous features we considered, which had been computed on the whole image. Mahotas supports computing a type of these features, **Speeded Up Robust Features** (**SURF**). There are several others, the most well-known being the original proposal of SIFT. These features are designed to be robust against rotational or illumination changes (that is, they only change their value slightly when illumination changes).

When using these features, we have to decide where to compute them. There are three possibilities that are commonly used:

- Randomly
- In a grid
- Detecting interesting areas of the image (a technique known as keypoint detection or interest point detection)

All of these are valid and will, under the right circumstances, give good results. Mahotas supports all three. Using interest point detection works best if you have a reason to expect that your interest point will correspond to areas of importance in the image.

We will be using the interest point method. Computing the features with mahotas is easy: import the right submodule and call the `surf.surf` function as follows:

```
>>> from mahotas.features import surf
>>> image = mh.demos.load('lena')
>>> image = mh.colors.rgb2gray(im, dtype=np.uint8)
>>> descriptors = surf.surf(image, descriptor_only=True)
```

The `descriptors_only=True` flag means that we are only interested in the descriptors themselves, and not in their pixel location, size, or orientation. Alternatively, we could have used the dense sampling method, using the `surf.dense` function as follows:

```
>>> from mahotas.features import surf
>>> descriptors = surf.dense(image, spacing=16)
```

This returns the value of the descriptors computed on points that are at a distance of 16 pixels from each other. Since the position of the points is fixed, the metainformation on the interest points is not very interesting and is not returned by default. In either case, the result (descriptors) is an n-times-64 array, where *n* is the number of points sampled. The number of points depends on the size of your images, their content, and the parameters you pass to the functions. In this example, we are using the default settings, and we obtain a few hundred descriptors per image.

We cannot directly feed these descriptors to a support vector machine, logistic regressor, or similar classification system. In order to use the descriptors from the images, there are several solutions. We could just average them, but the results of doing so are not very good as they throw away all location specific information. In that case, we would have just another global feature set based on edge measurements.

The solution we will use here is the **bag of words** model, which is a very recent idea. It was published in this form first in 2004. This is one of those obvious-in-hindsight ideas: it is very simple to implement and achieves very good results.

It may seem strange to speak of *words* when dealing with images. It may be easier to understand if you think that you have not written words, which are easy to distinguish from each other, but orally spoken audio. Now, each time a word is spoken, it will sound slightly different, and different speakers will have their own pronunciation. Thus, a word's waveform will not be identical every time it is spoken. However, by using clustering on these waveforms, we can hope to recover most of the structure so that all the instances of a given word are in the same cluster. Even if the process is not perfect (and it will not be), we can still talk of grouping the waveforms into words.

We perform the same operation with image data: we cluster together similar looking regions from all images and call these **visual words**.

> The number of words used does not usually have a big impact on the final performance of the algorithm. Naturally, if the number is extremely small (10 or 20, when you have a few thousand images), then the overall system will not perform well. Similarly, if you have too many words (many more than the number of images, for example), the system will also not perform well. However, in between these two extremes, there is often a very large plateau, where you can choose the number of words without a big impact on the result. As a rule of thumb, using a value such as 256, 512, or 1,024 if you have very many images should give you a good result.

We are going to start by computing the features as follows:

```
>>> alldescriptors = []
>>> for im in images:
...     im = mh.imread(im, as_grey=True)
...     im = im.astype(np.uint8)
...     alldescriptors.append(surf.dense(image, spacing=16))
>>> # get all descriptors into a single array
>>> concatenated = np.concatenate(alldescriptors)
>>> print('Number of descriptors: {}'.format(
...         len(concatenated)))
Number of descriptors: 2489031
```

This results in over 2 million local descriptors. Now, we use k-means clustering to obtain the centroids. We could use all the descriptors, but we are going to use a smaller sample for extra speed, as shown in the following:

```
>>> # use only every 64th vector
>>> concatenated = concatenated[::64]
>>> from sklearn.cluster import KMeans
>>> k = 256
>>> km = KMeans(k)
>>> km.fit(concatenated)
```

After this is done (which will take a while), the km object contains information about the centroids. We now go back to the descriptors and build feature vectors as follows:

```
>>> sfeatures = []
>>> for d in alldescriptors:
...     c = km.predict(d)
...     sfeatures.append(
...         np.array([np.sum(c == ci) for ci in range(k)])
...     )
>>> # build single array and convert to float
>>> sfeatures = np.array(sfeatures, dtype=float)
```

The end result of this loop is that `sfeatures[fi, fj]` is the number of times that the image `fi` contains the element `fj`. The same could have been computed faster with the `np.histogram` function, but getting the arguments just right is a little tricky. We convert the result to floating point as we do not want integer arithmetic (with its rounding semantics).

The result is that each image is now represented by a single array of features, of the same size (the number of clusters, in our case 256). Therefore, we can use our standard classification methods as follows:

```
>>> scores = cross_validation.cross_val_score(
...     clf, sfeatures, labels, cv=cv)
>>> print('Accuracy: {:.1%}'.format(scores.mean()))
Accuracy: 62.6%
```

This is worse than before! Have we gained nothing?

In fact, we have, as we can combine all features together to obtain 76.1 percent accuracy, as follows:

```
>>> combined = np.hstack([features, features])
>>> scores = cross_validation.cross_val_score(
...     clf, combined, labels, cv=cv)
>>> print('Accuracy: {:.1%}'.format(scores.mean()))
Accuracy: 76.1%
```

This is the best result we have, better than any single feature set. This is due to the fact that the local SURF features are different enough to add new information to the global image features we had before and improve the combined result.

Summary

We learned the classical feature-based approach to handling images in a machine learning context: by converting from a million pixels to a few numeric features, we are able to directly use a logistic regression classifier. All of the technologies that we learned in the other chapters suddenly become directly applicable to image problems. We saw one example in the use of image features to find similar images in a dataset.

We also learned how to use local features, in a bag of words model, for classification. This is a very modern approach to computer vision and achieves good results while being robust to many irrelevant aspects of the image, such as illumination, and even uneven illumination in the same image. We also used clustering as a useful intermediate step in classification rather than as an end in itself.

We focused on mahotas, which is one of the major computer vision libraries in Python. There are others that are equally well maintained. Skimage (scikit-image) is similar in spirit, but has a different set of features. OpenCV is a very good C++ library with a Python interface. All of these can work with NumPy arrays and you can mix and match functions from different libraries to build complex computer vision pipelines.

In the next chapter, you will learn a different form of machine learning: dimensionality reduction. As we saw in several earlier chapters, including when using images in this chapter, it is very easy to computationally generate many features. However, often we want to have a reduced number of features for speed and visualization, or to improve our results. In the next chapter, we will see how to achieve this.

11
Dimensionality Reduction

Garbage in, garbage out—throughout the book, we saw this pattern also holds true when applying machine learning methods to training data. Looking back, we realize that the most interesting machine learning challenges always involved some sort of feature engineering, where we tried to use our insight into the problem to carefully crafted additional features that the machine learner hopefully picks up.

In this chapter, we will go in the opposite direction with dimensionality reduction involving cutting away features that are irrelevant or redundant. Removing features might seem counter-intuitive at first thought, as more information should always be better than less information. Also, even if we had redundant features in our dataset, would not the learning algorithm be able to quickly figure it out and set their weights to 0? The following are several good reasons that are still in practice for trimming down the dimensions as much as possible:

- Superfluous features can irritate or mislead the learner. This is not the case with all machine learning methods (for example, Support Vector Machines love high dimensional spaces). However, most of the models feel safer with fewer dimensions.

- Another argument against high dimensional feature spaces is that more features mean more parameters to tune and a higher risk to overfit.

- The data we retrieved to solve our task might have just artificially high dimensionality, whereas the real dimension might be small.

- Fewer dimensions = faster training = more parameter variations to try out in the same time frame = better end result.

- Visualization—if we want to visualize the data we are restricted to two or three dimensions.

So, here we will show how to get rid of the garbage within our data while keeping the real valuable part of it.

Sketching our roadmap

Dimensionality reduction can be roughly grouped into feature selection and feature extraction methods. We already employed some kind of feature selection in almost every chapter when we invented, analyzed, and then probably dropped some features. In this chapter, we will present some ways that use statistical methods, namely correlation and mutual information, to be able to do so in vast feature spaces. Feature extraction tries to transform the original feature space into a lower-dimensional feature space. This is especially useful when we cannot get rid of features using selection methods, but still we have too many features for our learner. We will demonstrate this using **principal component analysis (PCA)**, **linear discriminant analysis (LDA)**, and **multidimensional scaling (MDS)**.

Selecting features

If we want to be nice to our machine learning algorithm, we provide it with features that are not dependent on each other, yet highly dependent on the value to be predicted. This means that each feature adds salient information. Removing any of the features will lead to a drop in performance.

If we have only a handful of features, we could draw a matrix of scatter plots (one scatter plot for every feature pair combination). Relationships between the features could then be easily spotted. For every feature pair showing an obvious dependence, we would then think of whether we should remove one of them or better design a newer, cleaner feature out of both.

Most of the time, however, we have more than a handful of features to choose from. Just think of the classification task where we had a bag of words to classify the quality of an answer, which would require a 1,000 by 1,000 scatter plot. In this case, we need a more automated way to detect overlapping features and to resolve them. We will present two general ways to do so in the following subsections, namely filters and wrappers.

Detecting redundant features using filters

Filters try to clean up the feature forest independent of any later used machine learning method. They rely on statistical methods to find which of the features are redundant or irrelevant. In case of redundant features, it keeps only one per redundant feature group. Irrelevant features will simply be removed. In general, the filter works as depicted in the following workflow:

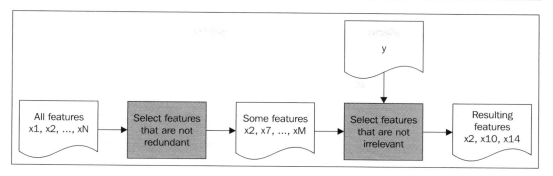

Correlation

Using correlation, we can easily see linear relationships between pairs of features. In the following graphs, we can see different degrees of correlation, together with a potential linear dependency plotted as a red-dashed line (fitted 1-dimensional polynomial). The correlation coefficient $Cor(X_1, X_2)$ at the top of the individual graphs is calculated using the common Pearson correlation coefficient (Pearson r value) by means of the `pearsonr()` function of `scipy.stat`.

Given two equal-sized data series, it returns a tuple of the correlation coefficient value and the p-value. The p-value describes how likely it is that the data series has been generated by an uncorrelated system. In other words, the higher the p-value, the less we should trust the correlation coefficient:

```
>>> from scipy.stats import pearsonr
>>> pearsonr([1,2,3], [1,2,3.1])
>>> (0.99962228516121843, 0.017498096813278487)
>>> pearsonr([1,2,3], [1,20,6])
>>> (0.25383654128340477, 0.83661493668227405)
```

In the first case, we have a clear indication that both series are correlated. In the second case, we still have a clearly non-zero r value.

However, the p-value of 0.84 tells us that the correlation coefficient is not significant and we should not pay too close attention to it. Have a look at the following graphs:

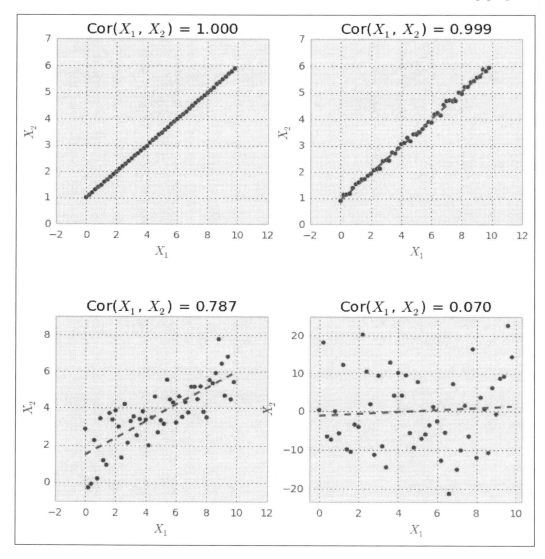

In the first three cases that have high correlation coefficients, we would probably want to throw out either X_1 or X_2 because they seem to convey similar, if not the same, information.

In the last case, however, we should keep both features. In our application, this decision would, of course, be driven by this p-value.

Although, it worked nicely in the preceding example, reality is seldom nice to us. One big disadvantage of correlation-based feature selection is that it only detects linear relationships (a relationship that can be modelled by a straight line). If we use correlation on a non-linear data, we see the problem. In the following example, we have a quadratic relationship:

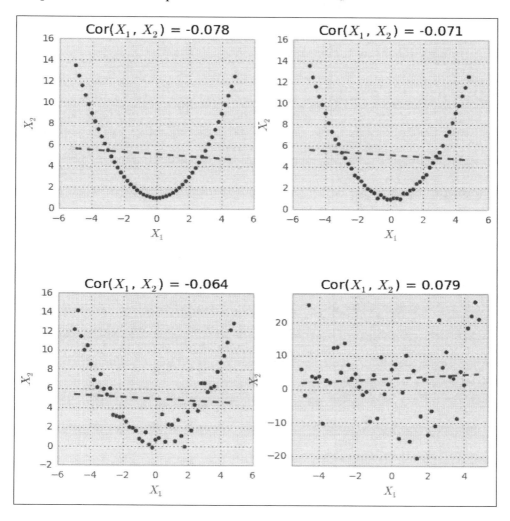

Although, the human eye immediately sees the relationship between X_1 and X_2 in all but the bottom-right graph, the correlation coefficient does not. It's obvious that correlation is useful to detect linear relationships, but fails for everything else. Sometimes, it already helps to apply simple transformations to get a linear relationship. For instance, in the preceding plot, we would have got a high correlation coefficient if we had drawn X_2 over X_1 squared. Normal data, however, does not often offer this opportunity.

Luckily, for non-linear relationships, mutual information comes to the rescue.

Mutual information

When looking at the feature selection, we should not focus on the type of relationship as we did in the previous section (linear relationships). Instead, we should think in terms of how much information one feature provides (given that we already have another).

To understand this, let's pretend that we want to use features from `house_size`, `number_of_levels`, and `avg_rent_price` feature set to train a classifier that outputs whether the house has an elevator or not. In this example, we intuitively see that knowing `house_size` we don't need to know `number_of_levels` anymore, as it contains, somehow, redundant information. With `avg_rent_price`, it's different because we cannot infer the value of rental space simply from the size of the house or the number of levels it has. Thus, it would be wise to keep only one of them in addition to the average price of rental space.

Mutual information formalizes the aforementioned reasoning by calculating how much information two features have in common. However, unlike correlation, it does not rely on a sequence of data, but on the distribution. To understand how it works, we have to dive a bit into information entropy.

Let's assume we have a fair coin. Before we flip it, we will have maximum uncertainty as to whether it will show heads or tails, as both have an equal probability of 50 percent. This uncertainty can be measured by means of Claude Shannon's information entropy:

$$H(X) = -\sum_{i=1}^{n} p(X_i)\log_2 p(X_i)$$

In our fair coin case, we have two cases: Let x_0 be the case of head and x_1 the case of tail with $p(X_0) = p(X_1) = 0.5$.

Thus, it concludes to:

$$H(X) = -p(x_0)\log_2 p(x_0) - p(x_1)\log_2 p(x_1) = -0.5 \cdot \log_2(0.5) - 0.5$$
$$\cdot \log_2(0.5) = 1.0$$

> For convenience, we can also use `scipy.stats.entropy([0.5, 0.5], base=2)`. We set the base parameter to 2 to get the same result as earlier. Otherwise, the function will use the natural logarithm via `np.log()`. In general, the base does not matter (as long as you use it consistently).

Now, imagine we knew upfront that the coin is actually not that fair with heads having a chance of 60 percent showing up after flipping:

$$H(X) = -0.6 \cdot \log_2(0.6) - 0.4 \cdot \log_2(0.4) = 0.97$$

We see that this situation is less uncertain. The uncertainty will decrease the farther away we get from 0.5 reaching the extreme value of 0 for either 0 percent or 100 percent of heads showing up, as we can see in the following graph:

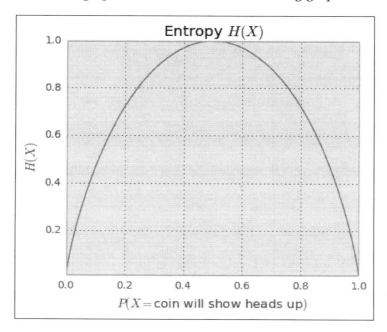

We will now modify entropy $H(X)$ by applying it to two features instead of one in such a way that it measures how much uncertainty is removed from X when we learn about Y. Then, we can catch how one feature reduces the uncertainty of another.

For example, without having any further information about the weather, we are totally uncertain whether it's raining outside or not. If we now learn that the grass outside is wet, the uncertainty has been reduced (we will still have to check whether the sprinkler had been turned on).

More formally, mutual information is defined as:

$$I(X;Y) = \sum_{i=1}^{m} \sum_{j=1}^{n} P(X_i, Y_j) \log_2 \frac{P(X_i, Y_j)}{P(X_i) P(Y_j)}$$

This looks a bit intimidating, but is really not more than sums and products. For instance, the calculation of $P()$ is done by binning the feature values and then calculating the fraction of values in each bin. In the following plots, we have set the number of bins to ten.

In order to restrict mutual information to the interval [0,1], we have to divide it by their added individual entropy, which gives us the normalized mutual information:

$$NI(X;Y) = \frac{I(X;Y)}{H(X) + H(Y)}$$

The nice thing about mutual information is that unlike correlation, it does not look only at linear relationships, as we can see in the following graphs:

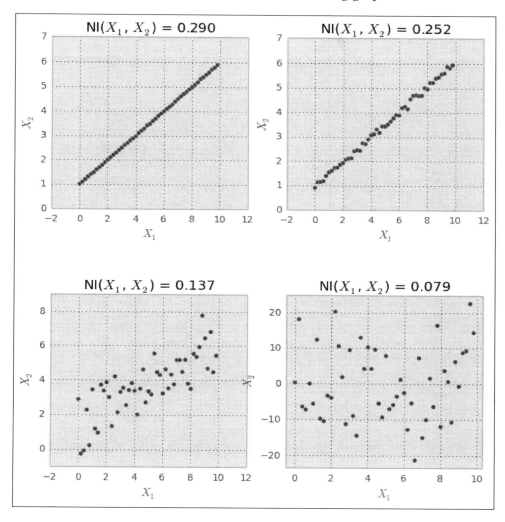

As we can see, mutual information is able to indicate the strength of a linear relationship. The following diagram shows that, it also works for squared relationships:

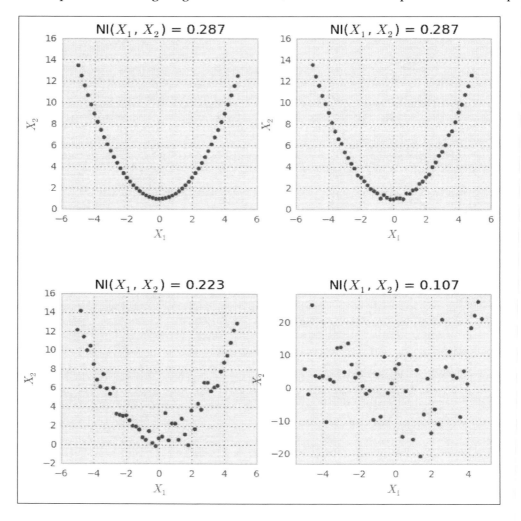

So, what we would have to do is to calculate the normalized mutual information for all feature pairs. For every pair having too high value (we would have to determine what this means), we would then drop one of them. In case of regression, we could drop this feature that has too low mutual information with the desired result value.

This might work for a not too-big set of features. At some point, however, this procedure can be really expensive, because the amount of calculation grows quadratically (as we are computing the mutual information between feature pairs).

Another huge disadvantage of filters is that they drop features that seem to be not useful in isolation. More often than not, there are a handful of features that seem to be totally independent of the target variable, yet when combined together they rock. To keep these, we need wrappers.

Asking the model about the features using wrappers

While filters can help tremendously in getting rid of useless features, they can go only so far. After all the filtering, there might still be some features that are independent among themselves and show some degree of dependence with the result variable, but yet they are totally useless from the model's point of view. Just think of the following data that describes the XOR function. Individually, neither A nor B would show any signs of dependence on Y, whereas together they clearly do:

A	B	Y
0	0	0
0	1	1
1	0	1
1	1	0

So, why not ask the model itself to give its vote on the individual features? This is what wrappers do, as we can see in the following process chart:

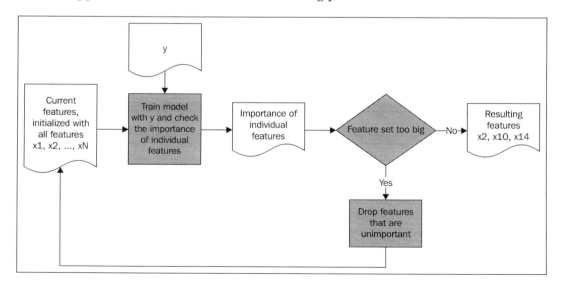

Here, we pushed the calculation of feature importance to the model training process. Unfortunately (but understandably), feature importance is not determined as a binary, but as a ranking value. So, we still have to specify where to make the cut, what part of the features are we willing to take, and what part do we want to drop?

Coming back to scikit-learn, we find various excellent wrapper classes in the `sklearn.feature_selection` package. A real workhorse in this field is `RFE`, which stands for recursive feature elimination. It takes an estimator and the desired number of features to keep as parameters and then trains the estimator with various feature sets as long as it has found a subset of features that is small enough. The `RFE` instance itself pretends to be like an estimator, thereby, indeed, wrapping the provided estimator.

In the following example, we create an artificial classification problem of 100 samples using datasets' convenient `make_classification()` function. It lets us specify the creation of 10 features, out of which only three are really valuable to solve the classification problem:

```
>>> from sklearn.feature_selection import RFE
>>> from sklearn.linear_model import LogisticRegression
>>> from sklearn.datasets import make_classification
>>> X,y = make_classification(n_samples=100, n_features=10,
n_informative=3, random_state=0)
>>> clf = LogisticRegression()
>>> clf.fit(X, y)
>>> selector = RFE(clf, n_features_to_select=3)
>>> selector = selector.fit(X, y)
>>> print(selector.support_)
[False  True False  True False False False False  True False]
>>> print(selector.ranking_)
[4 1 3 1 8 5 7 6 1 2]
```

The problem in real-world scenarios is, of course, how can we know the right value for `n_features_to_select`? Truth is, we can't. However, most of the time we can use a sample of the data and play with it using different settings to quickly get a feeling for the right ballpark.

The good thing is that we don't have to be that exact using wrappers. Let's try different values for `n_features_to_select` to see how `support_` and `ranking_` change:

n_features_ to_select	support_	ranking_
1	[False False False True False False False False False False]	[6 3 5 1 10 7 9 8 2 4]
2	[False False False True False False False False True False]	[5 2 4 1 9 6 8 7 1 3]
3	[False True False True False False False False True False]	[4 1 3 1 8 5 7 6 1 2]
4	[False True False True False False False False True True]	[3 1 2 1 7 4 6 5 1 1]
5	[False True True True False False False False True True]	[2 1 1 1 6 3 5 4 1 1]
6	[True True True True False False False False True True]	[1 1 1 1 5 2 4 3 1 1]
7	[True True True True False True False False True True]	[1 1 1 1 4 1 3 2 1 1]
8	[True True True True False True False True True True]	[1 1 1 1 3 1 2 1 1 1]
9	[True True True True False True True True True True]	[1 1 1 1 2 1 1 1 1 1]
10	[True True True True True True True True True True]	[1 1 1 1 1 1 1 1 1 1]

We see that the result is very stable. Features that have been used when requesting smaller feature sets keep on getting selected when letting more features in. At last, we rely on our train/test set splitting to warn us when we go the wrong way.

Other feature selection methods

There are several other feature selection methods that you will discover while reading through machine learning literature. Some even don't look like being a feature selection method because they are embedded into the learning process (not to be confused with the aforementioned wrappers). Decision trees, for instance, have a feature selection mechanism implanted deep in their core. Other learning methods employ some kind of regularization that punishes model complexity, thus driving the learning process towards good performing models that are still "simple". They do this by decreasing the less impactful features importance to zero and then dropping them (L1-regularization).

So watch out! Often, the power of machine learning methods has to be attributed to their implanted feature selection method to a great degree.

Feature extraction

At some point, after we have removed redundant features and dropped irrelevant ones, we, often, still find that we have too many features. No matter what learning method we use, they all perform badly and given the huge feature space we understand that they actually cannot do better. We realize that we have to cut living flesh; we have to get rid of features, for which all common sense tells us that they are valuable. Another situation when we need to reduce the dimensions and feature selection does not help much is when we want to visualize data. Then, we need to have at most three dimensions at the end to provide any meaningful graphs.

Enter feature extraction methods. They restructure the feature space to make it more accessible to the model or simply cut down the dimensions to two or three so that we can show dependencies visually.

Again, we can distinguish feature extraction methods as being linear or non-linear ones. Also, as seen before in the *Selecting features* section, we will present one method for each type (principal component analysis as a linear and non-linear version of multidimensional scaling). Although, they are widely known and used, they are only representatives for many more interesting and powerful feature extraction methods.

About principal component analysis

Principal component analysis (PCA) is often the first thing to try out if you want to cut down the number of features and do not know what feature extraction method to use. PCA is limited as it's a linear method, but chances are that it already goes far enough for your model to learn well enough. Add to this the strong mathematical properties it offers and the speed at which it finds the transformed feature space and is later able to transform between original and transformed features; we can almost guarantee that it also will become one of your frequently used machine learning tools.

Summarizing it, given the original feature space, PCA finds a linear projection of itself in a lower dimensional space that has the following properties:

- The conserved variance is maximized.
- The final reconstruction error (when trying to go back from transformed features to original ones) is minimized.

As PCA simply transforms the input data, it can be applied both to classification and regression problems. In this section, we will use a classification task to discuss the method.

Sketching PCA

PCA involves a lot of linear algebra, which we do not want to go into. Nevertheless, the basic algorithm can be easily described as follows:

1. Center the data by subtracting the mean from it.
2. Calculate the covariance matrix.
3. Calculate the eigenvectors of the covariance matrix.

If we start with N features, then the algorithm will return a transformed feature space again with N dimensions (we gained nothing so far). The nice thing about this algorithm, however, is that the eigenvalues indicate how much of the variance is described by the corresponding eigenvector.

Let's assume we start with $N = 1000$ features and we know that our model does not work well with more than 20 features. Then, we simply pick the 20 eigenvectors with the highest eigenvalues.

Applying PCA

Let's consider the following artificial dataset, which is visualized in the following left plot diagram:

```
>>> x1 = np.arange(0, 10, .2)
>>> x2 = x1+np.random.normal(loc=0, scale=1, size=len(x1))
>>> X = np.c_[(x1, x2)]
>>> good = (x1>5) | (x2>5) # some arbitrary classes
>>> bad = ~good # to make the example look good
```

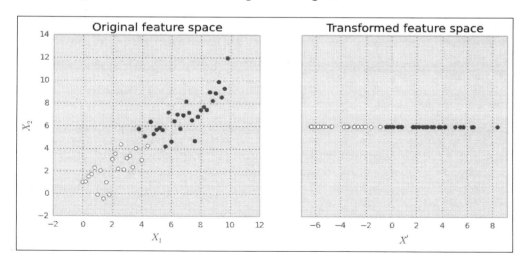

Scikit-learn provides the PCA class in its decomposition package. In this example, we can clearly see that one dimension should be enough to describe the data. We can specify this using the n_components parameter:

```
>>> from sklearn import linear_model, decomposition, datasets
>>> pca = decomposition.PCA(n_components=1)
```

Also, here we can use the fit() and transform() methods of pca (or its fit_transform() combination) to analyze the data and project it in the transformed feature space:

```
>>> Xtrans = pca.fit_transform(X)
```

As we have specified, Xtrans contains only one dimension. You can see the result in the preceding right plot diagram. The outcome is even linearly separable in this case. We would not even need a complex classifier to distinguish between both classes.

To get an understanding of the reconstruction error, we can have a look at the variance of the data that we have retained in the transformation:

```
>>> print(pca.explained_variance_ratio_)
>>> [ 0.96393127]
```

This means that after going from two to one dimension, we are still left with 96 percent of the variance.

Of course, it's not always this simple. Oftentimes, we don't know what number of dimensions is advisable upfront. In that case, we leave n_components parameter unspecified when initializing PCA to let it calculate the full transformation. After fitting the data, explained_variance_ratio_ contains an array of ratios in decreasing order: The first value is the ratio of the basis vector describing the direction of the highest variance, the second value is the ratio of the direction of the second highest variance, and so on. After plotting this array, we quickly get a feel of how many components we would need: the number of components immediately before the chart has its elbow is often a good guess.

Plots displaying the explained variance over the number of components is called a Scree plot. A nice example of combining a Scree plot with a grid search to find the best setting for the classification problem can be found at http://scikit-learn.sourceforge. net/stable/auto_examples/plot_digits_pipe.html.

Limitations of PCA and how LDA can help

Being a linear method, PCA has, of course, its limitations when we are faced with data that has non-linear relationships. We won't go into details here, but it's sufficient to say that there are extensions of PCA, for example, Kernel PCA, which introduces a non-linear transformation so that we can still use the PCA approach.

Another interesting weakness of PCA, which we will cover here, is when it's being applied to special classification problems. Let's replace good = (x1 > 5) | (x2 > 5) with good = x1 > x2 to simulate such a special case and we quickly see the problem:

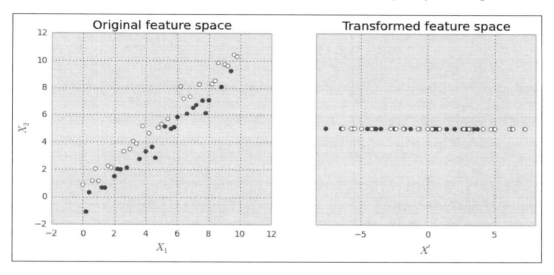

Here, the classes are not distributed according to the axis with the highest variance, but the second highest variance. Clearly, PCA falls flat on its face. As we don't provide PCA with any cues regarding the class labels, it cannot do any better.

Linear Discriminant Analysis (LDA) comes to the rescue here. It's a method that tries to maximize the distance of points belonging to different classes, while minimizing the distances of points of the same class. We won't give any more details regarding how in particular the underlying theory works, just a quick tutorial on how to use it:

```
>>> from sklearn import lda
>>> lda_inst = lda.LDA(n_components=1)
>>> Xtrans = lda_inst.fit_transform(X, good)
```

That's all. Note that in contrast to the previous PCA example, we provide the class labels to the `fit_transform()` method. Thus, PCA is an unsupervised feature extraction method, whereas LDA is a supervised one. The result looks as expected:

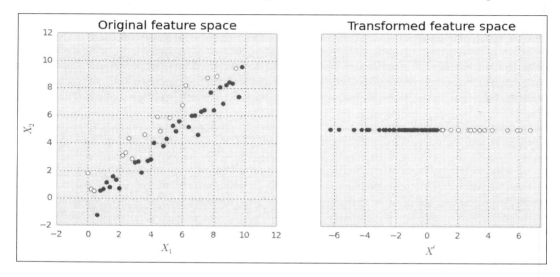

So, why then consider PCA at all and not simply use LDA? Well, it's not that simple. With an increasing number of classes and fewer samples per class, LDA does not look that well any more. Also, PCA seems to be not as sensitive to different training sets as LDA. So, when we have to advise which method to use, we can only suggest a clear "it depends".

Multidimensional scaling

Although, PCA tries to use optimization for retained variance, **multidimensional scaling (MDS)** tries to retain the relative distances as much as possible when reducing the dimensions. This is useful when we have a high-dimensional dataset and want to get a visual impression.

MDS does not care about the data points themselves; instead, it's interested in the dissimilarities between pairs of data points and interprets these as distances. The first thing the MDS algorithm is doing is, therefore, taking all the N datapoints of dimension k and calculates a distance matrix using a distance function d_o, which measures the (most of the time, Euclidean) distance in the original feature space:

$$\begin{pmatrix} X_{11} & \cdots & X_{N1} \\ \vdots & \ddots & \vdots \\ X_{1k} & \cdots & X_{Nk} \end{pmatrix} \rightarrow \begin{pmatrix} d_o(X_1,X_1) & \cdots & d_o(X_N,X_1) \\ \vdots & \ddots & \vdots \\ d_o(X_1,X_N) & \cdots & d_o(X_N,X_N) \end{pmatrix}$$

Now, MDS tries to position the individual datapoints in the lower dimensional space such that the new distance there resembles the distances in the original space as much as possible. As MDS is often used for visualization, the choice of the lower dimension is most of the time two or three.

Let's have a look at the following simple data consisting of three datapoints in five-dimensional space. Two of the datapoints are close by and one is very distinct and we want to visualize this in three and two dimensions:

```
>>> X = np.c_[np.ones(5), 2 * np.ones(5), 10 * np.ones(5)].T
>>> print(X)
[[  1.   1.   1.   1.   1.]
 [  2.   2.   2.   2.   2.]
 [ 10.  10.  10.  10.  10.]]
```

Using the MDS class in scikit-learn's manifold package, we first specify that we want to transform X into a three-dimensional Euclidean space:

```
>>> from sklearn import manifold
>>> mds = manifold.MDS(n_components=3)
>>> Xtrans = mds.fit_transform(X)
```

To visualize it in two dimensions, we would need to set n_components accordingly.

The results can be seen in the following two graphs. The triangle and circle are both close together, whereas the star is far away:

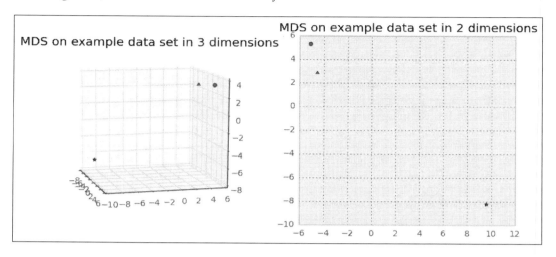

Let's have a look at the slightly more complex Iris dataset. We will use it later to contrast LDA with PCA. The Iris dataset contains four attributes per flower. With the preceding code, we would project it into three-dimensional space while keeping the relative distances between the individual flowers as much as possible. In the previous example, we did not specify any metric, so MDS will default to Euclidean. This means that flowers that were "different" according to their four attributes should also be far away in the MDS-scaled three-dimensional space and flowers that were similar should be near together now, as shown in the following diagram:

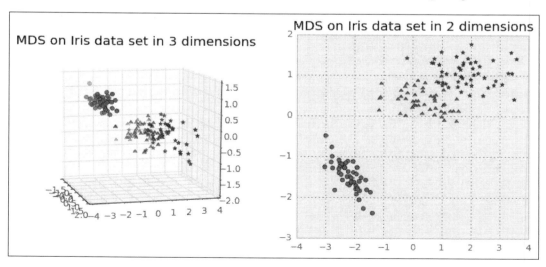

Reducing the dimensional reduction to three and two dimensions with PCA instead, we see the expected bigger spread of the flowers belonging to the same class, as shown in the following diagram:

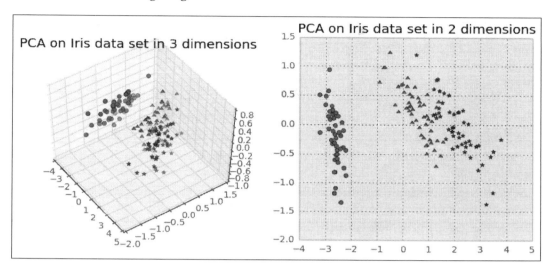

Of course, using MDS requires an understanding of the individual feature's units; maybe we are using features that cannot be compared using the Euclidean metric. For instance, a categorical variable, even when encoded as an integer (0= circle, 1= star, 2= triangle, and so on), cannot be compared using Euclidean (is circle closer to star than to triangle?).

However, once we are aware of this issue, MDS is a useful tool that reveals similarities in our data that otherwise would be difficult to see in the original feature space.

Looking a bit deeper into MDS, we realize that it's not a single algorithm, but rather a family of different algorithms, of which we have used just one. The same was true for PCA. Also, in case you realize that neither PCA nor MDS solves your problem, just look at the many other manifold learning algorithms that are available in the scikit-learn toolkit.

However, before you get overwhelmed by the many different algorithms, it's always best to start with the simplest one and see how far you get with it. Then, take the next more complex one and continue from there.

Summary

You learned that sometimes you can get rid of complete features using feature selection methods. We also saw that in some cases, this is not enough and we have to employ feature extraction methods that reveal the real and the lower-dimensional structure in our data, hoping that the model has an easier game with it.

For sure, we only scratched the surface of the huge body of available dimensionality reduction methods. Still, we hope that we got you interested in this whole field, as there are lots of other methods waiting for you to be picked up. At the end, feature selection and extraction is an art, just like choosing the right learning method or training model.

The next chapter covers the use of Jug, a little Python framework to manage computations in a way that takes advantage of multiple cores or multiple machines. You will also learn about AWS, the Amazon Cloud.

12
Bigger Data

It's not easy to say what big data is. We will adopt an operational definition: when data is so large that it becomes cumbersome to work with, we will talk about **big data**. In some areas, this might mean petabytes of data or trillions of transactions: data which will not fit into a single hard drive. In other cases, it may be one hundred times smaller, but still difficult to work with.

Why has data itself become an issue? While computers keep getting faster and have more memory, the size of the data has grown as well. In fact, data has grown faster than computational speed and few algorithms scale linearly with the size of the input data—taken together, this means that data has grown faster than our ability to process it.

We will first build on some of the experience of the previous chapters and work with what we can call medium data setting (not quite big data, but not small either). For this, we will use a package called **jug**, which allows us to perform the following tasks:

- Break up your pipeline into tasks
- Cache (memoize) intermediate results
- Make use of multiple cores, including multiple computers on a grid

The next step is to move to true *big data* and we will see how to use the cloud for computation purpose. In particular, you will learn about the Amazon Web Services infrastructure. In this section, we introduce another Python package called StarCluster to manage clusters.

Learning about big data

The expression "big data" does not mean a specific amount of data, neither in the number of examples nor in the number of gigabytes, terabytes, or petabytes occupied by the data. It means that data has been growing faster than processing power. This implies the following:

- Some of the methods and techniques that worked well in the past now need to be redone or replaced as they do not scale well to the new size of the input data

- Algorithms cannot assume that all the input data can fit in RAM

- Managing data becomes a major task in itself

- Using computer clusters or multicore machines becomes a necessity and not a luxury

This chapter will focus on this last piece of the puzzle: how to use multiple cores (either on the same machine or on separate machines) to speed up and organize your computations. This will also be useful in other medium-sized data tasks.

Using jug to break up your pipeline into tasks

Often, we have a simple pipeline: we preprocess the initial data, compute features, and then call a machine learning algorithm with the resulting features.

Jug is a package developed by Luis Pedro Coelho, one of the authors of this book. It's open source (using the liberal MIT License) and can be useful in many areas, but was designed specifically around data analysis problems. It simultaneously solves several problems, for example:

- It can *memoize* results to disk (or a database), which means that if you ask it to compute something you have already computed before, the result is instead read from disk.

- It can use multiple cores or even multiple computers on a cluster. Jug was also designed to work very well in batch computing environments, which use queuing systems such as **PBS** (**Portable Batch System**), **LSF** (**Load Sharing Facility**), or **Grid Engine**. This will be used in the second half of the chapter as we build online clusters and dispatch jobs to them.

An introduction to tasks in jug

Tasks are the basic building block of jug. A task is composed of a function and values for its arguments. Consider this simple example:

```
def double(x):

    return 2*x
```

In this chapter, the code examples will generally have to be typed in script files. Thus, they will not be shown with the >>> marker. Commands that should be typed at the shell will be indicated by preceding them with $.

A task could be "call double with argument 3". Another task would be "call double with argument 642.34". Using jug, we can build these tasks as follows:

```
from jug import Task
t1 = Task(double, 3)
t2 = Task(double, 642.34)
```

Save this to a file called jugfile.py (which is just a regular Python file). Now, we can run jug execute to run the tasks. This is something you type on the command line, not at the Python prompt, so we show it marked with a dollar sign ($):

```
$ jug execute
```

You will also get some feedback on the tasks (jug will say that two tasks named double were run). Run jug execute again and it will tell you that it did nothing! It does not need to. In this case, we gained little, but if the tasks took a long time to compute, it would have been very useful.

You may notice that a new directory also appeared on your hard drive named jugfile.jugdata with a few weirdly named files. This is the memoization cache. If you remove it, jug execute will run all your tasks again.

Often, it's good to distinguish between pure functions, which simply take their inputs and return a result, from more general functions that can perform actions (such as reading from files, writing to files, accessing global variables, modify their arguments, or anything that the language allows). Some programming languages, such as Haskell, even have syntactic ways to distinguish pure from impure functions.

With jug, your tasks do not need to be perfectly pure. It's even recommended that you use tasks to read in your data or write out your results. However, accessing and modifying global variables will not work well: the tasks may be run in any order in different processors. The exceptions are global constants, but even this may confuse the memoization system (if the value is changed between runs). Similarly, you should not modify the input values. Jug has a debug mode (use `jug execute --debug`), which slows down your computation, but will give you useful error messages if you make this sort of mistake.

The preceding code works, but is a bit cumbersome. You are always repeating the `Task(function, argument)` construct. Using a bit of Python magic, we can make the code even more natural as follows:

```
from jug import TaskGenerator
from time import sleep


@TaskGenerator
def double(x):
    sleep(4)
    return 2*x


@TaskGenerator
def add(a, b):
    return a + b


@TaskGenerator
def print_final_result(oname, value):
    with open(oname, 'w') as output:
        output.write('Final result: {}\n'.format(value))



y = double(2)
z = double(y)


y2 = double(7)
z2 = double(y2)
print_final_result('output.txt', add(z,z2))
```

Except for the use of `TaskGenerator`, the preceding code could be a standard Python file! However, using `TaskGenerator`, it actually creates a series of tasks and it is now possible to run it in a way that takes advantage of multiple processors. Behind the scenes, the decorator transforms your functions so that they do not actually execute when called, but create a `Task` object. We also take advantage of the fact that we can pass tasks to other tasks and this results in a dependency being generated.

You may have noticed that we added a few `sleep(4)` calls in the preceding code. This simulates running a long computation. Otherwise, this example is so fast that there is no point in using multiple processors.

We start by running `jug status`, which results in the output shown in the following screenshot:

Waiting	Ready	Finished	Running	Task name
1	0	0	0	jugfile.print_final_result
1	0	0	0	jugfile.add
2	2	0	0	jugfile.double
4	2	0	0	Total

Now, we start two processes simultaneously (using the `&` operator in the background):

```
$ jug execute &
$ jug execute &
```

Now, we run `jug status` again:

Waiting	Ready	Finished	Running	Task name
1	0	0	0	jugfile.print_final_result
2	0	0	2	jugfile.double
1	0	0	0	jugfile.add
4	2	0	0	Total

We can see that the two initial double operators are running at the same time. After about 8 seconds, the whole process will finish and the `output.txt` file will be written.

By the way, if your file was called anything other than `jugfile.py`, you would then have to specify it explicitly on the command line. For example, if your file was called `analysis.py`, you would run the following command:

```
$ jug execute analysis.py
```

This is the only disadvantage of not using the name `jugfile.py`. So, feel free to use more meaningful names.

Looking under the hood

How does jug work? At the basic level, it's very simple. A `Task` is a function plus its argument. Its arguments may be either values or other tasks. If a task takes other tasks, there is a dependency between the two tasks (and the second one cannot be run until the results of the first task are available).

Based on this, jug recursively computes a hash for each task. This hash value encodes the whole computation to get the result. When you run `jug execute`, for each task, there is a little loop that runs the logic depicted in the following flowchart:

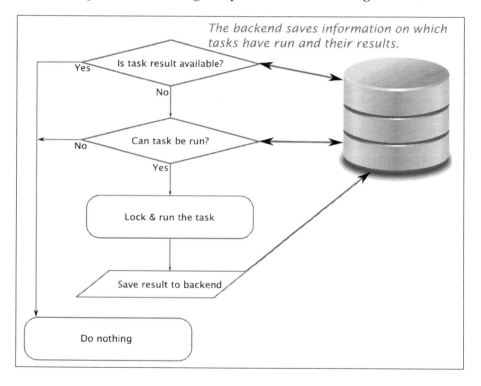

The default backend writes the file to disk (in this funny directory named `jugfile.jugdata/`). Another backend is available, which uses a Redis database. With proper locking, which jug takes care of, this also allows for many processors to execute tasks; each process will independently look at all the tasks and run the ones that have not run yet and then write them back to the shared backend. This works on either the same machine (using multicore processors) or in multiple machines as long as they all have access to the same backend (for example, using a network disk or the Redis databases). In the second half of this chapter, we will discuss computer clusters, but for now let's focus on multiple cores.

You can also understand why it's able to memoize intermediate results. If the backend already has the result of a task, it's not run again. On the other hand, if you change the task, even in minute ways (by altering one of the parameters), its hash will change. Therefore, it will be rerun. Furthermore, all tasks that depend on it will also have their hashes changed and they will be rerun as well.

Using jug for data analysis

Jug is a generic framework, but it's ideally suited for medium-scale data analysis. As you develop your analysis pipeline, it's good to have intermediate results automatically saved. If you have already computed the preprocessing step before and are only changing the features you compute, you do not want to recompute the preprocessing step. If you have already computed the features, but want to try combining a few new ones into the mix, you also do not want to recompute all your other features.

Jug is also specifically optimized to work with NumPy arrays. Whenever your tasks return or receive NumPy arrays, you are taking advantage of this optimization. Jug is another piece of this ecosystem where everything works together.

We will now look back at *Chapter 10, Computer Vision*. In that chapter, we learned how to compute features on images. Remember that the basic pipeline consisted of the following features:

- Loading image files
- Computing features
- Combining these features
- Normalizing the features
- Creating a classifier

We are going to redo this exercise, but this time with the use of jug. The advantage of this version is that it's now possible to add a new feature or classifier without having to recompute all of the pipeline.

We start with a few imports as follows:

```
from jug import TaskGenerator
import mahotas as mh
from glob import glob
```

Now, we define the first task generators and feature computation functions:

```
@TaskGenerator
def compute_texture(im):
    from features import texture
    imc = mh.imread(im)
    return texture(mh.colors.rgb2gray(imc))


@TaskGenerator
def chist_file(fname):
    from features import chist
    im = mh.imread(fname)
    return chist(im)
```

The `features` module we import is the one from *Chapter 10, Computer Vision*.

 We write functions that take the filename as input instead of the image array. Using the full images would also work, of course, but this is a small optimization. A filename is a string, which is small if it gets written to the backend. It's also very fast to compute a hash if needed. It also ensures that the images are only loaded by the processes that need them.

We can use `TaskGenerator` on any function. This is true even for functions, which we did not write, such as `np.array`, `np.hstack`, or the following command:

```
import numpy as np
to_array = TaskGenerator(np.array)
hstack = TaskGenerator(np.hstack)


haralicks = []
chists = []
```

```
labels = []


# Change this variable to point to
# the location of the dataset on disk
basedir = '../SimpleImageDataset/'
# Use glob to get all the images
images = glob('{}/*.jpg'.format(basedir))


for fname in sorted(images):
    haralicks.append(compute_texture(fname))
    chists.append(chist_file(fname))
    # The class is encoded in the filename as xxxx00.jpg
    labels.append(fname[:-len('00.jpg')])


haralicks = to_array(haralicks)
chists = to_array(chists)
labels = to_array(labels)
```

One small inconvenience of using jug is that we must always write functions to output the results to files, as shown in the preceding examples. This is a small price to pay for the extra convenience of using jug.

```
@TaskGenerator
def accuracy(features, labels):
    from sklearn.linear_model import LogisticRegression
    from sklearn.pipeline import Pipeline
    from sklearn.preprocessing import StandardScaler
    from sklearn import cross_validation

    clf = Pipeline([('preproc', StandardScaler()),
                ('classifier', LogisticRegression())])
    cv = cross_validation.LeaveOneOut(len(features))
    scores = cross_validation.cross_val_score(
        clf, features, labels, cv=cv)
    return scores.mean()
```

Note that we are only importing `sklearn` inside this function. This is a small optimization. This way, `sklearn` is only imported when it's really needed:

```
scores_base = accuracy(haralicks, labels)
scores_chist = accuracy(chists, labels)


combined = hstack([chists, haralicks])
scores_combined = accuracy(combined, labels)
```

Finally, we write and call a function to print out all results. It expects its argument to be a list of pairs with the name of the algorithm and the results:

```
@TaskGenerator
def print_results(scores):
    with open('results.image.txt', 'w') as output:
        for k,v in scores:
            output.write('Accuracy [{}]: {:.1%}\n'.format(
                k, v.mean()))


print_results([
        ('base', scores_base),
        ('chists', scores_chist),
        ('combined' , scores_combined),
        ])
```

That's it. Now, on the shell, run the following command to run this pipeline using jug:

```
$ jug execute image-classification.py
```

Reusing partial results

For example, let's say you want to add a new feature (or even a set of features). As we saw in *Chapter 10*, *Computer Vision*, this is easy to do by changing the feature computation code. However, this would imply recomputing all the features again, which is wasteful, particularly, if you want to test new features and techniques quickly.

We now add a set of features, that is, another type of texture feature called linear binary patterns. This is implemented in mahotas; we just need to call a function, but we wrap it in `TaskGenerator`:

```
@TaskGenerator
def compute_lbp(fname):
    from mahotas.features import lbp
    imc = mh.imread(fname)
    im = mh.colors.rgb2grey(imc)
    # The parameters 'radius' and 'points' are set to typical values
    # check the documentation for their exact meaning
    return lbp(im, radius=8, points=6)
```

We replace the previous loop to have an extra function call:

```
lbps = []
for fname in sorted(images):
    # the rest of the loop as before
    lbps.append(compute_lbp(fname))
lbps = to_array(lbps)
```

We call accuracy with these newer features:

```
scores_lbps = accuracy(lbps, labels)
combined_all = hstack([chists, haralicks, lbps])
scores_combined_all = accuracy(combined_all, labels)


print_results([
        ('base', scores_base),
        ('chists', scores_chist),
        ('lbps', scores_lbps),
        ('combined' , scores_combined),
        ('combined_all' , scores_combined_all),
        ])
```

Now, when you run `jug execute` again, the new features will be computed, but the old features will be loaded from the cache. This is when jug can be very powerful. It ensures that you always get the results you want while saving you from unnecessarily recomputing cached results. You will also see that adding this feature set improves on the previous methods.

Not all features of jug could be mentioned in this chapter, but here is a summary of the most potentially interesting ones we didn't cover in the main text:

- `jug invalidate`: This declares that all results from a given function should be considered invalid and in need of recomputation. This will also recompute any downstream computation, which depended (even indirectly) on the invalidated results.

- `jug status --cache`: If `jug status` takes too long, you can use the `--cache` flag to cache the status and speed it up. Note that this will not detect any changes to the jugfile, but you can always use `--cache --clear` to remove the cache and start again.

- `jug cleanup`: This removes any extra files in the memoization cache. This is a garbage collection operation.

 There are other, more advanced features, which allow you to look at values that have been computed inside the jugfile. Read up on features such as barriers in the jug documentation online at http://jug.rtfd.org.

Using Amazon Web Services

When you have a lot of data and a lot of computation to be performed, you might start to crave more computing power. Amazon (http://aws.amazon.com) allows you to rent computing power by the hour. Thus, you can access a large amount of computing power without having to precommit by purchasing a large number of machines (including the costs of managing the infrastructure). There are other competitors in this market, but Amazon is the largest player, so we briefly cover it here.

Amazon Web Services (**AWS**) is a large set of services. We will focus only on the **Elastic Compute Cloud** (**EC2**) service. This service offers you virtual machines and disk space, which can be allocated and deallocated quickly.

There are three modes of use. First is a reserved mode, whereby you prepay to have cheaper per-hour access, a fixed per-hour rate, and a variable rate, which depends on the overall compute market (when there is less demand, the costs are lower; when there is more demand, the prices go up).

On top of this general system, there are several types of machines available with varying costs, from a single core to a multicore system with a lot of RAM or even graphical processing units (GPUs). We will later see that you can also get several of the cheaper machines and build yourself a virtual cluster. You can also choose to get a Linux or Windows server (with Linux being slightly cheaper). In this chapter, we will work on our examples on Linux, but most of this information will be valid for Windows machines as well.

For testing, you can use a single machine in the **free tier**. This allows you to play around with the system, get used to the interface, and so on. Note, though, that this machine contains a slow CPU.

The resources can be managed through a web interface. However, it's also possible to do so programmatically and to write scripts that allocate virtual machines, format hard disks, and perform all operations that are possible through the web interface. In fact, while the web interface changes very frequently (and some of the screenshots we show in the book may be out of date by the time it goes to press), the programmatic interface is more stable and the general architecture has remained stable since the service was introduced.

Access to AWS services is performed through a traditional username/password system, although Amazon calls the username an *access key* and the password a *secret key*. They probably do so to keep it separate from the username/password you use to access the web interface. In fact, you can create as many access/secret key pairs as you wish and give them different permissions. This is helpful for a larger team where a senior user with access to the full web panel can create other keys for developers with fewer privileges.

Amazon.com has several regions. These correspond to physical regions of the world: West coast US, East coast US, several Asian locations, a South American one, and two European ones. If you will be transferring data, it's best to keep it close to where you will be transferring to and from. Additionally, keep in mind that if you are handling user information, there may be regulatory issues regulating their transfer to another jurisdiction. In this case, do check with an informed counsel on the implications of transferring data about European customers to the US or any other similar transfer.

Amazon Web Services is a very large topic and there are various books exclusively available to cover AWS. The purpose of this chapter is to give you an overall impression of what is available and what is possible with AWS. In the practical spirit of this book, we do this by working through examples, but we will not exhaust all possibilities.

Creating your first virtual machines

The first step is to go to `http://aws.amazon.com/` and create an account. These steps are similar to any other online service. A single machine is free, but to get more, you will need a credit card. In this example, we will use a few machines, so it may cost you a few dollars if you want to run through it. If you are not ready to take out a credit card just yet, you can certainly read the chapter to learn what AWS provides without going through the examples. Then you can make a more informed decision on whether to sign up.

Once you sign up for AWS and log in, you will be taken to the console. Here, you will see the many services that AWS provides, as depicted in the following screenshot:

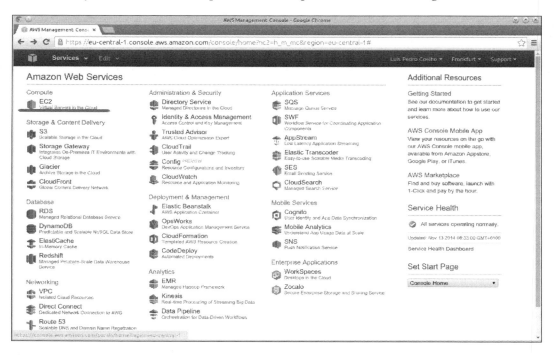

We pick and click on **EC2** (the top element on the leftmost column—this is the panel shown as it was when this book was written. Amazon regularly makes minor changes, so you may see something slightly different from what we present in the book). We now see the EC2 management console, as shown in the following screenshot:

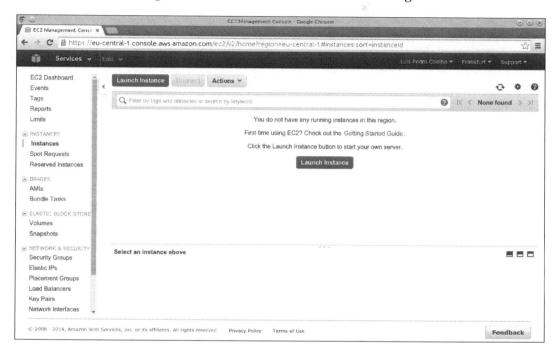

In the top-right corner, you can pick your region (see the Amazon regions information box). Note that *you will only see information about the region that you have selected at the moment*. Thus, if you mistakenly select the wrong region (or have machines running in multiple regions), your machines may not appear (this seems to be a common pitfall of using the EC2 web management console).

In EC2 parlance, a running server is called an **instance**. We select **Launch Instance**, which leads to the following screen asking us to select the operating system to use:

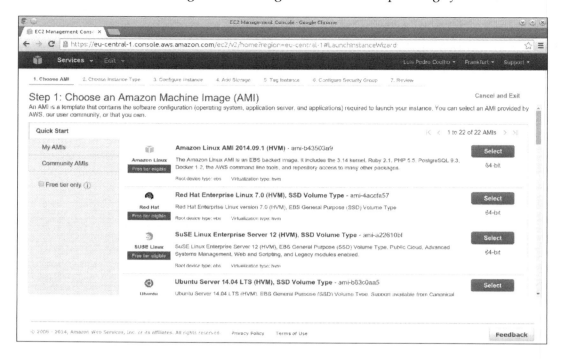

Select the **Amazon Linux** option (if you are familiar with one of the other offered Linux distributions, such as Red Hat, SUSE, or Ubuntu, you can also select one of these, but the configurations will be slightly different). Now that you have selected the software, you will need to select the hardware. In the next screen, you will be asked to select which type of machine to use:

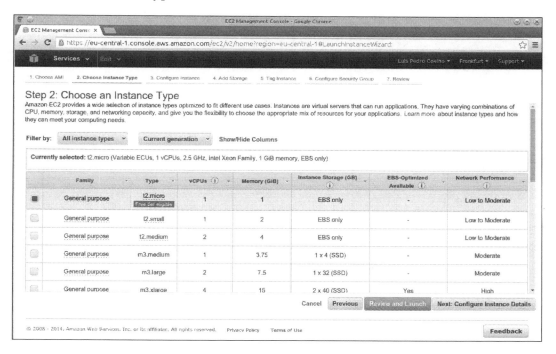

We will start with one instance of the **t2.micro** type (the **t1.micro** type was an older, even less powerful machine). This is the smallest possible machine and it's free. Keep clicking on **Next** and accept all of the defaults until you come to the screen mentioning a key pair:

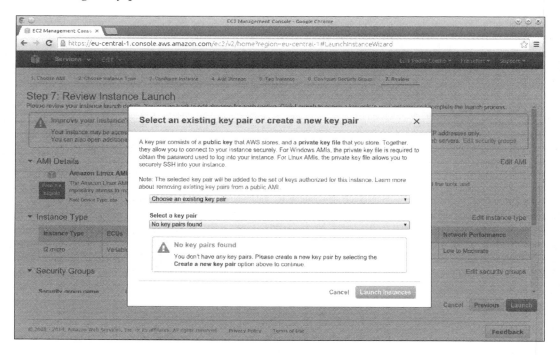

We will pick the name `awskeys` for the key pair. Then check **Create a new key pair**. Name the key pair file `awskeys.pem`. Download and save this file somewhere safe! This is the SSH (Secure Shell) key that will enable you to log in to your cloud machine. Accept the remaining defaults and your instance will launch.

You will now need to wait a few minutes for your instance to come up. Eventually, the instance will be shown in green with the status as **running**:

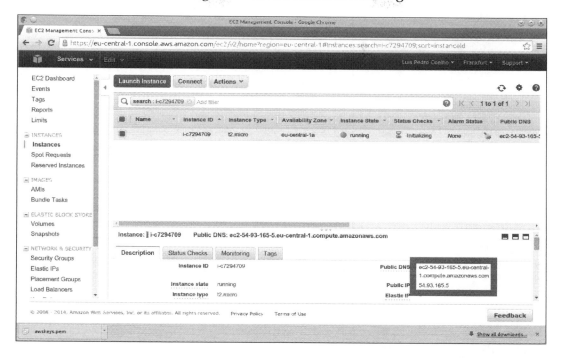

In the preceding screenshot, you should see the Public IP which can be used to log in to the instance as follows:

```
$ ssh -i awskeys.pem ec2-user@54.93.165.5
```

Therefore, we will be calling the ssh command and passing it the key files that we downloaded earlier as the identity (using the -i option). We are logging in as user ec2-user at the machine with the IP address as 54.93.165.5. This address will, of course, be different in your case. If you choose another distribution for your instance, the username may also change. In this case, try logging in as root, ubuntu (for Ubuntu distribution), or fedora (for fedora distribution).

Finally, if you are running a Unix-style operating system (including Mac OS), you may have to tweak its permissions by calling the following command:

```
$ chmod 600 awskeys.pem
```

This sets the read/write permission for the current user only. SSH will otherwise give you an ugly warning.

Now you should be able to log in to your machine. If everything is okay, you should see the banner, as shown in the following screenshot:

```
$ ssh -i awskeys.pem ec2-user@ec2-54-93-165-5.eu-central-1.compute.amazonaws.com
Last login: Thu Nov 13 07:43:33 2014 from embln.embl.de

    __|  __|_  )
    _|  (     /     Amazon Linux AMI
   ___|\___|___|

https://aws.amazon.com/amazon-linux-ami/2014.09-release-notes/
7 package(s) needed for security, out of 18 available
Run "sudo yum update" to apply all updates.
[ec2-user@ip-172-31-26-129 ~]$ █
```

This is a regular Linux box where you have sudo permission: you can run any command as the superuser by prefixing it with sudo. You can run the update command it recommends to get your machine up to speed.

Installing Python packages on Amazon Linux

If you prefer another distribution, you can use your knowledge of that distribution to install Python, NumPy, and others. Here, we will do it on the standard Amazon distribution. We start by installing several basic Python packages as follows:

```
$ sudo yum -y install python-devel \
    python-pip numpy scipy python-matplotlib
```

To compile mahotas, we will also need a C++ compiler:

```
$ sudo yum -y install gcc-c++
```

Finally, we install git to make sure that we can get the latest version of the code for the book:

```
$ sudo yum -y install git
```

In this system, pip is installed as python-pip. For convenience, we will use pip to upgrade itself. We will then use pip to install the necessary packages as follows:

```
$ sudo pip-python install -U pip
$ sudo pip install scikit-learn jug mahotas
```

At this point, you can install any other package you wish using pip.

Running jug on our cloud machine

We can now download the data and code for the book using this sequence of commands:

```
$ git clone \
https://github.com/luispedro/BuildingMachineLearningSystemsWithPython
$ cd BuildingMachineLearningSystemsWithPython
$ cd ch12
```

Finally, we run this following command:

```
$ jug execute
```

This would work just fine, but we would have to wait a long time for the results. Our free tier machine (of type t2.micro) is not very fast and only has a single processor. So, we will *upgrade our machine*!

We go back to the EC2 console, and right-click on the running instance to get the pop-up menu. We need to first stop the instance. This is the virtual machine equivalent to powering off. You can stop your machines at any time. At this point, you stop paying for them. Note that you are still using disk space, which also has a cost, billed separately. You can terminate the instance, which will also destroy the disk. This loses any information saved on the machine.

Once the machine is stopped, the **Change instance type** option becomes available. Now, we can select a more powerful instance, for example, a **c1.xlarge** instance with eight cores. The machine is still off, so you need to start it again (the virtual equivalent to booting up).

> AWS offers several instance types at different price points. As this information is constantly being revised as more powerful options are introduced and prices change (generally, getting cheaper), we cannot give you many details in the book, but you can find the most up-to-date information on Amazon's website.

We need to wait for the instance to come back up. Once it has, look up its IP address in the same fashion as we did before. When you change instance types, your instance will get a new address assigned to it.

You can assign a fixed IP to an instance using Amazon.com's Elastic IPs functionality, which you will find on the left-hand side of the EC2 console. This is useful if you find yourself creating and modifying instances very often. There is a small cost associated with this feature.

With eight cores, you can run eight jug processes simultaneously, as illustrated in the following code:

```
$ # the loop below runs 8 times
$ for counter in $(seq 8); do
>    jug execute &
> done
```

Use `jug status` to check whether these eight jobs are, in fact, running. After your jobs are finished (which should now happen pretty fast), you can stop the machine and downgrade it again to a **t2.micro** instance to save money. The micro instance can be used for free (within certain limits), while the **c1.xlarge** one we used costs 0.064 US dollars per hour (as of February 2015 — check the AWS website for up-to-date information).

Automating the generation of clusters with StarCluster

As we just learned, we can spawn machines using the web interface, but it quickly becomes tedious and error prone. Fortunately, Amazon has an API. This means that we can write scripts, which perform all the operations we discussed earlier, automatically. Even better, others have already developed tools that can be used to mechanize and automate many of the processes you want to perform with AWS.

A group at MIT developed exactly such a tool called StarCluster. It happens to be a Python package, so you can install it with Python tools as follows:

```
$ sudo pip install starcluster
```

You can run this from an Amazon machine or from your local machine. Either option will work.

We will need to specify what our cluster will look like. We do so by editing a configuration file. We generate a template configuration file by running the following command:

```
$ starcluster help
```

Then pick the option of generating the configuration file in `~/.starcluster/config`. Once this is done, we will manually edit it.

Keys, keys, and more keys

There are three completely different types of keys that are important when dealing with AWS. First, there is a standard username/password combination, which you use to log in to the website. Second, there is the SSH key system, which is a public/private key system implemented with files; with your public key file, you can log in to remote machines. Third, there is the AWS access key/secret key system, which is just a form of username/password that allows you to have multiple users on the same account (including adding different permissions to each one, but we will not cover these advanced features in this book).

To look up our access/secret keys, we go back to the AWS Console, click on our name on the top-right, and select **Security Credentials**. Now at the bottom of the screen, there should be our access key, which may look something like **AAKIIT7HHF6IUSN3OCAA**, which we will use as an example in this chapter.

Now, edit the configuration file. This is a standard `.ini` file: a text file where sections start by having their names in brackets and options are specified in the `name=value` format. The first section is the `aws info` section and you should copy and paste your keys here:

```
[aws info]
AWS_ACCESS_KEY_ID = AAKIIT7HHF6IUSN3OCAA
AWS_SECRET_ACCESS_KEY = <your secret key>
```

Now we come to the fun part, that is, defining a cluster. StarCluster allows you to define as many different clusters as you wish. The starting file has one called smallcluster. It's defined in the `cluster smallcluster` section. We will edit it to read as follows:

```
[cluster smallcluster]
KEYNAME = mykey
CLUSTER_SIZE = 16
```

This changes the number of nodes to 16 instead of the default of two. We can additionally specify which type of instance each node will be and what the initial image is (remember, an image is used to initialized the virtual hard disk, which defines what operating system you will be running and what software is installed). StarCluster has a few predefined images, but you can also build your own.

We need to create a new SSH key with the following command:

```
$ starcluster createkey mykey -o ~/.ssh/mykey.rsa
```

Now that we have configured a sixteen node cluster and set up the keys, let's try it out:

```
$ starcluster start smallcluster
```

This may take a few minutes as it allocates seventeen new machines. Why seventeen when our cluster is only sixteen nodes? StarCluster always creates a master node. All of these nodes have the same filesystem, so anything we create on the master node will also be seen by the worker nodes. This also means that we can use jug on these clusters.

These clusters can be used as you wish, but they come preequipped with a job queue engine, which makes it ideal for batch processing. The process of using them is simple:

1. You log in to the master node.
2. You prepare your scripts on the master (or better yet, have them prepared before hand).
3. You submit jobs to the queue. A job can be any Unix command.
    The scheduler will find free nodes and run your job.
4. You wait for the jobs to finish.
5. You read the results on the master node. You can also now kill all the slave nodes to save money. In any case, do not leave your system running when you do not need it anymore! Otherwise, this will cost you (in dollars-and-cents).

Before logging in to the cluster, we will copy our data to it (remember we had earlier cloned the repository onto BuildingMachineLearningSystemsWithPython):

```
$ dir=BuildingMachineLearningSystemsWithPython
$ starcluster put smallcluster $dir $dir
```

We used the $dir variable to make the command line fit in a single line. We can log in to the master node with a single command:

```
$ starcluster sshmaster smallcluster
```

We could also have looked up the address of the machine that was generated and used an ssh command as we did earlier, but using the preceding command, it does not matter what the address was, as StarCluster takes care of it behind the scenes for us.

As we said earlier, StarCluster provides a batch queuing system for its clusters; you write a script to perform your actions, put it on the queue, and it will run in any available node.

At this point, we need to install some packages again. Fortunately, StarCluster has already done half the work. If this was a real project, we would set up a script to perform all the initialization for us. StarCluster can do this. As this is a tutorial, we just run the installation step again:

```
$ pip install jug mahotas scikit-learn
```

We can use the same jugfile system as before, except that now, instead of running it directly on the master, we schedule it on the cluster.

First, write a very simple wrapper script as follows:

```
#!/usr/bin/env bash
jug execute jugfile.py
```

Call it `run-jugfile.sh` and use `chmod +x run-jugfile.sh` to give it executable permission. Now, we can schedule sixteen jobs on the cluster by using the following command:

```
$ for c in $(seq 16); do
>     qsub -cwd run-jugfile.sh
> done
```

This will create 16 jobs, each of which will run the `run-jugfile.sh` script, which we will simply call jug. You can still use the master as you wish. In particular, you can, at any moment, run `jug status` and see the status of the computation. In fact, jug was developed in exactly such an environment, so it works very well in it.

Eventually, the computation will finish. At this point, we need to first save our results. Then, we can kill off all the nodes. We create a directory `~/results` and copy our results here:

```
# mkdir ~/results
# cp results.image.txt ~/results
```

Now, log off the cluster back to our worker machine:

```
# exit
```

Now, we are back at our AWS machine (notice the $ sign in the next code examples). First, we copy the results back to this computer using the `starcluster get` command (which is the mirror image of `put` we used before):

```
$ starcluster get smallcluster results results
```

Finally, we should kill all the nodes to save money as follows:

```
$ starcluster stop smallcluster
$ starcluster terminate smallcluster
```

> Note that terminating will really destroy the filesystem and all your results. In our case, we have copied the final results to safety manually. Another possibility is to have the cluster write to a filesystem, which is not allocated and destroyed by StarCluster, but is available to you on a regular instance; in fact, the flexibility of these tools is immense. However, these advanced manipulations could not all fit in this chapter.
>
> StarCluster has excellent documentation online at http://star.mit. edu/cluster/, which you should read for more information about all the possibilities of this tool. We have seen only a small fraction of the functionality and used only the default settings here.

Summary

We saw how to use jug, a little Python framework to manage computations in a way that takes advantage of multiple cores or multiple machines. Although this framework is generic, it was built specifically to address the data analysis needs of its author (who is also an author of this book). Therefore, it has several aspects that make it fit in with the rest of the Python machine learning environment.

You also learned about AWS, the Amazon Cloud. Using cloud computing is often a more effective use of resources than building in-house computing capacity. This is particularly true if your needs are not constant and are changing. StarCluster even allows for clusters that automatically grow as you launch more jobs and shrink as they terminate.

This is the end of the book. We have come a long way. You learned how to perform classification when we labeled data and clustering when we do not. You learned about dimensionality reduction and topic modeling to make sense of large datasets. Towards the end, we looked at some specific applications (such as music genre classification and computer vision). For implementations, we relied on Python. This language has an increasingly expanding ecosystem of numeric computing packages built on top of NumPy. Whenever possible, we relied on scikit-learn, but used other packages when necessary. Due to the fact that they all use the same basic data structure (the NumPy multidimensional array), it's possible to mix functionality from different packages seamlessly. All of the packages used in this book are open source and available for use in any project.

Naturally, we did not cover every machine learning topic. In the Appendix, we provide pointers to a selection of other resources that will help interested readers learn more about machine learning.

Where to Learn More Machine Learning

We are at the end of our book and now take a moment to look at what else is out there that could be useful for our readers.

There are many wonderful resources out there to learn more about machine learning — way too much to cover them all here. The following list can therefore represent only a small, and very biased, sampling of the resources the authors think are best at the time of writing.

Online courses

Andrew Ng is a professor at Stanford who runs an online course in machine learning as a massive open online course at Coursera (http://www.coursera.org). It is free of charge, but may represent a significant time investment.

Books

This book is focused on the practical side of machine learning. We did not present the thinking behind the algorithms or the theory that justifies them. If you are interested in that aspect of machine learning, then we recommend *Pattern Recognition and Machine Learning* by Christopher Bishop. This is a classical introductory text in the field. It will teach you the nitty-gritty of most of the algorithms we used in this book.

If you want to move beyond the introduction and learn all the gory mathematical details, then *Machine Learning: A Probabilistic Perspective* by Kevin P. Murphy is an excellent option (www.cs.ubc.ca/~murphyk/MLbook). It's very recent (published in 2012) and contains the cutting edge of ML research. This 1100 page book can also serve as a reference as very little of machine learning has been left out.

Question and answer sites

MetaOptimize (`http://metaoptimize.com/qa`) is a machine learning question and answer website where many very knowledgeable researchers and practitioners interact.

Cross Validated (`http://stats.stackexchange.com`) is a general statistics question and answer site, which often features machine learning questions as well.

As mentioned in the beginning of the book, if you have questions specific to particular parts of the book, feel free to ask them at TwoToReal (`http://www.twotoreal.com`). We try to be as quick as possible to jump in and help as best as we can.

Blogs

Here is an obviously non-exhaustive list of blogs, which are interesting to someone working in machine learning:

- Machine Learning Theory: `http://hunch.net`

  The average pace is approximately one post per month. Posts are more theoretical. They offer additional value in brain teasers.

- Text & Data Mining by practical means: `http://textanddatamining.blogspot.de`

  Average pace is one post per month, very practical, always surprising approaches.

- Edwin Chen's Blog: `http://blog.echen.me`

  The average pace is one post per month, providing more applied topics.

- Machined Learnings: `http://www.machinedlearnings.com`

  The average pace is one post per month, providing more applied topics.

- FlowingData: `http://flowingdata.com`

  The average pace is one post per day, with the posts revolving more around statistics.

- Simply Statistics: `http://simplystatistics.org`

  Several posts per month, focusing on statistics and big data.

- Statistical Modeling, Causal Inference, and Social Science: `http://andrewgelman.com`

  One post per day with often funny reads when the author points out flaws in popular media, using statistics.

Data sources

If you want to play around with algorithms, you can obtain many datasets from the Machine Learning Repository at the University of California at Irvine (UCI). You can find it at `http://archive.ics.uci.edu/ml`.

Getting competitive

An excellent way to learn more about machine learning is by trying out a competition! Kaggle (`http://www.kaggle.com`) is a marketplace of ML competitions and was already mentioned in the introduction. On the website, you will find several different competitions with different structures and often cash prizes.

The supervised learning competitions almost always follow the following format: you (and every other competitor) are given access to labeled training data and testing data (without labels). Your task is to submit predictions for testing data. When the competition closes, whoever has the best accuracy wins. The prizes range from glory to cash.

Of course, winning something is nice, but you can gain a lot of useful experience just by participating. So, you have to stay tuned after the competition is over as participants start sharing their approaches in the forum. Most of the time, winning is not about developing a new algorithm, but cleverly preprocessing, normalizing, and combining existing methods.

All that was left out

We did not cover every machine learning package available for Python. Given the limited space, we chose to focus on scikit-learn. However, there are other options and we list a few of them here:

- MDP toolkit (`http://mdp-toolkit.sourceforge.net`): Modular toolkit for data processing

- PyBrain (`http://pybrain.org`): Python-based Reinforcement Learning, Artificial Intelligence, and Neural Network Library

- Machine Learning Toolkit (Milk) (`http://luispedro.org/software/milk`): This package was developed by one of the authors of this book and covers some algorithms and techniques that are not included in scikit-learn

- Pattern (`http://www.clips.ua.ac.be/pattern`): A package that combines web mining, natural language processing, and machine learning, having wrapper APIs for Google, Twitter, and Wikipedia.

A more general resource is `http://mloss.org`, which is a repository of open source machine learning software. As is usually the case with repositories such as this one, the quality varies between excellent well maintained software and projects that were one-offs and then abandoned. It may be worth checking out whether your problem is very specific and none of the more general packages address it.

Summary

We are now truly at the end. We hope you enjoyed the book and feel well equipped to start your own machine learning adventure.

We also hope you learned the importance of carefully testing your methods. In particular, the importance of using correct cross-validation method and not report training test results, which are an over-inflated estimate of how good your method really is.

Index

A

B

C

Thank you for buying
Building Machine Learning Systems
with Python
Second Edition

About Packt Publishing

Packt, pronounced 'packed', published its first book, *Mastering phpMyAdmin for Effective MySQL Management*, in April 2004, and subsequently continued to specialize in publishing highly focused books on specific technologies and solutions.

Our books and publications share the experiences of your fellow IT professionals in adapting and customizing today's systems, applications, and frameworks. Our solution-based books give you the knowledge and power to customize the software and technologies you're using to get the job done. Packt books are more specific and less general than the IT books you have seen in the past. Our unique business model allows us to bring you more focused information, giving you more of what you need to know, and less of what you don't.

Packt is a modern yet unique publishing company that focuses on producing quality, cutting-edge books for communities of developers, administrators, and newbies alike. For more information, please visit our website at www.packtpub.com.

About Packt Open Source

In 2010, Packt launched two new brands, Packt Open Source and Packt Enterprise, in order to continue its focus on specialization. This book is part of the Packt Open Source brand, home to books published on software built around open source licenses, and offering information to anybody from advanced developers to budding web designers. The Open Source brand also runs Packt's Open Source Royalty Scheme, by which Packt gives a royalty to each open source project about whose software a book is sold.

Writing for Packt

We welcome all inquiries from people who are interested in authoring. Book proposals should be sent to author@packtpub.com. If your book idea is still at an early stage and you would like to discuss it first before writing a formal book proposal, then please contact us; one of our commissioning editors will get in touch with you.

We're not just looking for published authors; if you have strong technical skills but no writing experience, our experienced editors can help you develop a writing career, or simply get some additional reward for your expertise.

Mastering Machine Learning with scikit-learn

ISBN: 978-1-78398-836-5   Paperback: 238 pages

Apply effective learning algorithms to real-world problems using scikit-learn

1. Design and troubleshoot machine learning systems for common tasks including regression, classification, and clustering.

2. Acquaint yourself with popular machine learning algorithms, including decision trees, logistic regression, and support vector machines.

3. A practical example-based guide to help you gain expertise in implementing and evaluating machine learning systems using scikit-learn.

Scala for Machine Learning

ISBN: 978-1-78355-874-2   Paperback: 520 pages

Leverage Scala and Machine Learning to construct and study systems that can learn from data

1. Explore a broad variety of data processing, machine learning, and genetic algorithms through diagrams, mathematical formulation, and source code.

2. Leverage your expertise in Scala programming to create and customize AI applications with your own scalable machine learning algorithms.

3. Experiment with different techniques, and evaluate their benefits and limitations using real-world financial applications, in a tutorial style.

Please check **www.PacktPub.com** for information on our titles

R Machine Learning Essentials

ISBN: 978-1-78398-774-0   Paperback: 218 pages

Gain quick access to the machine learning concepts and practical applications using the R development environment

1. Build machine learning algorithms using the most powerful tools in R.

2. Identify business problems and solve them by developing effective solutions.

3. Hands-on tutorial explaining the concepts through lots of practical examples, tips and tricks.

Clojure for Machine Learning

ISBN: 978-1-78328-435-1   Paperback: 292 pages

Successfully leverage advanced machine learning techniques using the Clojure ecosystem

1. Covers a lot of machine learning techniques with Clojure programming.

2. Encompasses precise patterns in data to predict future outcomes using various machine learning techniques.

3. Packed with several machine learning libraries available in the Clojure ecosystem.

Please check **www.PacktPub.com** for information on our titles